Shakespeare's
Life and
Stage

Shakespeare's Life and Stage

(S) H. Burton

Chambers

Published by W & R Chambers Ltd, Edinburgh 1989

Acknowledgements

The author and publisher would like to thank the following for
permission to reproduce the illustrations:

Winter's Plan of Stratford *c*. 1768, The Shakespeare Birthplace
Trust, Stratford-upon-Avon. Shakespeare's Birthplace, earliest
known representation of the Birthplace from an engraving by R.
Greene, The British Library. London showing the Globe from
Wenceslaus Hollar's 'Long View' of London from Bankside, 1647,
Guildhall Library, City of London. George Vertue's sketch of New
Place, 1737, The British Library, London. Shakespeare's Will and
Signature, The Controller of Her Majesty's Stationery Office. A
plan of London in about 1630, showing the playhouses in use after
1574, reproduced from Andrew Gurr: *The Shakespearean Stage*
1574-1642, Cambridge University Press, Second Edition 1985. A
playhouse *c*. 1595, adapted from C Walter Hodges: *The Globe
Restored*, Ernest Benn Ltd, 1953.

Front cover illustration, the Chandos portrait of Shakespeare,
reproduced with the permission of The National Portrait Gallery,
London.

British Library Cataloguing in Publication Data *A16434*

Burton, S.H. (Samuel Holroyd)
    Shakespeare's life and stage.
    1. Drama in English. Shakespeare, William, 1564-1616
    I. Title
    822.3'3

045976 .822.332
BSR

ISBN 0-550-21003-2
ISBN 0-550-21002-4 pbk

Cover design by James Hutcheson
Typeset by Bookworm Typesetting Ltd, Edinburgh
Printed in Great Britain by J. W. Arrowsmith Ltd, Bristol

Contents

Preface   vii

List of Illustrations   ix

PART I   HIS LIFE

1   Fact and Fiction   3
2   Shakespeare's Stratford   9
3   Shakespeare's Parents   21
4   Early Years and Education   27
5   Troubled Times and a New Life   45
6   'Now in London Place Him'   62
7   'A Fellowship in a Cry of Players'   79
8   'The Great Globe Itself'   93
9   'These Our Servants'   115
10 'I, William Shakespeare'   133

PART II   HIS STAGE

11 The Theatres and their Stages   161
12 The Actors and their Companies   179
13 The Audiences   191
14 Foul Papers and Printed Books   199

Appendix 1   Shakespeare's Family Tree   213

Appendix 2   A Chronological Table of Events   214

Reading List   218

Index   219

Preface

The biographical information provided in Part I has been compiled from the most reliable sources currently available. It incorporates the work of the many recent researchers who have unearthed some long-buried facts and, in so doing, have exploded some hoary legends. In telling the story of Shakespeare's life, I have relied on their learning. Where there is still room for conjecture about important matters – 'the Lancashire connection', for example, (see Chapter 5) – I have set down the conflicting opinions as fully and as fairly as possible.

While nowhere departing from the facts, I have in some instances put forward my own interpretations of them. When it seemed to me that my reading of certain events in Shakespeare's life was correct, and when I believed that I could usefully suggest new ways of looking at well-known material, I did not hesitate to do so. At all such times I have been careful to provide the evidence on which I have formed my opinions, so that my readers can decide how much weight to give them.

Shakespeare was essentially a man of the theatre. Only by placing him in that context can we attempt to understand the course his life took and the nature of his achievement. That is why Part II provides detailed descriptions of the theatres and stages for which he wrote, the acting companies that gave him his opportunities and structured his career, and the audiences who paid to see his plays. It ends with an account of what happened to Shakespeare's manuscripts after he handed them over to his theatre company and describes how, in the end, they found their way into print.

The Reading List at the end of the book is itself an acknowledgement of my debts to scholars on whose work I have drawn. I must, however, make special mention of two here. S. Schoenbaum's *William Shakespeare, A Documentary Life* was first published in 1975, since when, like all its readers, I have found it a treasure house of fact and a lasting inspiration. We owe its author further gratitude for his *Compact Documentary Life*, published in a revised edition in 1987. Andrew Gurr's *The Shakespearian Stage, 1574-1642* is an invaluable guide. Most of the information about this important subject lies scattered in multi-volume reference works and in specialist journals. Professor Gurr steers his readers safely and enjoyably through a vast mass of essential material.

Shakespeare and his contemporaries spelt their names as the fancy took them. I have standardised the spelling according to the modern fashion. I have also modernised both the spelling and the punctuation of quoted material.

S. H. Burton

List of Illustrations

1   Samuel Winter's Plan of Stratford   13

2   Shakespeare's Birthplace by Richard Greene   25

3   'Long View' of London: Wenceslaus Hollar   99

4   New Place: a sketch by George Vertue   110

5   Shakespeare's Will   149

6   Playhouse Sites in London between 1574 and 1630   167

7   A Public Playhouse of Shakespeare's day   175

Part I
HIS LIFE

1

Fact and Fiction

MUCH OF William Shakespeare's life was lived in the public eye and many of its events were recorded in legal documents and other official papers. In consequence, a great deal is known about what he did and about what happened to him. Many facts have been established beyond dispute and some episodes in his life can be described in considerable and trustworthy detail.

Yet it is often said that we know little about him; and in a sense that is true. Because he is so famous we want to know more than the bare facts can tell us. Hoping to discover what sort of a man he was, we ask questions to which there can be no certain answers. What was he like as a son, as a husband, as a father? Was he a religious man? How did he react to success and to misfortune? What were his views on the great issues of his day?

If we knew the answers to such questions we could get closer to him. We could describe his personality and analyse his character with some confidence.

But there is no material for a reliable account of Shakespeare's private life. He left behind no diaries, no letters, no personal papers of any kind. Or, if he did, they have not yet been found. Nor did his family or his friends hand down their intimate memories of him. The colleagues who wrote about him in the first collected edition of his plays (the First Folio, 1623) were writing about Shakespeare the great playwright, not about Will Shakespeare their former companion. True, they refer to him affectionately ('gentle Shakespeare . . . so worthy a friend and fellow') and they tell us that he wrote swiftly and fluently. There is no reason to doubt the sincerity of their tributes, but they are worded in general terms. The introductory pages of the First Folio were not written to provide details of Shakespeare's personal life.

All our positive information about him comes from official documents recording the public events of his life. For example, the records tell us, among many other things, that he bought property in Stratford and in London; that he became a shareholder in the leading acting company of the day; that he went to law several times; that he married in haste; that he received four-and-a-half yards of scarlet-red

3

cloth from King James I for a royal uniform to wear on State occasions. Yet his thoughts and feelings about these matters are hidden from us. They can only be guessed at.

Often, his actions, as recorded in the public documents, enable us to arrive at a broad understanding of his motives. For instance, his property transactions in Stratford show that he was determined to provide his family with a secure position in his native town. That fairly obvious conclusion is as far as we can safely go in trying to explore his state of mind at that time. Nor do the other factual records allow us any depth of insight.

That is why so many of his biographers attempt to discover 'the real man' in his works. Arguing that he must have expressed his own ideas and emotions in his plays and poems, they interpret them as personal statements and search them for self-revelations. They see Shakespeare's writings as his commentary on life – his intellectual, emotional and spiritual autobiography.

Many well-known books have been based on this approach, and it is easy to understand its popularity. It seems to offer a reliable way of discovering what Shakespeare was like. Surely what he wrote must be a reflection of his own thoughts and feelings? Surely he must have 'unlocked his heart' in all he wrote, as Wordsworth believed he did in the Sonnets? Can we doubt that in *Macbeth* he expressed his deepest convictions about the nature of evil? Does not *Much Ado* present his own ideal of true love?

It *may* be so: but where is the proof? Shakespeare was a dramatist. The words of the plays are not his direct, personal statements. They are spoken by characters he created in situations he invented. If we claim that a particular character or speech or, indeed, a whole play is an expression of the dramatist's own emotions or beliefs we are soon in trouble.

Consider just one example. In *King Lear*, Gloucester utters a profoundly pessimistic view of human life:

> As flies to wanton boys, are we to the gods;
> They kill us for their sport.

In the same play, Edgar expresses a stern faith in heavenly justice:

> The gods are just, and of our pleasant vices
> Make instruments to plague us.

Which of those two pronouncements represents 'Shakespeare's own view of life'? Does either? We cannot possibly know. They are spoken by two very different characters in very different situations. Uttered by those two people at those moments in the play, they ring true. They are psychologically and dramatically convincing. As for Shakespeare 'himself', all we can say is that he may well have been of Gloucester's opinion at times and shared Edgar's view at others. Since that would be true of most feeling and thinking human beings, it is not a very remarkable 'discovery' to make about the 'inner life' of William Shakespeare.

Any autobiographical interpretation of Shakespeare's work is bound to be subjective. Each attempt produces a different portrait of 'the man himself'. To give just three notable examples: Edward Dowden's *Shakespeare* (1877) is quite unlike John Dover Wilson's (1932); and Dover Wilson's is very different from A.L. Rowse's (1963). Even writers who know the facts about Shakespeare's life (as Dover Wilson and Rowse did) plunge headlong into speculation when they search through the plays and poems to find 'his true character'.

Interpretative biographers look for the Shakespeare they personally hope to find; they are also influenced by the spirit of the age in which they are writing. His Victorian biographers, for example, were quite sure that when he created the character of King Henry V he revealed his own admiration for warriors and empire builders. More recent writers have taken another view claiming that, in his portrayal of that same king, Shakespeare questioned the morality of patriotic war and asked by what right a monarch led men to their deaths.

Even the best of these 'interpreters' can do no more than make their own guesses about what kind of a man Shakespeare *may* have been. For that reason their work, though often of great interest, is not a reliable introduction to the story of Shakespeare's life. For that, we must turn to an objective account of the established facts contained in the historical records.

No reliable biography of Shakespeare was published until many years after his death. There were two reasons for this. First, much of the documentary evidence now available lay undiscovered in various archives. Second, what facts were known were so entangled with fiction that nobody was sure which was which.

Soon after he died, stories began to be told about him. Some of them found their way into print and got passed on from book to book. (A few of the old chestnuts still appear from time to time!) Many of these traditional tales are wild inventions; others may contain specks of truth. They are all second-hand, for there is no proof that any of them were told in Shakespeare's lifetime. Certainly, none of them appeared in print until long after his death. He died in 1616, and it was not until near the end of the century that these biographical stories began to appear in books. After that, they accumulated into a Shakespeare legend that became accepted as a truthful account of his life.

When Nicholas Rowe published a biography of Shakespeare in 1709 he used a lot of this misleading ready-made material. Rowe's was the first attempt to write a full account of Shakespeare's life, but it was neither full nor reliable. Short of facts, he padded it out with stories that had already appeared in print or were circulating in manuscripts. He made some attempt to discover historical facts, but he was careless. For example, he realised that the church registers at Stratford must contain important information but he did not inspect them himself. The man he employed to look at them made several mistakes which Rowe included in his *Life*.

For the next hundred years, Rowe's mixture of half fact and pure fiction was regarded as being an authentic account of Shakespeare's life. Later biographers simply followed Rowe, adding a few stories of their own to those he had printed.

It is not surprising that the pioneers relied so much on mere gossip. The legal and other official records that provide modern biographers with the facts are not all in one place. They are kept in Stratford, in London, and in other English locations. Some, indeed, have gone abroad; private collectors and university libraries in many countries have bought documents dating from Shakespeare's day and containing information about him. Consequently, it has taken a great many scholars a very long time to piece together all the facts we now have.

No wonder then that the first enquirers discovered so little hard evidence. They did not know where to find a lot of it; and when they did look in a few of the right places they were not able to make use of what they found. They lacked the necessary research skills and historical knowledge.

There was no shortage of old wives' tales to take the place of facts. Enquiring in Stratford and the countryside round about, these Shakespeare collectors found what they wanted – stories that fitted in with their own ideas of the kind of man Shakespeare must have been and of the kind of upbringing he must have had. It did not worry them that the tellers of these stories could not possibly guarantee their truth. They lapped up anecdotes and treated them as reliable evidence. Many of the yarns they heard were based on nothing but rambling and out-of-date hearsay: 'My grandfather knew a man who knew one of Shakespeare's sons-in-law, and this man told my grandfather that . . .'.

It was not until the end of the eighteenth century that scholars began to strip away the myths and uncover the facts. Edmond Malone was the greatest of these true researchers, and all the work done since has built on his patient and skilful labours. The mistakes he made have been corrected, and a great deal of information that he could not know has been discovered.

The work is not yet complete – perhaps it never will be. Fresh documents bearing on Shakespeare's life are discovered from time to time. When that happens, the material is put through well-tried tests and compared with known facts before it is accepted as a genuine addition to Shakespearian knowledge.

Yet some of the hoary old stories are occasionally repeated as being true. For example: that Shakespeare's father was a butcher and that young Will recited poetic laments about the slaughter of innocent calves before he killed them. Then there is the wholly false assertion that Shakespeare must have been ill-educated because he started life in a small town and did not go to a university. These and other fairy tales are still passed on.

And the story-telling does not stop with the repetition of ancient yarns. Shakespeare's fame is so immense that there is a ready market for sensational inventions. It is not difficult for an ingenious writer to concoct a *Life* that is mainly fiction, and buyers can always be found for the latest 'fresh interpretation' or 'startling revelations of Shakespeare's secret life'.

Though it flies in the face of all the facts, one particular untruth, the myth of the 'ignorant Shakespeare' (referred to earlier), is quite often resurrected and used to prop up some wild notion or other. It has been the linchpin of the theory that Shakespeare was not the author of the plays and poems that bear his name.

Starting from the assumption that Shakespeare was ill-educated, the argument proceeds like this. The plays and poems were obviously the work of a writer who had read widely and whose mind was well-stocked and subtle. The ignoramus from Stratford could not have possessed that knowledge or those intellectual qualities. Therefore, he could not have written those works.

The 'anti-Stratfordians' (the people who deny Shakespeare's authorship) propose various claimants to his place. Marlowe, Bacon and the Earl of Oxford are each favoured by different sects. Even Queen Elizabeth I has been put forward! The arguments used to support her 'authorship' are no worse than those used on behalf of the other substitute Shakespeares.

All the evidence is against their belief that 'the man from Stratford', as they call Shakespeare, was ignorant (see Chapter 4), and the anti-Stratfordian theories would not be worth the space given to them here if you were not bound to come across them sometime. They keep cropping up, and whenever they do they attract a lot of attention because Shakespeare is still news. Any story about him will create a stir, especially when time and money are available to publicise it. Neither the 'Baconians' nor any of the other anti-Stratfordians have ever been able to produce reliable evidence to support their arguments, yet they have generated a vague suspicion in the minds of ill-informed people that Shakespeare's authorship is doubtful. It is not. The historical record of his life – and that record includes the testimony of men who were his colleagues and companions for years – proves conclusively that the plays and poems to which his name is given were indeed the work of William Shakespeare.

Biographies of Shakespeare are plentiful, but (for the reasons set out in this preliminary chapter) some are unreliable. However, most of the false statements published about Shakespeare have now been discredited by a weighty – and growing – body of well-established documentary evidence. Students who have read an account of his life based on and confined to that evidence will not be misled by books in which old stories are uncritically repeated and new theories are rashly propounded.

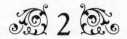

Shakespeare's Stratford

WILLIAM SHAKESPEARE was born in Stratford-upon-Avon in 1564 and he died there in 1616. For most of his working life he spent the greater part of each year in London, where his success was achieved and his fortune was made. As the records show, however, his attachment to his native town was never broken.

His purchase of New Place was one of many steps he took to preserve and strengthen his links with Stratford. Aged thirty-three at the time, he had become a leading figure in the London theatre world and he could have bought a house there had he wanted to. Instead, he put his money into a fine house in Stratford, a short walk away from his Henley Street birthplace where his father and mother still lived.

Writing, acting and managing, he had to live where his work was and occupy lodgings in London during the long theatrical season; but his wife and children lived in New Place and he was able to spend part of each year at home with them in Stratford.

From then on, as his London career flourished, he took every opportunity of multiplying his Stratford connections, acquiring more property and land in and near to that town. By the time he was forty-six he was more often to be seen in Stratford than in London. Still active in the affairs of the King's Men – the great theatre company for which he was the principal dramatist, as well as being one of its chief shareholders and managers – he had certainly not yet retired. His commitments in London necessitated travelling to and from the capital, but he considered that the attractions of a Stratford-based life outweighed the disadvantages of the long journeys.

During one of his London visits – in May 1612 – he was required to give written evidence to be used in a lawsuit. The dispute (known as the Belott-Mountjoy suit) had no connection with Shakespeare's own affairs, so the details do not matter here; but the legal preamble to his sworn statement illuminates his attitude to Stratford and to his life there. The document begins with the declaration that it is the record of testimony provided by:

> William Shakespeare of Stratford-upon-Avon in the County of Warwick, gentleman of the age of 48 years.

The phrasing of that declaration may have been suggested by the lawyer who took down his evidence, but its factual content must have been supplied by Shakespeare himself. He certainly regarded it as being accurate and appropriate, for he signed the statement that it introduced. Clearly, it was important to him to be identified as a Stratford man of good social standing.

As those facts show – and the public records contain others of similar import – his relationship with Stratford was a major influence in his life. Many people have a strong feeling for the place of their birth, but few are as determined to return to live there as he was, or as single-minded in mastering circumstances to bring it about.

In London he achieved fame and prosperity. He enjoyed the applause of audiences, the admiration and affection of colleagues. The arbiters of taste sang his praises. Noblemen honoured him. The court gave him its favour. Two monarchs esteemed him. Yet throughout his crowded and triumphant years in the capital he consistently planned his personal affairs to establish for himself and his family a secure home in Stratford and an honoured position in its life.

It is because the place exerted a lifelong pull on him that information about Shakespeare's Stratford and its people is of more than purely historical interest. Some of those closest to him were deeply involved in its affairs; and events that occurred in Stratford changed their lives and his. An account of those events and a description of the town in which they happened play an essential part in any biography of William Shakespeare.

Many years after Shakespeare's death, another Warwickshire-born author, George Eliot, wrote of the wholesome and enduring influence of a childhood spent in a well-loved place. That belief, expressed in the following passage (from Chapter 3 of *Daniel Deronda*), harmonises with everything that is known about Shakespeare's life in Stratford and helps us to understand why it mattered so much to him.

A human life, I think, should be well rooted in some spot of a native land, where it may get the love of tender kinship for the face of the earth, for the labours that men go forth to, for the sounds and accents that haunt it, for whatever will give that early home a familiar unmistakable difference amidst the future widening of knowledge.

All the evidence indicates that Shakespeare's life was 'well rooted'; and the enduring effects of his early environment are as apparent in his writing as in his actions. Many of the descriptive details and images used in his plays and poems are derived from sources familiar to him in the part-urban, part-rural surroundings in which his

Stratford home was set. From first to last, he drew material from that copious store – its sights, sounds and scents, its animal and plant life, its landscape, its streets, its domestic round and daily tasks, its holiday feasts and rituals.

One particularly striking example typifies his habitual and detailed recall of Stratford scenes and events. It occurs in *Hamlet*, where Gertrude's description of Ophelia's death by drowning begins with these words:

> There is a willow grows aslant a brook,
> That shows his hoar leaves in the glassy stream;
> There with fantastic garlands did she come,
> Of crow-flowers, nettles, daisies, and long purples . . . .

More than twenty years before Shakespeare wrote that description, a girl from a village near Stratford was drowned in the Avon, at a spot where willow trees and wild flowers crowded its banks. The close similarity between the scenes where the real and the imagined deaths occurred might be dismissed as coincidental but for the fact that the drowned girl's name was Katherine Hamlet. Shakespeare was a boy of fifteen when she died, but the title of the play he was writing brought her surname back into his mind, and with it a vivid recollection of the bygone event and the well-known riverside.

Again, many of the people in his plays were transposed from the street life, the markets and fairs and the countryside of Stratford: tradespeople, craftsmen, watchmen, citizens, farmers, tinkers, labourers, schoolmasters, parsons, magistrates, landowners and squires. Indeed, the very names of people and places in and around his native town found their way into his plays, sometimes a little disguised, and often spelt as they were pronounced in the local dialect: 'Marian Hacket, the fat ale-wife of Wincot'; 'Old Sly's son of Burtonheath'; 'William Visor of Woncot'; 'Clement Perkes o' the Hill'. Throughout his career, 'Stratford types' mingled with creations that sprang from the 'future widening of his knowledge' – the Eastcheap Londoners, the court ladies and gallants, the princes and nobles, the Romans and kings, whose origins lay outside the familiar Stratford scene.

Well over four hundred years have gone by since William Shakespeare was born, but ample records have survived to provide a detailed description of the Stratford he knew.

The history of the town is recorded in legal and ecclesiastical documents, in corporation account books and in the minutes of council meetings. There are private papers too which supplement the records of public business with information about events in the lives of individual people and families. Some refer to property transactions and tell us much about Stratford houses, streets and gardens and about the nearby farms and villages. Others give details of the finances, occupations, relationships and interests of Stratford people. Matters mentioned in others include religion and church-going, marriage contracts, domestic life, good and bad neighbours, the price of bread and ale, education, disease and death, births and festivities. All these sources afford vivid glimpses of Shakespeare's Stratford, telling us what the town looked like and how life went on there in his day.

The information provided by the written records of the past is supplemented by the appearance and character of present-day Stratford, which retains many of the features that it had in Shakespeare's lifetime. Buildings with which he was familiar are still there and the ground plan of the place has been little changed. Streets bearing the names he knew still mark out the ways he went to school, to church, to the houses of relatives and neighbours, and over Clopton Bridge on the road to London.

Though Stratford is now, as it has long been, a world-famous tourist attraction visited by thousands every year, its thriving 'Shakespeare industry' has not altered its essential character. It remains what it was in his day – a market town set in rural Warwickshire in the southern half of the English Midlands.

Its name explains its origins. 'Strat' comes from the Old English word *straet*, meaning 'road' or 'highway', so 'Stratford-upon-Avon' is the name of the place where, in Anglo-Saxon England (and, indeed, long before), travellers along the *straet* crossed the River Avon by means of a ford. Two long-distance and much-used routes, one from east to west and the other from north to south, met here, where the water was shallow enough to be safely waded unless the river was in flood.

From early times, people got their living and made their homes near this river crossing. As the centuries passed, the primitive settlement developed into a busy staging post and trading centre. Travellers paused there for rest and refreshment at its inns. Dealers came from far and near to attend its fairs. Local farmers sold their produce at its market and bought necessities – such as cloth, yarn, leather goods, domestic utensils and agricultural tools – made by Stratford craftsmen.

The right to hold a weekly market dated back to 1196, and charters establishing four annual fairs were granted at various times in the next hundred years. These invaluable commercial privileges were obtained from the Crown for Stratford by successive bishops of Worcester, in whose diocese the town lay. They were also its manorial lords, so it was to their own advantage that Stratford should flourish. They conferred another important benefit on its people by allowing their tenants there to lease property on very favourable terms. This did much to encourage in its citizens the confidence and enterprise that marked their management both of their own business affairs and those of the town.

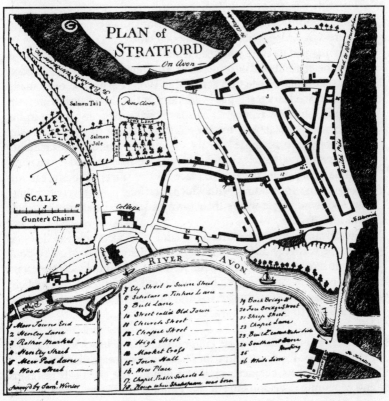

Samuel Winter's Plan of Stratford (*c.* 1768)
the lay-out had changed little since Shakespeare lived there

Their horizons were not bounded by their immediate surroundings, for they extended their activities into the wider world that good communications opened for them. Throughout the Middle Ages, and for many years afterwards, the Avon was a busy waterway along which goods were carried from Stratford to Tewkesbury (where the Avon joins the Severn) and beyond. The road from Coventry, then a famous cloth-making centre, passed through Stratford on its way to the great port of Bristol. London itself, though distant, was by no means out of range. As we know from the records, Stratford's leading men (Shakespeare's father and his close associates, for example) did not hesitate to make the journey whenever they considered that their own business affairs or those of the town could be best served by dealing directly with merchants or lawyers in the capital.

Two other features contributed to Stratford's development into a bustling and prosperous trading place. Immediately to the north lay the Forest of Arden, still thickly wooded when Shakespeare knew it, though many of its trees had been felled. Arden provided timbers for the roof beams and wall posts of Stratford's houses and for the wooden bridge that replaced the ford across the Avon. Farms had been made in the forest clearances, but wild deer and other game were still plentiful. We know from *As You Like It* what Arden was like in his day, for it is the setting for the country scenes in that play. His dramatic purposes required the introduction of some exotic elements – a lioness and olive trees – but, overall, the background is realistic. The imaginary events that take place 'in the skirts of the forest' are played out in surroundings with which Stratford people were familiar. The woodland began where their town ended, and a short walk took them into Arden.

Southwards, between Stratford and the Cotswold Hills, the landscape was very different. Here, in the district known as Feldon, an extensive stretch of open and fertile land supported numerous farms, hamlets and villages. This was good farming country, where sheep grazed and corn grew. Its products made a handsome contribution to Stratford's trade.

By 1485, when the first of the Tudor monarchs – Henry VII – became king, the basic features of Stratford had long been established; and the town retained its characteristics throughout the political, religious and economic developments of the Tudor period. The working lives and deep-seated attitudes of its people were not fundamentally changed by the decrees of government, far-reaching though they were. Getting their living by their trade and their workshops, Stratford's citizens adjusted to fresh circumstances and seized the new opportunities that came along, but without greatly disturbing the underlying pattern of their accustomed ways or calling into question their habitual values.

Their continuing belief in those values was confirmed by the prosperity of their town and by the successful careers of local people, most notably that of Sir Hugh Clopton. For many years after his death in 1496, ambitious men in Stratford were inspired to emulate his deeds. His life was spent in activities with which they were familiar and reflected personal qualities and aspirations of which they approved. In the Stratford of the 1550s, its citizens – Shakespeare's father among them – saw in Clopton's well-remembered career the kind of triumph they too might enjoy, if not perhaps in such ample measure.

Clopton was born in a manor house a mile away from Stratford. He was not the eldest son, so he had to make his own way in the world. He went to London where, as a mercer (a dealer in textiles, especially silk and other fine fabrics), he acquired a very large fortune. He was active in the government of the city, becoming an alderman and then sheriff. In 1492 he was elected Lord Mayor and knighted.

Although his birthplace was just outside Stratford and his wealth was London-made, Sir Hugh Clopton always thought of himself as a Stratford man, and he made the welfare of that town one of his chief concerns. His greatest benefaction was the building of the fine stone bridge that spans the Avon to this day and still bears his name. The old wooden bridge, narrow and decaying, had become a hazard. It was described as being 'very hard to pass by', and travellers were 'in jeopardy of life' when the river was in flood. Clopton's great new bridge ensured the safe passage of people and goods into and out of the town.

He also rebuilt the Guild Chapel; and just opposite, at the corner of Chapel Street and Chapel Lane, he built a big town house. Eventually, that same house (New Place) came into the ownership of another successful Stratford man. William Shakespeare, like Hugh Clopton before him, became wealthy in London; and he too, in his turn, laid out his money in ways that enhanced his local reputation and won him a respected position in his native place. The working lives of these two eminent Stratfordians were spent in very different occupations, but it is evident that, in some respects at least, they shared the same values.

It is also evident that both William Shakespeare and his father, John, were thoroughly representative of their fellow townspeople in their attitude to possessions and social status, accepting it as a fact of life that wealth and rank commanded public esteem. They conducted their worldly affairs accordingly. When, as a young man, John Shakespeare set himself up in business in Stratford, he was well aware of the excellent prospects that the town had to offer.

Like several other prominent buildings in Stratford, the Guild Chapel originally belonged to the Guild of the Holy Cross, an organisation that dated back to 1296. Founded to serve religious and charitable purposes, the guild played an important part in the town's development. Its members enriched the guild with donations and bequests, and it used its resources for the general good. It provided four priests to serve the chapel. It built a guildhall and almshouses, established a school and paid the master. It busied itself with social welfare and public amenities, relieving the poor, contributing to the upkeep of the bridge, and seeing that the town clocks were kept in good repair.

The Guild of the Holy Cross, a Roman Catholic foundation, was dissolved in 1547. There was no place for it in the Protestant England of Edward VI. Then, in 1553, when the town became a self-governing borough, the guild's property, income, and many of its functions were taken over by the newly-established Corporation of Stratford.

From then on, the town's affairs were very largely in the control of its leading citizens. Corporation business was conducted by the town council. It consisted of fourteen aldermen and fourteen burgesses, and its powers were greater than those of the guild had ever been.

It was a self-electing body. Any vacancies that arose were filled by citizens voted in by the existing aldermen and burgesses. They also elected one of the aldermen to serve for twelve months as their bailiff. The bailiff of Stratford (the equivalent of a mayor) presided over the council and was in a strong position to influence its decisions, for he was responsible for carrying out its policies. He also negotiated with the lord of the manor on the council's behalf, discussing not only rents and leases but other important matters, such as the appointment of the vicar of Holy Trinity Church and the master of Stratford school. In both cases, the right of appointment lay with the lord of the manor, but a skilful and determined bailiff could ensure that the council's views carried weight when a new vicar had to be found. As for the schoolmaster, the council usually got the man it wanted. After all, it paid his salary, provided his house and footed the bill for his removal expenses to Stratford.

The council dominated every aspect of the town's business and civic life. It had the power to make byelaws that applied to everyone who lived in the borough. Its bailiff was a justice of the peace. It regulated the conduct of the market and the fairs. It fixed the price and quality of bread and ale. It made public health orders applying to alehouses, butchers' premises and the cleanliness of the streets. It appointed officials – for example, ale-tasters, bread-weighers, constables and chamberlains – whose duties and powers affected every citizen.

Like many another Tudor town, Stratford was a largely self-regulated community which offered plenty of scope to ambitious and enterprising people – especially to those whose ambition and enterprise got them a seat in the council chamber, where policy was decided and regulations were made. The fact that John Shakespeare rose up the council ladder until he became bailiff of Stratford tells us quite a lot about his attitude to life and about the kind of home in which his son William grew up.

But if the citizens of Stratford had a good deal of freedom to manage their local affairs, they had no control at all over one important aspect of their daily lives. Their religion was determined for them by the reigning monarch and the national parliament. Throughout William Shakespeare's lifetime – first under Queen Elizabeth I and then under her successor King James I – all the people of England were commanded by law to conform to the doctrines and the forms of worship of the Church of England. At Shakespeare's christening in Holy Trinity Church in 1564 and at his burial there in 1616, the rites used were those set down in the Anglican Book of Common Prayer.

One of the chief reasons for the loyalty that the vast majority of her subjects gave to Queen Elizabeth was that she had settled the religious strife of previous years by establishing the Church of England. By doing so, she had created an orderly environment in which ordinary people could go about their daily affairs without wondering what the next upheaval would be.

In religious matters, the steadiness of national policy throughout William Shakespeare's lifetime was in sharp contrast to the violent fluctuations that had occurred during his father's youth and early manhood. John Shakespeare was born in the reign of Henry VIII. That king originated the break with Rome by rejecting the Pope's authority over the English church, though it remained Roman Catholic in doctrine and ritual. In the reign of his successor (Edward VI), when John Shakespeare was in his late teens and early twenties, the pace of religious change quickened. The English church was rapidly reformed in accordance with Protestant theory and practice. By law, the Roman Catholic Mass could no longer be said. All worship in English churches followed the Book of Common Prayer. When Edward VI died in 1553 the Church of England had been established.

Queen Mary then set about returning her country to the Roman Catholic Church. The Act of Uniformity (which compelled the use of the Book of Common Prayer) was repealed. Priests and the Mass were brought back. The Queen accepted the supremacy of the Pope in all church matters. She married King Philip II of Spain, hoping to have by him a child who, as her successor, would keep England free from Protestantism.

Mary's hopes were not fulfilled. She died childless. Her attempt to restore Roman Catholicism had caused widespread fear, bitterness and much suffering. Her Spanish marriage was deeply unpopular, for many English people regarded Spain as England's enemy. Her reign had brought nothing but defeat abroad and strife at home.

Queen Elizabeth I, daughter of Henry VIII, succeeded Mary in 1558; and she at once reversed Mary's pro-Catholic policies. In the first year of her reign the Book of Common Prayer was declared to be the sole legal form of worship in 'any Cathedral, or Parish Church, or other place within this realm of England'. Roman Catholic priests and services were once more proscribed by law, and the Protestant Church of England was again established as the national church which all English people must attend, or be punished for not doing so.

Both John and William Shakespeare lived in times when religion affected daily life in many ways. People then were used to church-going, and they were used to being compelled to attend services regularly. They were used to church courts which tried a wide variety of offences. In this respect it made no difference whether the state religion was Roman Catholic or Protestant. During William Shakespeare's lifetime the Stratford church court tried people for opening shops on Sundays, for spreading malicious gossip, for playing games or drinking in taverns during the hours of church services, for non-attendance at church for whatever reason, for failing to contribute to the poor or the upkeep of the parish church, for adultery and other kinds of sexual misbehaviour. These were just some of the offences for which those found guilty were punished by fines, excommunication, or public penance performed in church or at the market cross.

Such a degree of government control over religion and of church interference in personal behaviour would be intolerable to us, but in Shakespeare's day it was accepted as a fact of life. People expected the monarch and parliament to settle the state religion, and they accepted the state church as a busy and powerful presence in everyday affairs.

When Queen Elizabeth restored Protestantism in 1558/9 she judged the mood of the English people well. By that time, most of them preferred the Protestant Church and they approved of the queen's decision. For some, of course, adherence to one side or the other – Protestant or Catholic – was a matter of conscience on which their personal salvation depended. In Mary's reign devout believers had been ready to die for the Protestant faith, just as in Elizabeth's reign some proved ready to die for Roman Catholicism – but martyrs are always exceptional people. Most of Elizabeth's subjects were content with their new queen's Protestant policy and, sick of religious upheavals, looked forward to being left in peace to get on with their worldly concerns. They wanted what Elizabeth gave them: a Protestant settlement that would last.

In Stratford, as in many another English town, the general support for the queen's policy was reinforced by some strong financial interests. During Mary's reign, the corporation held on to the power and the property granted to it by Edward VI's charter, but her pro-Catholic measures were always seen as a threat. Under a Catholic monarch, the Guild of the Holy Cross might be restored. If that happened, the corporation would lose its wealth, and the aldermen and burgesses would lose their influence over the town's business, civic and educational life.

For John Shakespeare, an up-and-coming citizen of Stratford when Queen Elizabeth I was crowned, a religious settlement that removed the threat to the corporation was an assurance that his own civic ambitions and worldly progress would not be thwarted. There has been a lot of speculation about his religion (see Chapter 5), so it is worth stressing here that, whatever his own personal inclinations may or may not have been, John Shakespeare's material interests were bound up with the Protestantism that Elizabeth established and maintained.

Certainly, it was a time of hope when, at the beginning of the new reign, the merchants, shopkeepers, dealers and craftsmen of Stratford were energetically developing their trade.

It is misleading to think of Shakespeare's Stratford as being a small town when he lived there. By modern standards it was; but it was not small by Tudor reckoning. England was then a rural country with a total population of about five million, of which only about one million were town-dwellers. The rest – the vast majority – lived in villages, hamlets and isolated farms. London, with half a million people (one-tenth of the total population of England), was the only city that we should consider really big. The cities of Bristol, York and Norwich each had between 25 000 and 30 000 inhabitants. Then there were the ten 'great towns', as they were called – Coventry was one – that topped the 18 000 mark. Stratford, with about 2000 people, had well above the average population of the other places then recognised as towns.

With its market, fairs, cornmill, workplaces, shops and inns, its bridge, roads and river, its guildhall, chapel and almshouses, its big school and fine parish church, Stratford was a busy, bustling, important place. It was not at all the kind of quiet, out-of-the-way, sleepy backwater which we nowadays describe as 'a small town'.

It was also a pleasant place in which to live. Contemporary surveys described its wide streets and its quiet back lanes, its well-built houses and good gardens. A thousand elms grew in its open spaces. Just outside the borough boundary lay the woodland of Arden and the farmland of Feldon, affording country sports and pastimes as well as commodities. The River Avon turned the town mill-wheel and carried the laden barges, but it had its recreational uses too: fishing, swimming and boating.

All in all, Stratford was a good place for an enterprising man when the new reign began. It shared to the full in the national mood of optimism and it offered its citizens fine prospects now that things were settled. Certainly, John Shakespeare, not yet thirty, and with good hopes of success in his business and civic career, entered a thriving period of his life.

More than fifty years afterwards, his son dramatised the christening of the infant Elizabeth in *Henry VIII*. In the last scene of that play, Archbishop Cranmer foretells the benefits that she will bring to England when she is queen:

> Her own shall bless her:
> Her foes shake like a field of beaten corn
> And hang their heads with sorrow. Good grows with her;
> In her days every man shall eat in safety
> Under his own vine what he plants, and sing
> The merry songs of peace to all his neighbours.

Not all the queen's days were to prove safe, peaceful and prosperous, but those words, written nine years after her death, were in tune with the feelings of those who saw the play. During and after her reign, most of the people of England considered that she had brought her country much good.

In 1558, and for some time to come, the outlook was bright, and though for the queen and the nation – and for John Shakespeare himself – storm-clouds later gathered, optimism prevailed during the years when young William Shakespeare was growing up in his father's house in Stratford.

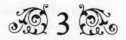

Shakespeare's Parents

JOHN SHAKESPEARE was born in Snitterfield, a small village near Stratford. The exact date of his birth is not known, but as he was in his early seventies when he died in September 1601 he must have been born in 1530 or a year or so before.

John's father, Richard Shakespeare, was a tenant farmer. He rented land in and around Snitterfield and, judging by the official valuation of his goods at his death in 1561, he made a more than adequate living. The records show that he was fined for various minor farming offences – putting too many of his beasts out to graze on common land, and turning them loose in the parish meadows – but there was nothing unusual about that. His neighbours did the same and, like Richard Shakespeare, sometimes got away with it and sometimes paid the penalty. At any rate, he had the reputation of being 'an honest and skilful person' for he helped to value the property of several people in the parish, and only a man answering that description was qualified to act as an 'appraisor'.

One of Richard Shakespeare's sons, Henry, farmed in Snitterfield and nearby all his life, but John Shakespeare chose a different course. At the age of fourteen he started a seven-year apprenticeship to a Stratford glover and whittawer.

Whittawers made 'white leather' from the skins of deer, sheep and goats. It was a skilful job and one that was in great demand. The skins, soaked in a solution of alum and salt, were stretched and beaten out and pared down with sharp knives until they were soft and pliant. Gloves, belts, purses and aprons were made from this pale-coloured, supple leather.

Gloves were an essential item of dress in those days – and not just for keeping hands warm. They were fashionable and expensive. Often richly embroidered or beaded – even jewelled – and sometimes cunningly perfumed, they were badges of rank for great people and signs of prosperity for citizens. Frequent as gifts, they were marks of esteem or tokens of love.

So, when John Shakespeare finished his long apprenticeship he was master of a good trade; and one in which he made rapid progress. By 1552 he was already occupying the house in Henley Street to which he later brought his wife and in which all his children were born and brought up. 'The Birthplace', as it has long been called, consisted then of two adjoining parts, subsequently made into one big house. The western wing housed the family. The workshop and store were in the next-door building.

John's name first appears in the Stratford records in that same year. He was fined one shilling for piling rubbish in the street instead of carting it away to the 'common muckhill' that was situated at the western end of Henley Street, where the open country began. John Shakespeare was not the only offender. Two of his neighbours, Humphrey Reynolds and Adrian Quiney, were also fined. The size of the fine (one shilling was then a two-day wage for a skilled workman) shows that the corporation took a serious view of this particular breach of its public health regulations.

Evidently, his offence was not held against him for long. In 1556 he was chosen as one of the corporation's two ale-tasters. This was an unpaid but important official post for which 'able persons and discreet' were selected. Each week during their term of office the ale-tasters checked the price and quality of the ale and bread sold in the town, making sure that the ale was good and sold in sealed pots and that loaves were not underweight. It was not an easy job. The ale-tasters had to decide whether a warning would suffice or whether sterner action was called for. Some brewers and bakers played sharp tricks, and downright dishonesty had to be reported even when a neighbour or friend was caught out. It took a fair man to make good decisions and a strong-minded man to resist threats or to refuse bribes. A good record as an ale-taster marked out a reliable and resourceful person. In John Shakespeare's case, it proved to be the first step towards high civic office.

By this time his business was well established and he had money to invest in town property. He bought a house in Greenhill Street, together with the land ('garden and croft') that surrounded it. He also bought the workshop wing of the Henley Street house which, until then, he had rented. He now owned the whole substantial building, part family house, part business premises.

Now in his late twenties and doing well, he turned his thoughts to marriage. He did not need to look very long or to look very far for his bride. Her name was Mary Arden and she lived in the hamlet of Wilmcote, close to Snitterfield and about three miles from Stratford. She was six or seven years younger than John.

Her father, Robert Arden, was well-to-do; owner of a big farmhouse and land in Wilmcote as well as two other farmhouses and more land in Snitterfield. He also had eight daughters for whom suitable husbands had to be found, and Mary was the youngest of the eight.

The two fathers knew each other well, for Robert Arden was Richard Shakespeare's landlord. He owned the farmhouse in which Richard lived and some of the land he farmed. Socially, the Ardens of Wilmcote were a cut above the Shakespeares of Snitterfield; and social distinction came into the reckoning when marriages were arranged in Tudor times. The name of Arden had long been famous in Warwickshire, and though Robert himself was not prominent in public affairs, he was respected as belonging to a 'most ancient and worthy family'. In the language of the day, Mary's father and his offspring were 'of gentle blood'.

John Shakespeare married well. Mary brought him a good dowry; and the Arden connection advanced his social standing. Many years later, when he obtained a grant of arms from the College of Heralds, his claim to the rank of 'Gentleman' was greatly strengthened because of his marriage to 'the daughter and one of the heirs of Robert Arden of Wilmcote, Esquire'.

However, the advantages of the match were not all on one side. Robert Arden's dealings with Richard Shakespeare and his knowledge of John's character and prospects encouraged him to take a favourable view of the proposed marriage. He died before it took place, but the courtship was under way when he made his will in 1556. Although Mary was his youngest daughter, he appointed her one of his two executors and he left her a handsome inheritance: the valuable Wilmcote estate and part of his Snitterfield land. If he had been opposed to her marrying John Shakespeare he would not have endowed her with so large a share of his wealth.

They were married late in 1557, after Mary had attended to the legal business of settling her father's estate. Exactly when or where the ceremony was performed we do not know. Robert Arden had asked to be buried in the churchyard at Aston Cantlow, a neighbouring parish with which the Ardens had close family connections, so it is likely that John and Mary were married in that church. The register for that period has not survived.

Mary's inheritance was a considerable addition to her husband's assets, but she brought him more than property. Young as she was, she had helped to run a large household, and her upbringing and family background had accustomed her to the management of material resources. A level-headed and practical woman, the daughter of Robert Arden was well qualified to make a success of her new life as the wife of an ambitious citizen.

There was plenty for her to do, and scope for her talents. The Henley Street household was a typical master craftsman's establishment. It was both a family home and a workplace. There were then no factories or firms, as we know them now. Day-labourers and journeymen went out to work; but for a citizen and his family their household was their workplace. They, their apprentices and their domestic servants formed a close-knit working unit. The home was 'the factory' and the family was 'the firm'.

By custom, by religious teaching, and by law, the husband was the head of the house, the family and the business. Legally, his wife was his inferior in all things; but his worldly success depended very much on her ability to help him in his working life. Her share in that was no less important than her skilful organisation of purely domestic matters for which she was solely responsible. The letter of the law decreed the woman's subordination, but the efficient running of a citizen's household called for a daily and practical partnership between husband and wife.

Not that Mary Shakespeare in taking up her new duties was expected to share in the labour of the Henley Street workshop. She was not required to prepare leather or to make gloves; but she needed to learn enough about the processes and skills of the craft to be able to keep an eye on things in her husband's absence. When he was at his stall in the weekly market, or trading at fairs, or travelling on borough business, he relied on her to deal with any problems that arose in the workshop wing of the house. That responsibility was, of course, additional to her everyday duty of supervising and sharing in the domestic tasks of a large household.

In legal matters too (and it was an age in which people often went to law) John Shakespeare's wife had advice to give and experience on which to draw. As the records show, she twice participated directly in the family's legal business. When land was mortgaged to raise ready money, she was a party to the transaction. She was again involved when the Shakespeares tried to regain possession of the mortgaged estate.

Thirty years after Mary Arden became the wife of John Shakespeare, her son William wrote *The Merry Wives of Windsor*, a play in which two citizens' wives have leading roles. It would be absurd to attempt to see either Mistress Ford or Mistress Page as a 'portrait' of the playwright's mother. He was writing a comic drama, not a biography. By then, too, keen observation of people and life in London as well as in Stratford had provided him with abundant material for his characters. Nevertheless, the energy and enterprise with which he endowed those two imaginary women were qualities familiar to him in his boyhood.

They were the mental and temperamental traits a woman needed to make a success of her key position in the kind of household in which he grew up.

A woman of Mary Shakespeare's station in life could hope for financial security and a respected place in the social hierarchy if her husband thrived; but she recognised that the attainment of those prospective benefits depended on her efforts as well as on his. When she married she knew that her life's work was beginning. She accepted shared responsibility for the welfare of 'the family firm'.

All the available evidence indicates that John Shakespeare's wife proved more than equal to the demands that life made on her. The public records tell us something of her story, but she left behind no personal papers to supplement the bare facts. It is not likely that she could write. Few women of the day could – not even those who, like her, grew up in a well-to-do home – though many could read. Her lack of schooling was not in any way unusual (see Chapter 4).

Between 1557 and 1580 she bore eight children. (See the Family Tree – Appendix 1.) Except the last, all these births occurred during the period in which the family was prospering and John Shakespeare was becoming increasingly influential in Stratford life. In 1576, things began to go badly wrong for the Shakespeares (see Chapters 4 and 5), and it was not until twenty years later that their position was restored by the triumphant career of their third-born child and eldest son.

Shakespeare's Birthplace as it was in 1769
the first printed view of the house in Henley Street

'The Birthplace', the Shakespeare house in Henley Street, provides a present-day visitor with vivid impressions of the lives spent there so long ago. It speaks with special eloquence of the woman on whom they all depended and whose responsibility for their welfare was unremitting in good and bad times alike.

The parlour, comfortable and spacious by Tudor standards, was reserved for use on Sundays and Saints' Days. The kitchen was the heart of the household. Here, meat was dressed and cooked; flour sieved, bread baked; husband, children, servants and apprentices fed; herbs from the garden, simples from the fields and hedgerows were dried and medicines were concocted; wine was made and beer brewed to stock the cool stone cellar; clothes were made, mended, washed and pressed – and all this by the labour of skilful hands.

John Shakespeare's workshop – now a museum – adjoined the family quarters, so his wife did not have far to go when she was needed there in his absence. Nor did food have time to cool when she summoned her husband and his assistants to the family meals.

From the kitchen, a staircase gives access to the upper rooms. Here, all the children were born; and here, some of them died, preceding their father and mother on the last journey to Stratford parish church.

After John's death in 1601 Mary continued to live in the family house. Grandchildren soon took the place of the children she had borne and brought up, for her married daughter Joan (her fifth child) and her husband, William Hart, moved in to share her home.

In September 1608 Mary died in the house in which she had lived for more than fifty years. She was buried in Holy Trinity churchyard; and a terse entry in the register rounded off her long and busy life: 'Mayry Shaxspere, wydowe'.

4

Early Years and Education

BY A LONG established and pleasant custom, Shakespeare's birthday is celebrated on 23 April – St George's Day. We cannot be sure that this traditional birth date is right, but we know by his baptismal record that it cannot be far wrong.

The register of Holy Trinity Church records the christening of *Gulielmus, filius Johannes Shakspere* (William, son of John Shakespeare) on 26 April 1564 – a Wednesday. If his parents observed the Prayer Book's recommended interval between birth and baptism (and there is no reason to believe that they did not) christening on a Wednesday would follow birth on the previous Friday, Saturday or Sunday. Therefore, since Sunday 23 April 1564 is just as likely to have been the date of his birth as either of the other two possible dates, we can happily accept the tradition that he was born on St George's Day.

He was the third child of John and Mary Shakespeare to be baptised in Stratford church, but Joan (1558) and Margaret (1562) died in infancy, a common fate then. (Later – in 1569 – another of their daughters was also christened Joan. She lived to be an old woman.) Their son William was lucky to survive his first summer, for the town was visited by the plague in July 1564. Before the cold weather came to check the pestilence two hundred Stratford people died of that highly infectious disease. A Henley Street neighbour, Roger Green, lost four children in that year's epidemic, but the Shakespeare family escaped the sickness.

For John and Mary Shakespeare the year of their first son's birth was marked by the good fortune that attended them through most of the first twenty years of their married life. John's business enterprises were flourishing. He was trading in barley, timber and wool, as well as processing leather and making gloves. (His wool dealing got him into a lot of trouble later on – see Chapter 5 – but he did well out of it for a time.) When his father died in the winter of 1561, he carried on the farming business at Snitterfield until he had the opportunity of disposing of the leased land on favourable terms. Fully occupied with his Stratford-based activities, he passed the Snitterfield lease to his brother-in-law, Alexander Webbe, who had married Mary's sister, Margaret Arden. Tightly-knit bonds linked the Henley Street establishment with relatives and neighbours in the surrounding countryside as well as in the town.

It was a hard-working but comfortable household for a child to grow up in; a buoyant place, in which signs of the father's growing importance were part of daily life. In the years before William's birth, John Shakespeare had advanced steadily through the lower ranks of borough offices, playing a more and more active part in civic life. His successful term as ale-taster was followed by service as one of Stratford's four constables. He and his three colleagues were responsible for organising and supervising the watchmen, whose duties included the unpopular night patrol and the enforcement of fire precautions. When turbulence erupted, as it often did, the constables and their men had to deal with street brawls and alehouse fights.

Just how dangerous things could get is illustrated by a fatal wounding that took place in 1602. Richard Quiney was then bailiff and, therefore, ultimately answerable for maintaining the Queen's Peace. While assisting the constables to quieten a band of armed and intoxicated men, he was so severely wounded that he later died of his injuries. Though nothing quite as bad occurred during John Shakespeare's spell as constable, on several occasions weapon-carrying and violent drunks had to be disarmed and arrested.

Jokes about lazy or stupid or corrupt constables and senile watchmen were popular in Elizabethan England. Nevertheless, everyday law and order depended on this rudimentary and locally organised 'police force'. It was the comic aspect of 'the Watch' that William Shakespeare exploited in *Much Ado About Nothing*, but he knew very well from family stories that Constable Dogberry's command to his reluctant subordinates – 'You are to bid any man stand, in the prince's name' – was often taken seriously, and obeyed.

Service as constable done, John Shakespeare was rapidly promoted. Five years before William's birth, he was elected a burgess. From 1561 to 1563 he was one of the two chamberlains who supervised the management of the property and income vested in the town council after the suppression of the Guild of the Holy Cross. Deputy at first, he then became the senior chamberlain and discharged his duties so well that he was asked to stay on as acting chamberlain when his term of office expired. He was at the centre of council business during a period when change was in the air. The new reign and the restoration of Protestantism presented the corporation with fresh tasks which it was diligent in performing and with increased opportunities which it was eager to seize.

There was a lot for him to do. Regular and frequent council meetings were held in the guildhall, starting at nine in the morning. While the plague was raging, the burgesses and the aldermen met in the guildhall garden to reduce the risk of infection, discussing there, among many other matters, ways of helping fellow townspeople made poor by the sickness.

Extra duties came his way on top of routine council business. Several expensive projects were in hand at the time. Work was being done in the Guild Chapel to make it suitable for Protestant services. Repairs were needed to the vicarage of Holy Trinity Church, and the buildings of Stratford school were being improved and extended. As chamberlain, John Shakespeare was responsible for the accounts and for seeing that the corporation got value for its money.

He did the work well and was rewarded for his efforts. The council had expelled one of its fourteen aldermen in 1564, and John Shakespeare was elected to fill the vacancy. His installation took place in September 1565, with all the pomp and ceremony usual on those grand occasions. From then on, he was no longer plain 'John Shakespeare'. As an alderman, he was entitled to be referred to in speech and in writing as '*Master* Shakespeare'. (Our modern 'Mr' is a contraction of 'Master', an honorific title to which in those days comparatively few could lay claim.) Other marks of dignity went with the office: an alderman's thumb-ring, and a black cloth gown faced with fur, worn in the guildhall, at church, and on all public occasions.

Then, in 1568 (when his son William was four), the council chose him as their bailiff. He was now Stratford's chief citizen, presiding at council meetings and influential in all civic business. He represented the town's interests in negotiations with the lord of the manor. He was responsible for the efficient working of the market and the fairs, taking final decisions on commercial matters that affected everybody, such as fixing the price at which corn was to be traded and bread and ale sold.

By virtue of his office, he became a Justice of the Peace, issuing warrants for the arrest of debtors and offenders against the corporation's byelaws. He presided over the Court of Record, which ranked as a Crown Court. He was Stratford's coroner and almoner too.

Master Shakespeare, who had now exchanged his alderman's black gown for the splendour of the bailiff's scarlet robe, was accorded all those ceremonial shows of public esteem that went with his position. On his official appearances and journeys – in the guildhall, at the market and the fairs, to and from church, where he and his wife occupied the bailiff's pew at the front of the nave – he was attended by the corporation's uniformed and mace-bearing serjeants. On the corporation's behalf, he entertained visiting preachers and other dignitaries. When the acting companies from London came to Stratford on tour he issued them with a licence to perform and, with his family, sat in the front row when they staged their plays.

Nor did he retreat into obscurity when his term of office as bailiff expired. His successor was his close friend and Henley Street neighbour Adrian Quiney, a mercer. The council elected Master John Shakespeare chief alderman and deputy bailiff to assist Quiney in what proved to be an efficient and harmonious partnership. In January 1572, for example, when William was getting on for eight years old, his father and Adrian Quiney set off for London to conduct borough business in the capital. They were given a free hand to proceed 'according to their discretion'.

Until 1576, John Shakespeare continued to play a leading and highly respected part in the civic life of Stratford. It is clear from the borough records that nobody worked more tirelessly or more successfully than he to advance the corporation's status and to increase its resources.

In telling the story of William Shakespeare's life it is essential to keep his father's remarkable career in mind. During his most impressionable years the boy grew up in a secure and prosperous household headed by a successful father busy with public affairs. Surrounded by tangible signs of dignity, his judgements respected, his opinions sought, his position acknowledged, Master Shakespeare was an impressive and influential man. Then, abruptly, when his son was in his thirteenth year, everything changed. Honours and security vanished as shadows do when the sun goes in.

It is evident from the public records of William Shakespeare's later life that this sudden reversal of his father's career (the details of which are set out in Chapter 5) made a long-lasting impression on him. As soon as he was in a position to do so, he used his own resources to restore to his father and mother the prosperity and esteem that had been theirs during the earliest years of his life. That accomplished, he steadily established for himself, his wife and his children a position of respect in the town in which his father had once been so eminent. The provisions of his will, made when his life was ending, demonstrate his concern to safeguard that position for his descendants.

It is not surprising that William Shakespeare's later conduct of his worldly affairs was influenced by his early experience of misfortune. Common knowledge of human nature is all we need to realise how deeply shocked the twelve-year-old boy would be when his secure home was threatened and his father was humbled. Diaries or letters, if we had them, might add to our understanding; but the plain, well-documented facts speak for themselves. At one period in the years of trouble, John Shakespeare, who in his heyday had been ceremonially escorted through the streets of Stratford, was reduced to hiding at home behind locked doors, in danger of arrest for debt if he ventured out.

It was not only on William Shakespeare's later actions that early experience of family misfortune left its mark. Its influence can be traced in his writings too. Without forgetting the dangers of attempting to discover the dramatist's 'real self' in his works (see Chapter 1), we can sometimes catch a glimpse of that elusive being if we keep the biographical facts firmly in mind as we consider what he wrote. In this particular matter, without indulging in flights of fancy, we can safely use our knowledge of what happened to Shakespeare's family when he was young to account for certain threads that persist throughout his works.

Impressions associated with his father's rise and fall surface in references and images used in his plays. For example, there is a memory of the splendid years in *Henry IV Part 1* where Falstaff protests that when he was Prince Hal's age he was so slender that he could have 'crept in any alderman's thumb-ring'. In *Romeo and Juliet* Mercutio describes the fairy Queen Mab as appearing 'in shape no bigger than an agate stone on the forefinger of an alderman'.

Certain habitual themes which run like deep undercurrents through his writing – comedies, histories, tragedies, poems, all alike – reflect attitudes implanted in an impressionable mind by youthful experience of change and loss. Many of the characters he created, young and old, princes and commoners, in happiness and in sorrow – it makes no difference – are acutely aware of the mutability of the human lot. Frequent images of inevitable change ('Fortune's wheel', 'the book of fate', 'the cup of alteration' – to give but three examples) represent the fragility of hopes always vulnerable to the unforeseen. People see themselves as 'Time's subjects' at the mercy of his 'fell hand'. They reflect on the hollowness of success; on the painful contrast between what we intend and what we achieve, between what things seem to be and what they really are; on the arbitrary bestowal of rewards and punishments; on the licence afforded to the great by a world that punishes the poor.

Such recurrent musings testify that the lessons learnt in his teens were never forgotten. The language in which King Lear denounces hypocrisy and injustice springs out of Shakespeare's memories of family misfortune thirty years before he wrote the play.

> Through tattered clothes small vices do appear;
> Robes and furred gowns hide all. Plate sin with gold,
> And the strong lance of justice hurtless breaks;
> Arm it in rags, a pigmy's straw does pierce it.

Though the Shakespeares of Henley Street never experienced the abject poverty of 'tattered clothes' and 'rags', they discovered the bitter consequences of no longer being entitled to 'robes and furred gowns'.

Some years after the family's decline began, William Shakespeare took up the career for which his genius so strikingly fitted him. A long period of very hard work and the shrewd employment of its rewards enabled him to put things right for his parents. The records of his actions tell us quite plainly what his motives were; and the personal attitude required to make such a sustained and single-minded effort is no mystery, either. To recover from that early blow, he had to maintain in all his dealings, both in London and in Stratford, the calmness and balance which Prince Hamlet – acutely aware of his own lack of those qualities – found so admirable in his friend Horatio:

> for thou hast been
> As one, in suffering all, that suffers nothing;
> A man that fortune's buffets and rewards
> Has ta'en with equal thanks; and bless'd are those
> Whose blood and judgement are so well commingled
> That they are not a pipe for fortune's finger
> To sound what stop she please. Give me that man
> That is not passion's slave, and I will wear him
> In my heart's core, ay, in my heart of heart,
> As I do thee.

Most young men find it not unattractive to be 'passion's slave' – for a time, at any rate; and William Shakespeare was no exception. It took him some effort to develop the remarkable degree of self-discipline evident in his maturity. The recorded events of his early manhood in Stratford suggest that his own 'blood and judgement' were far from being 'well commingled' at that period of his life. Then, pressed by adversity – in part of his own making – he found his way out, and the resolution to take it.

That same unwavering strength of purpose underpinned all that he achieved in the theatre. We are so dazzled by his creative genius that we overlook the hard slog and unremitting attention to detail without which he could not have sustained his prodigious output – and busy all the time with theatre management and personal business.

Before we follow him through his initial uncertainties and his years of success, we must return to the story of his childhood in his father's house, taking it up again in 1569, at a time when all was well with the family in Henley Street. Bailiff John Shakespeare's son is five – and ready for school.

The burgesses and aldermen of Stratford were entitled to send their sons to the town's excellent grammar school free of charge. The school – it still exists and still uses some of the buildings it occupied then – does not possess admission registers for the period of William Shakespeare's schooldays, but we know from other sources that sons of John Shakespeare's fellow councillors were there at that time – Adrian Quiney's son Richard among them. It is not rational to suppose that the bailiff of Stratford did not exercise this valuable privilege on his son's behalf. Moreover – and this fact clinches the argument – there is ample evidence in the works of William Shakespeare that their author had received the standard classical education provided by a Elizabethan grammar school. For a Stratford boy there was only one available source of an academic training of that kind – the town's own school.

Like other such schools in other English towns of that day, 'the King's New School of Stratford-upon-Avon' was an ancient establishment. It was called the 'new' school because it had been re-founded in 1553, in the reign of King Edward VI. The Guild of the Holy Cross had maintained a school there since at least 1403, but the town councillors took it over when the guild was suppressed. They maintained its buildings, paid the schoolmaster's salary and provided him with a house. That was why when John Shakespeare was chamberlain he had so much to do with the affairs of the school. He arranged for a new schoolmaster to move from Warwick to the well-paid Stratford post. He converted the old school into a residence for the master and his family, and he made a new schoolroom on the upper floor of the guildhall.

The grammar school offered many advantages to the children of the better-off townspeople. (The children of the poor – the vast majority – continued to receive little or no schooling of any kind.) Stratford's leading citizens, like their counterparts elsewhere, wanted the best possible education for their sons. The education of their daughters was quite a different matter. With marriage as the only 'career' open to them, most remained at home and were trained in domestic skills to fit them to run their own household in due course. They might be taught to read, if there was anybody in the family competent and willing to teach them, but if they grew up illiterate nobody worried. A few lucky ones went to a local 'charge-school' where, in return for a very modest weekly fee, they received a brief and rudimentary education.

Boys, however, had to make their way in a world that was offering new opportunities to well-educated people. The sons of men of John Shakespeare's generation needed an academic education of a kind that had neither been necessary for nor available to their fathers. Whether John Shakespeare himself could write, we do not know. He had to witness many borough documents and legal papers, but he never signed them with his name. Instead, he made his mark, using either a cross, or a symbol representing a glover's 'donkey' (a clamp on which gloves were stitched), or a drawing of a pair of compasses (used in designing patterns on gloves). This does not prove that he could not write. People who could write – Adrian Quiney is one known example – sometimes made their mark instead of signing their names. Professional writers (scriveners) were always on hand, so it may be that because John Shakespeare did not have to write much, he found it easier to draw a symbol than to write his name. However, it is very likely that as a child he was taught to read, but not to write. It was a common practice to insist that reading was mastered before writing was begun, and he would have had only a brief schooling at Snitterfield.

At any rate, his lack of formal education was no handicap to him in his career. His son may well have had a family joke in mind when, in *Much Ado About Nothing*, he caused Constable Dogberry to warn the literate watchman George Seacoal not to be proud of his accomplishments: '. . . for your reading and writing', says Dogberry, 'let it appear when there is no need of such vanity'.

But in 1569, in changing times, Stratford's chief citizens took a very different attitude to education. The sons of ambitious fathers were required to become fluent readers and writers – in Latin as well as in English. At the age of eleven, Richard Quiney wrote his father a letter in excellent Latin. Though it is unlikely that his proud parent could understand a word of it, at least it proved to him that the boy was being well taught.

The masters of Stratford school were good scholars, well qualified to provide a classical education and, since many of them were parsons as well, they gave their pupils a strict religious training too.

A scene in *The Merry Wives of Windsor* throws light on parental attitudes and on the teaching methods of the day. Mistress Page is taking her little son William to school when they meet Sir Hugh Evans, the schoolmaster. ('Sir' was a respectful form of address accorded to parsons, and Evans is a parson as well as a schoolmaster.) Rather annoyed when she discovers that the boys have been given 'a playing day', Mistress Page complains that her son is not making progress: 'Sir Hugh, my husband says my son profits nothing in the world at his book; I pray you ask him some questions in his accidence'.

There and then, in the street, the master puts his pupil through a test, asking him the sort of questions about accidence (Latin grammar) with which Elizabethan schoolboys were all too familiar. Not dissatisfied with his answers, Evans sends the boy off to play, but warns him to expect a flogging unless he improves his knowledge of pronouns. William Page's mother, who knows no Latin, is impressed by her son's ability to trot out answers she cannot understand to questions that mean nothing to her. Her complacent comment that William 'is a better scholar than I thought he was' signifies her approval of 'good Sir Hugh' (as she then calls him) and of his teaching.

It has often been suggested that the comic Welshman, Sir Hugh Evans, is Shakespeare's partly affectionate, partly mocking portrait of Thomas Jenkins, who taught him in the upper school. We cannot be sure of that. Like Evans, Jenkins was a parson, but he was not Welsh.

It is certain, however, that the Latin lesson in the play came straight out of Shakespeare's memories of his own schooldays. The questions the master asks and the answers he expects to get cover the same ground and are phrased in the same way as the questions and answers provided as models in the standard textbook (Lily's *Short Introduction to Grammar*), which the pupils had to learn by heart. The grammar drill that young William Page undergoes in the street in Windsor is the same grammar drill that young William Shakespeare learnt to master in the schoolroom at Stratford.

He spent his first two years in the 'petty class', where he was taught to read and write. In some towns, the beginners – 'the petties' – were taught in a separate 'petty school', but at Stratford they were taught in the grammar school buildings and put through their paces by an usher (under-master) who was sometimes assisted by one of the senior school pupils. As in the grammar school proper, the teaching methods were based on learning lessons by heart and then repeating them to the teacher. Failure to be word-perfect was severely punished. The usher's rod was used as frequently as the master's.

They began with the 'hornbook', so called because it had a thin sheet of transparent horn pasted over the printed text to protect it from rain and grubby fingers. From the hornbook they learnt the alphabet, printed in both capital and small letters, and the Lord's Prayer. They also learnt to build words from syllables, memorising vowel and consonant combinations.

Later, they practised reading and writing until they were fluent in

English. Many of their exercises were drawn from the Bible and the Book of Common Prayer, from both of which they learnt passages by heart, including the Catechism of the Church of England. They were also grounded in arithmetic and the rudiments of account-keeping.

To modern eyes, this basic education seems narrow; but it was thorough. What they were expected to learn, they learnt – the usher saw to that. Forced to pay close attention to the vocabulary and rhythms of passages of eloquent and vigorous English, they were challenged by models of prose composition when they practised their own writing.

Put through the protracted slog of the petty class, children of tender age and varied abilities would naturally respond in different ways. Since most of those who passed through it with William Shakespeare have left behind no record of their lives, we cannot generalise about its effects on them. We can, however, safely conclude that it did no harm to his creative potential.

On the positive side, we can trace throughout his work the influence of the great examples of written English which he was compelled to study, memorise, and take as his models. That part of his school training was reinforced by regular church-going. There, he heard readings from the Bible, recited responses, prayed aloud in Prayer Book English, and listened to the clear, direct language of the Homilies – official sermons read by the parson on Sundays and Holy Days 'by order of the Queen's Majesty' to inculcate religious conformity and political obedience.

Prepared by the petty class for the full rigours of the grammar school itself, he moved up into the first form of the lower school when he was seven. His school days began at six in the morning (an hour later in winter), starting with prayers in the Guild Chapel before the first school lesson. Morning school lasted until eleven. Afternoon school began at one and ended at five, with more prayers to round it off. There was a six-day school week. Holidays at Christmas and Easter were short, but there were occasional 'playing days' to break the grim routine.

Conditions were Spartan. The comfort of their pupils was not a consideration to which Elizabethan educators paid much attention. Hot in summer and cold in winter, the occupants of Stratford's big schoolroom pursued their studies in a cheerless environment. Heads bent over the books on their shared desks, they sat on rough benches. Candles provided a dim light in the dark winter months, each boy bringing one from home, just as he brought his day's contribution to the fuel for the one fireplace.

Discipline was rigid, and they had few opportunities for recreation.

There were no organised games, as we know them, but they were let out for brief and strictly supervised breaks when the younger boys whipped their tops while the older ones were made to compete in approved 'manly' pastimes, such as running and wrestling.

All the teaching was done in the one room. At one end, the master, his tall desk raised on a dais, presided over the upper school. At the other end, the usher taught the lower school. A curtain drawn across the middle of the room made an ineffective sound barrier between the two. Teachers and pupils alike were accustomed to working amid the drone of voices as the noisy succession of questions and answers rose and fell throughout the long school day. While the master and usher heard the answers of one form – sometimes given individually, sometimes chanted in unison by all its members – the other forms prepared their next lesson, getting ready for their own turn to be tested.

Young William Shakespeare spent four years in the lower school, getting down to the real business of his education, which was learning Latin. Like young William Page, he memorised Lily's *Grammar* and worked away at its drill until he was word-perfect. He acquired a copious Latin vocabulary by learning a dictionary by heart. He learnt Latin proverbs and moral sayings. He practised translation from Latin into English and from English into Latin, using biblical passages for the latter. He read Latin books, poetry as well as prose. He was taught to speak Latin – indeed, he was forbidden to speak anything but Latin in class and in the school yard. As a weekly exercise, he acted scenes from Latin plays. It is tempting to suppose that he found this the most enjoyable part of his gruelling lower school apprenticeship to learning.

In the upper school, Latin was still the dominant study. The master's teaching was based on the same methods as the usher's, so there was no escape from the daily demands of memorising and repetition. Even so, the advanced course offered lively-minded pupils some imaginative stimulus. Wider reading and more varied exercises were a welcome change after the monotonous grind of the lower school. They studied works by some of the greatest Latin authors: the satires of Juvenal; the narrative, reflective and lyric poetry of Virgil, Horace and Ovid. (Ovid was Shakespeare's favourite, to judge by the frequent echoes of that poet's work in his own writing.) Caesar and Sallust provided historical reading. Cicero was studied as a philosopher and a master of prose style.

Many hours of each school day were spent in learning to write good Latin prose. They composed letters, essays and speeches, modelling their grammatical constructions and rhetorical devices on those used by the authors they were reading. With constant practice and stern correction, many pupils were able to write correct and elegant Latin before their master had done with them.

They learnt to write verses in Latin too. Elizabethan teachers attached much importance to this exercise. They held that a scholar who was taught to write 'a smooth and pure verse' had been given a mental training that fitted him 'to comprehend a great deal of choice matter in a very little room'.

The same rigorous methods were later applied to teaching the boys Greek, which they started after they had proved themselves proficient in Latin. Their first textbook was the New Testament in Greek, passages from which were closely studied and translated. Few pupils attained in that language the high standard that most reached in Latin, but those who completed the final year in the upper school were well grounded.

Not surprisingly, the learning that Stratford school drilled into its pupils was not soon forgotten, even by those – and they formed the big majority – whose later careers were remote from academic interests. For the few in whose working lives a literary background was an asset, their time at school provided a sure and long-lasting foundation.

For example, Richard Field, son of a Stratford tanner, left school at fifteen and was sent to London to be apprenticed to the best printer in that city. When his master died, he took charge of the business and was himself recognised as outstanding in his craft by the time his former schoolfellow William Shakespeare arrived in the capital. (He printed Shakespeare's *Venus and Adonis* in 1593 and *The Rape of Lucrece* in the following year.) Field learnt the technical skills of printing during his apprenticeship, of course, but it was at Stratford school that he got the literary education required when dealing with authors' manuscripts.

An incident that occurred in the adult life of Richard Quiney provides more evidence of the school's efficient teaching. Quiney – whose schoolboy facility in writing Latin was mentioned earlier – was in London in 1598, negotiating with the Privy Council on behalf of Stratford corporation. Like his father, Adrian, and most of the Shakespeares' other friends he played a leading part in Stratford affairs. While he was there he received a letter from Abraham Sturley, another prominent Stratfordian, suggesting that he should try to interest 'our countryman Mr Shakespeare' (he was referring to William) in a Stratford property deal that Sturley and Quiney were planning. Sturley – a Cambridge graduate – wrote partly in Latin, a language that came easily to him and that he often used. The note-worthy point is that he did not hesitate to use it in an important business letter to Quiney who, as Sturley well knew, had received the whole of his education at Stratford school and had then set up as a draper (cloth dealer), spending all his working life in trade. Yet Sturley rightly assumed that Quiney would have no difficulty in understanding Latin, though some twenty years had gone by since he last sat in a classroom.

As that brief description of Shakespeare's education indicates, it was thorough. He was taught by scholarly men who followed the best theory and practice of the day and gave their pupils as good an education as was available anywhere at that time. As in all other Elizabethan grammar schools, the curriculum and teaching methods at Stratford were designed to fill boys with sound learning and to train them to be obedient and hardworking. Nowadays, it would be considered an intensely academic education, but the Elizabethans saw it in quite a different light. To them, it was an excellent preparation for life.

They did not expect pupils to go on from school to a university. Some did; but that was not the main aim. They believed that the long and disciplined labour required for a good grounding in classical studies was both intellectually and morally valuable. The mental effort needed to learn the Latin and Greek languages sharpened the boys' wits and made them industrious. The classical authors read at school were regarded as a fount of wisdom. Reinforced by biblical and prayer-book instruction, the close study of classical texts confronted young people with examples of virtue, noble thoughts about life and instructive instances of personal conduct and historical events – all expressed in language of unsurpassable eloquence, clarity and beauty. Exposed daily to such uplifting influences, how could able and willing pupils fail to benefit? And what could stupid or lazy pupils expect but a flogging to urge them on?

Quite simply, the educators intended to make their pupils better and more useful people. Nobody questioned the aim, and very few doubted the soundness of the methods used to achieve it. Elizabethan schoolboys were confidently expected to derive great benefits from the system. With a grammar school education behind them, they would be well fitted to occupy a respected place in society. They would be capable of conversing intelligently with their fellows, of understanding the laws of the land and the issues of the day. They would be aware of their duties to God and the Queen.

We need not suppose that all parents fully understood or bothered overmuch with the high terms in which the educators expressed their ideals. It was enough for them that the new grammar schools were available to their sons. They firmly believed that their children would be up to no good if they were allowed to be idle. They were quite sure that learning – even if they had little themselves – was a good thing for boys and that beating was an effective way of encouraging them to acquire it.

What is more, they understood very well that educational attainments had become a useful means of advancement. A man did not have to be high in the land or busy with great affairs to profit from a grammar school training. Educated citizens now had an advantage in trade and in a variety of skilled occupations. They were likely to become influential in local matters and adroit in civic business.

This very practical concern is well illustrated by a letter written to a schoolmaster of the day by the father of one of his pupils. Complaining that his son 'comes on never a whit', the aggrieved parent added: 'He also writes such false English that he is neither fit for trade nor any employment wherein to use his pen'.

Parents may not have understood all the values claimed by the educators for their system, but they went along very heartily with the belief expressed (in 1558) by the founder of one of the new schools: 'The wealth [of the] public is advanced and maintained . . . by virtuous education'. By sending their sons to grammar schools they reckoned that they were giving them a good chance of obtaining a personal share of the enhanced public wealth.

It is all very well for educators and parents to have firm opinions about what is good for schoolchildren, but the pupils themselves are more often aware of the disadvantages of school than of its theoretical blessings. Shakespeare's references to schooldays indicate that he did not recall his own with affection. Certainly, he resisted the common temptation to sentimentalise about them when they were over. His recollections are never nostalgic. They evoke the drudgery and harshness of the schoolboy's life with a realism that shows where his sympathies lay. When his allusions to pupils and their teachers are comical, the joke is usually at the expense of the latter.

The best-known of all his references comes in *As You Like It*, where Jacques describes

> . . . the whining schoolboy, with his satchel
> And shining morning face, creeping like snail
> Unwillingly to school.

A year before he wrote those words, William Shakespeare had taken possession of New Place. His fine house was separated from the Guild Chapel and the grammar school only by the narrow width of Chapel

Lane. Whenever he was at home, the 'shining morning faces' of schoolboys passing its windows were a reminder of the years when he and Richard Quiney made their daily journey from Henley Street to school. It was at most a ten-minute walk and, however slowly they went, they could not long put off the dreaded moment when they must present themselves for morning prayers and the beginning of yet another school day.

He generally displays teachers in an unflattering light. His pedagogues are fussy, self-important, ludicrous figures as a rule. Nor do their pupils' parents show up much better. They pack their sons off to school and encourage their masters to put them through the educational mill, complacently assuming that it must be good for them. The Latin lesson in *The Merry Wives of Windsor* is very funny, but it is the schoolmaster and the parent we laugh at, not the pupil. Their self-congratulatory behaviour is comic, but there is nothing funny in William Page's unenviable situation. Commanded to demonstrate that he has profited from his lessons, and in danger of a flogging if he fails to jump through the hoops his teacher holds up, he is not ridiculed, as the adults in the scene are.

To give just one more instance, *Love's Labour's Lost* is much concerned with the folly of those who confuse mere book-learning with wisdom. The pedagogue Holofernes (who 'teaches the boys the hornbook' and grounds them in Latin) is one of the characters used to get that theme across to the audience. Proud of his erudition, Holofernes has a comic trick of using Latin words instead of English. Then, for the benefit of the 'unlettered', he explains each of his learned expressions with a string of synonyms. His peculiar style of speaking parodies the method pupils had to use when making oral translations from Latin:

> The deer was, as you know, *sanguis*, in blood; ripe as a pomewater [a popular kind of apple], who now hangeth like a jewel in the ear of *coelo*, the sky, the welkin, the heaven; and anon falleth like a crab on the face of *terra*, the soil, the land, the earth.

Accustomed to ruling in his classroom, Holofernes is ludicrously unaware that his pedantic attitudes and habits, unchallenged there, make him a figure of fun when he steps outside his little kingdom.

A boy with a quick mind and a good memory could get through his education without frequent punishments, but it was often a doleful experience, even for apt pupils. To judge by the tone and content of his allusions to schooldays, Shakespeare recalled them as a time of tribulation. For example, in *The Two Gentlemen of Verona* Speed tells Valentine that he has learnt 'to sigh like a schoolboy that had lost his

ABC'. In *Coriolanus* the hero describes his blurred eyes as filled with 'schoolboys' tears'.

School life is associated with hardship, constraint and monotony. Schoolboys are little different from conscripts or beasts of burden, longing for freedom. Their happiness begins when school ends and they are released from servitude. All these ideas come together in this description of the dispersal of disbanded soldiers (in *Henry IV Part 2*):

> Like youthful steers unyoked, they take their courses
> East, west, north and south; or like a school broke up
> Each hurries toward his home and sporting-place.

Even so, William Shakespeare's schooldays were far from barren. He never refers to them with pleasure, but it was the teaching methods and the repressive regime that he disliked, rather than the content of his studies. By the time he left school he was proficient in the Latin language and well read in its literature. He could speak Latin, write it, and – most importantly – he had learnt to appreciate the great poets, dramatists, historians and philosophers whose works played so large a part in the upper school curriculum. With that academic and literary background, he was as well educated as most of the people who became his theatre colleagues or social acquaintances.

Ben Jonson's famous lines to Shakespeare's memory (printed in the prefatory pages of the First Folio) include the statement that he 'had small Latin and less Greek'. That remark has often been quoted as evidence that Shakespeare's education was deficient, but the argument is faulty. Jonson was a learned man. By his standards, few people then (or later, for that matter) were erudite in classical scholarship. There is a touch of complacency in Jonson's reference to the fact that his great rival had not attained his own lofty height of academic learning, but his tribute to Shakespeare lacks nothing in warmth and admiration. He salutes him as the

> Soul of the Age!
> The applause! delight! and wonder of our Stage!

Moreover, he expressly claims that Shakespeare outshines the mightiest authors of Greece and Rome, describing him as the dramatist 'To whom all Scenes of Europe homage show'. Had he regarded Shakespeare as being ill-educated, it is hardly likely that Ben Jonson, himself a most thorough scholar, would have drawn that particular comparison – and certainly not in those terms.

Jonson's awareness that Shakespeare's stock of academic learning was no greater than that of most educated people did not lead him to question the authorship of the plays; nor did he suppose that anyone could think it a plausible reason for doing so. Like all Shakespeare's other colleagues and associates in the theatre, and like all contemporary commentators on the literary scene, Jonson recognised that his works do not display any remarkable amount of learning. They include many references to the history of Greece and Rome (some of which were readily accessible in popular English books) and they contain numerous images and ideas that echo classical authors; but none of this book-learning was uncommon among people with a grammar school background. The classical writings on which Shakespeare drew were the standard texts of Elizabethan classrooms.

Yet, granted that Stratford school gave him no more – and no less – than the education such a school existed to provide, what he learned there was crucial to the later blossoming of his artistic life. Like all his schoolfellows, William Shakespeare was the first of his family to receive a thorough, formal, education. Like them, he came from a non-academic background, and entered a different world when he entered school – a world in which he was forced to concentrate all his mental faculties on the study of language and the development of linguistic skills. From an early age, daily practice in translation into and from English focussed his attention on vocabulary and syntax. Progressively, his studies demanded higher standards of precision, more sensitive responses to verbal subtleties, greater command of varied styles. No bad training that, for one whose life's work was to be the use of words. Close study of great writing instilled a love of literature and fed his imagination. The sources of his plays and his references to past and contemporary authors tell us that he remained a quick and eager reader all his life. All in all, whatever his criticism of it, he got a good deal out of school.

Furthermore, his education – working on what all the evidence shows was a genial temperament – brought him the priceless advantage of easy converse with people of varied social backgrounds. The Elizabethans valued civilised discourse and the arts. The Queen herself – exempt from the restrictions that denied academic education to women – was widely read. Her learning and her enthusiasm for music, poetry and plays set standards for her court and for theatrical London. Without his grammar school education, Shakespeare would have been hopelessly handicapped when he first attempted to make his way in the London theatre. Without it, indeed, such an enterprise would not have been open to him. No uneducated tyro could expect a hearing in that brilliant and sophisticated world, whatever talents – even genius – might be buried within his unlettered mind.

It is not known for certain when William Shakespeare left school. Most pupils left at the age of fifteen, but the evidence suggests that his father, needing his help at home, withdrew him at fourteen. By that time he had completed three years of the advanced curriculum in the upper school and, in the circumstances in which John Shakespeare was then placed, neither father nor son may have seen much point in his beginning the final year of study.

Judging by what we know of his attitude to the school regime, early leaving offered him release from much that he disliked. On the other hand, his prospects were not good. As far as could then be foreseen, his last walk back from school to his father's house in Henley Street led him into an uncertain and insecure future.

5

Troubled Times and a New Life

THE NATURE of John Shakespeare's misfortunes is plain. His business affairs became entangled, and he was short of the ready money he needed to sort them out. This prosaic explanation is firmly based on the evidence of mortgage deeds and court cases. The facts derived from these sources (some of them quite recently discovered) have discredited the romantic and once-popular theory that he was heavily fined for refusing to attend public worship out of loyalty to the old faith.

It is, of course, true that people who would not take part in the services of the Established Church for religious reasons – 'recusants', as they were called – could suffer crippling financial penalties. As the struggle with Spain intensified, fears of plots against the Queen increased. Roman Catholics were regarded as potential traitors, so attendance at Protestant worship became a test of political reliability.

It is also true that John Shakespeare's name did appear in a list of Stratfordians who had been absent from services at Holy Trinity Church. Religious scruples were not, however, the only reasons for non-attendance. The Stratford churchwardens listed John Shakespeare with some of the other offenders in a special category: 'We suspect that these nine persons next ensuing absent themselves for fear of processes'. In other words, he and the other eight special cases stayed away from church not on conscientious grounds but because they were afraid of being arrested for debt if they left the safety of their homes. They were insolvent, not subversive.

The notion that John Shakespeare voluntarily incurred financial hardship is not at all convincing. Everything we know about his career argues strongly that he was not the kind of person to jeopardise his worldly prospects by making idealistic gestures.

Nor can the supposition that he was a Roman Catholic and was penalised for it be a credible explanation of his abrupt withdrawal from civic life. That happened in 1576, when – having been for many years a most diligent and capable councillor – he ceased to attend council meetings. Yet fellow members of Stratford council who were known to be 'papists' continued to play an active part in borough affairs. They avoided disqualification by making token appearances at public worship, thus observing the letter if not the spirit of the law. There were no compelling religious reasons to prevent John Shakespeare from adopting that common course of action unless, quite out of character, he had suddenly become so strict in his beliefs that he was ready to sacrifice his material interests for his faith. In all his years of civic office, including his time as bailiff, he had never allowed his religious convictions – whatever they may have been – to keep him away from church or council when custom, ceremony, or the law of the land called for his presence.

His colleagues on the council knew perfectly well that it was financial embarrassments that prevented him from attending, and they tried to make things easier for him. For example, they let him off the fines that other absentees had to pay. They halved his contribution to the military levy. (A year later, he still could not pay it.) They excused him the weekly payment that aldermen made towards the relief of the poor, resolving that 'Mr John Shakespeare . . . shall not be taxed to pay anything'.

It is clear that his many friends on the town council hoped he could solve his business problems and resume public life, for they kept him on the list of aldermen for ten years. At last, in 1586, they decided that he must be replaced because, as they recorded in their minutes, 'Mr Shakespeare doth not come to the halls [attend council meetings] . . . nor hath not done of long time'.

John Shakespeare's financial difficulties did not become public knowledge until 1576, but they had been in the making for some time before that. His glover's business and his wife's inheritance had made him prosperous, but he outstretched his resources by getting involved in too many activities – and some of his enterprises were very risky.

An energetic and ambitious man, he gave a lot of time – more than most councillors felt able to give – to borough affairs. In addition to whittawing and gloving, he traded in timber and barley. He dealt in property too. (Only a short time before he was known to be in trouble, he bought two more houses in Stratford and leased fourteen acres of land near his brother Henry's farm.)

On top of all that, he became heavily committed to wool trading, a venture that strained his finances and trapped him into prolonged and expensive lawsuits. There was money to be made in the wool trade, but it had its own particular risks.

An early Stratford tradition described him as having been a wool dealer as well as a glover, and Stratfordians referred to the eastern wing of his Henley Street house as 'the Woolshop'. Proof that wool had been stored there came during nineteenth-century restorations of that building, when large quantities of wool combings were found under the floorboards. Documents that have come to light since then reveal the extent of his dealings. He was a wool trader in a big way.

For example, the records of the Court of Common Pleas show that in 1599 John Shakespeare sued John Walford, a clothier of Marlborough (in Wiltshire), for a debt of £21. That sum was owing to him for a consignment of wool he had supplied to Walford. It was a lot of money – just over half the price that John Shakespeare had paid for the two Stratford houses he bought in 1575. To make matters worse, Walford had kept him waiting for his money for thirty years! A debt of that size, outstanding for so long, was a serious drain on finances that were often stretched to their limit.

Further proof of large-scale wool dealing has been found in the Exchequer Court records. In 1572, John Shakespeare took the opportunity of buying 300 tods of wool at a price well below the going rate. (Wool was sold by 'the tod' – a bale weighing 28lbs. So, in present-day terms, he bought nearly four tonnes of this cut-price wool.) If all went well, of course, he stood to make a handsome profit when he sold it. Even so, he had to lay out £210. That was ten times the sum that Walford owed him. To put it another way, he could have bought another five houses for the money he risked on the wool.

In later life, William Shakespeare drew on his memories of his father's wool dealing and put them to comic use in *The Winter's Tale*. The Clown in that play is a shepherd's son, and when he first appears he is trying – unsuccessfully – to work out the value of the wool that has just been sheared from his father's flock.

> Let me see . . . every tod yields pound and odd shilling; fifteen hundred shorn, what comes the wool to?

'Pound and odd shilling' was the standard price of a tod throughout most of John Shakespeare's time in the trade. The secret of success was to buy below and sell above that mark.

There was one big difference between the shepherd's activities in the play and those of John Shakespeare in real life. The former – a producer – was selling wool legally. The latter – a dealer – was buying and selling wool illegally, because he was not 'a merchant of the Staple'. By Tudor law, only merchants of the Staple were permitted to deal in wool, and it was a serious offence to infringe their monopoly. This law, like most others then, could not be strictly enforced. John Shakespeare was just one of many people who made (or lost) money on illegal wool deals. They ran considerable risks. There was no civil service or police force (in the modern sense, that is) to keep an eye on traders, but 'private enterprise' informers were always ready to make money by denouncing offenders. They received half of any fines that were imposed. Quite often, they did a deal with the law breakers, collecting a bribe in return for keeping quiet. Either way, an informer could make a nasty hole in a trader's profit.

John Shakespeare's wool bargains of 1572 were reported to the Exchequer Court by a man called James Langrake, who got his living as an informer. He was not a Stratford man, but news of these large-scale deals reached him at his home in Northamptonshire.

In regulating the wool trade, as in other matters, Elizabethan law was inconsistent, haphazard and tardy. John Shakespeare finally took Walford to court for a thirty-year-old debt, but the business deal for which Walford owed him money was itself illegal. He was also involved in moneylending, another potentially profitable but precarious business. There were strict laws against 'usury' – lending money at interest. Yet people borrowed and people lent; and everybody knew that it went on. It had to. Traders of all kinds needed capital to finance their deals. Even so, moneylenders operated in a twilight world, providing an essential service but always liable to denunciation and prosecution.

In 1570 John Shakespeare was twice denounced for moneylending. In each case he had advanced large sums. On the first occasion the informer was Anthony Harrison of Evesham in Worcestershire, who swore that Shakespeare had made a loan of £100 at twenty per cent interest. On the second occasion the tireless busybody Langrake swore that he had lent out £80 at twenty-five per cent interest. The result of the first case is not on record, but Langrake's accusation cost John Shakespeare a heavy fine – forty times greater, in fact, than the fine he had paid for tipping rubbish in Henley Street in his less adventurous days.

To the Elizabethans, as to us, moneylending presented acute and unresolved moral problems. They were no better able than we are to settle the conflict between ethics and expediency. When William Shakespeare wrote *The Merchant of Venice* he dramatised a fiercely-debated public issue – and one that also lay very close to home.

It is an interesting reflection of those times – and a comment on how little some things change – that neither John Shakespeare's wool trading nor his moneylending harmed his reputation in Stratford, though everybody there knew about them. The wool deal with Walford took place quite openly while he was bailiff. He was denounced for moneylending just one year before he and Adrian

Quiney went to London on corporation business. Offences such as his in the grey areas of commercial life were far too common to damage his standing. He lost his eminent position in the town not because he was known to be cutting legal corners, but because he was known to be desperately short of money. The situation was well understood by everyone: while Mr John Shakespeare's finances were unsound he must make shift to live in obscurity as best he could. He was in the same predicament that Shylock was to face when stripped of his wealth:

> You take my house when you do take the prop
> That doth sustain my house; you take my life
> When you do take the means whereby I live.

Fortunately, John Shakespeare was never driven to such straits that he had to sell his Henley Street house, but he had to part with his house in Greenhill Street. He also had to mortgage most of his wife's inheritance to raise much-needed money: a house and land in Wilmcote; a share of two houses and land in Snitterfield. Nor, pushed as he was, did he get loans large enough to reflect the value of the mortgaged property or to give him more than a short breathing-space. All his creditors clamoured for their money as soon as he was known to be hard up. To add to his troubles, several people he had helped with financial guarantees got into difficulties. His pledges were called in, and he had to honour them or go to jail: £20 on behalf of a hatmaker in Nottingham; £10 forfeited bail for a Stratford tinker; another £10 for his brother Henry's debts.

He survived somehow. He had his glover's business to fall back on, though trade was not what it had been. The whole of the midland region was then experiencing a slump, and Stratford could not escape the consequences. In the circumstances, John Shakespeare could count himself lucky to hold on to what remained of his property. Things might have been worse for the Henley Street household; but at the time the fourteen-year-old William was taken away from school there was little reason to believe that they could get much better.

We do not know for certain what William Shakespeare did immediately after leaving school. The Stratford tradition that he became his father's apprentice was recorded by Nicholas Rowe as far back as 1709. Numerous references in the plays to the technicalities of leather-working and glove-making can be cited to support this belief; but, since he had heard talk of such matters from childhood, they do not prove that he had an apprentice's training. However, nothing has been discovered to cast serious doubts on the tradition. It would have been sensible for John to teach his son the craft by which he had himself prospered in earlier years. When trade picked up again, William would have the means of making his living. In the meantime, he could help out with the work, and he would be on hand to run errands when the risk of arrest kept his father indoors.

Bearing the attitudes of the day in mind (see Chapter 4), we should not imagine that either father or son would have regarded a craft apprenticeship as a poor outcome of a long academic education. William Shakespeare was simply following in the footsteps of most of his schoolfellows. To give just two examples: the after-school career of the apprentice draper Quiney and that of the apprentice printer Field were certainly not considered to be a waste of their excellent education.

The problem for the Shakespeares was whether William's apprenticeship could eventually help to pull the family's affairs round. In the circumstances, it was as good a start in life as he could hope for, but it would be years before he was able to stand on his own feet. Nor was it at all clear how, even when he had served his time, his assistance in the workshop would do much to improve John Shakespeare's own position, encumbered as it was with debts and lawsuits.

In the event, young William Shakespeare did not wait long enough to see what apprenticeship would lead to. He left home to embark on a daring venture, full of risk and excitement.

It was a rash act of his own that forced him to change course. At the end of 1582, when he was not yet able to keep himself, he became responsible for the support of a wife and – soon afterwards – a child. Having thus added more dependents to the already-burdened family, the young husband decided that he could not solve either his own or his father's financial problems by remaining in Stratford. He must try his luck elsewhere.

He was eighteen when he married Anne Hathaway. She was twenty-six, and pregnant by him – their first child, Susanna, was born six months later. It has been supposed that he was trapped into marriage by a woman eager to get herself a husband before it was too late. (Most Elizabethan women were much younger when they married.) That, however, is mere guesswork; and so is the often-repeated assertion that their marriage was unhappy.

The fact is that we know nothing about their feelings for each other at any time of their lives. Clearly, it was imprudent of him to marry when he did; but there is no point in raking through his plays and poems in search of 'evidence' that they did not (or did) get on well together. For every line that has been quoted to 'prove' that he repented of his hasty step another can be quoted to 'prove' that he did not. Even the famous 'second best bed' bequest to her in his will (see Chapter 10) is not conclusive either way. It has been trotted out to show that she lost his affection, but it can be used with equal plausibility to show that he continued to love her dearly. We do not know whether he was faithful to her or not, for it is by no means certain that the 'Dark Lady' of the Sonnets ever existed; and all the other stories about his supposed love affairs are mere anecdotes and of doubtful ancestry.

We do know that when he lived in London he returned frequently to join his wife in Stratford. We do know that he finally left London and lived with her in New Place, where she spent most of her married life. We do know that she continued to live there after his death, sharing the house with her daughter Susanna and her husband John Hall. We do know that on 8 August 1623 she was buried in a grave next to her husband's in the chancel of Holy Trinity Church.

Anne Hathaway lived at Shottery, a hamlet about a mile away from Stratford. She was the eldest daughter of Richard Hathaway, a farmer. Richard, who married twice and had children by both of his wives, died a year before Anne's marriage. He left her a useful sum of money to be paid out on her wedding day.

A visit to Anne Hathaway's Cottage is a pleasant part of the Stratford tourist ritual, but the term 'Cottage' is more romantic than accurate. The building is a substantial farmhouse in which a large family were able to live comfortably. The Hathaways were not as well connected as the Ardens – the family into which John Shakespeare had married – but they were of good standing. If, as has been freely conjectured, William's father objected to the courtship during the summer of 1582, it was not because the prospective bride came from an unsuitable family, but because the prospective bridegroom had no money – and no immediate likelihood of earning any. The legacy that Anne was to receive on her wedding day would not keep a married couple for long.

Before the year ended, however, Anne's pregnancy overcame whatever opposition there may have been. As a minor (under twenty-one in those days), William could not marry without his father's permission, so it was in John Shakespeare's power to prevent the marriage. Since neither he nor his wife wished to condemn their unborn grandchild to bastardy, he gave his consent.

Instead of waiting for their banns to be published in church on three successive Sundays or Saints' Days (the usual procedure), they obtained a marriage licence from the Bishop of Worcester. Marriage by licence was not uncommon. It was a quicker way to the altar, available to couples who had relatives or friends willing to act as sureties. The bishop's court would not issue a licence until those sureties signed a bond, promising to indemnify the bishop and his legal officers should the marriage prove to be unlawful.

Their marriage licence – which had to be given to the clergyman performing the ceremony – has not been found, but the marriage licence bond has been preserved in the archives at Worcester. Dated 28 November 1582, it states that William Shakespeare and Anne Hathaway have received the bishop's permission to marry after one 'asking' (publishing) of their banns. It names Fulk Sandells and John Rychardson as the sureties who will forfeit the large sum of £40 if the marriage is later proved to have been illegal. The two men named as sureties were Shottery farmers. Old friends of Anne's dead father, they now demonstrated their concern for his daughter in this very practical way.

The Worcester archives also contain a register in which the transactions of the bishop's court were recorded. The granting of the Shakespeare marriage licence was duly noted in that register, but the clerk made a careless mistake. To be fair to him, he had a great many matters to record. The court had been very busy that day, dealing with over forty cases – one of which concerned a person named William Whateley. When the clerk made the Shakespeare entry he confused the names. He got the bridegroom's name right, but he called the bride 'Anne Whateley'. It was not the only mistake he made when recording names on that occasion, and his blunder with Anne's surname was no worse than some of his others. (In one case he wrote 'Darby' instead of 'Bradeley'.)

Though it is in itself of no great importance, the clerk's error has excited a lot of attention and has been used to support a wholly fanciful theory about the marriage. According to this elaborate and much-publicised fantasy, woven around the scribe's easily-explained slip, William Shakespeare was trying to back out of his obligation to Anne Hathaway. 'Anne Whateley' – so the story goes – was the name of 'the woman he really loved', and he got a licence to marry her so that neither Anne Hathaway nor her Shottery friends, nor his own father, would be able to force him into a marriage he no longer desired.

Few, if any, guesses about William Shakespeare's feelings for Anne Hathaway can be given much credence, and this particularly silly bit of theorising collapses when it is set against the known facts. In the first place, there is no proof that 'Anne Whateley' ever existed. 'She' was created by a clerk's blunder. In the second place, because he was a minor, William Shakespeare could not himself get a marriage licence.

It had to be obtained for him by others, with proof of parental consent and the provision of sureties. In the third place, the marriage licence bond proves that John Shakespeare gave his consent to his son's marriage to Anne Hathaway – *not* to 'Anne Whateley'. (Since his motive was to ensure the legitimacy of his unborn grandchild, it is foolish to suppose that he would have assisted William to desert the pregnant Anne for some other bride.) Finally, the marriage bond proves that the two Shottery men stood sureties for William Shakespeare's marriage to Anne Hathaway. They would not have accepted that responsibility if they had any reason to doubt the bridegroom's good faith.

We do not know when or where the wedding took place, but the first big event of their married life was recorded in the register of Holy Trinity Church. 'Susanna daughter to William Shakespeare' was christened there on 26 May 1583. Within another two years their family was increased – and, as it proved, completed – by the birth of twins, a boy and a girl. On 2 February 1585 their christening was entered in the same register: 'Hamnet and Judith son and daughter to William Shakespeare'.

The twins were named after their parents' friends Hamnet Sadler, a Stratford baker, and his wife Judith. Later on, the Sadlers returned the compliment by naming their son William. The friendship was lifelong. When William Shakespeare died in 1616 he left Hamnet Sadler money to buy a mourning ring in his memory.

In 1585, however, money was a pressing problem for the young husband – not yet twenty-one when the twins were born. With no income of his own, he had a wife and three children to support. Even if John Shakespeare's finances had been sound, William would still have been in an awkward situation. In those days, a son was not expected to marry until he was able to leave his father's house to set up an independent household. A married man's place was at the head of his family, bringing up his children under his own roof. For everyone's sake, he had to find some way of ending his dependence on his harassed father.

Apart from one brief reference, his name does not appear in the public records during the seven years between 1585 and 1592 – 'the Lost Years', as they are often called. He is mentioned in a legal document dated 1588 as having joined with his parents the year before in an attempt to raise money by increasing the mortgage on the Wilmcote land his mother had inherited. As their eldest son, and by then of age, he was legally involved in the fate of the Shakespeare property. That fleeting glimpse reveals that the family was still in difficulties in 1587; but after that we are short of hard information until, in a publication dated 1592, he is clearly identified as a rising star of the London theatre.

The nature of that publication is described in Chapter 6, where its immense contribution to our knowledge of Shakespeare's life is explained. Before that, however, we must look at some of the attempts that have been made to fill in the gap of 'the Lost Years'. We begin with some of the myths that were once popular, but to which little credit is now given.

Early biographers told colourful stories about his supposed deeds between 1585 and 1592. According to some, he loafed about the Stratford countryside, associating with heavy drinkers and assorted ne'er-do-wells. Others told how he took to poaching and fled to London to escape punishment. Once there, said others, he organised a horse-minding service for theatre-goers and did so well that he was able to buy his way into an acting company. Two more recent guesses were that he became a lawyer's clerk, and that he enlisted as a soldier and fought against the Spanish army which was trying to subdue the rebellious Dutch. No reliable evidence has ever been found to support any of those stories.

Amid all this unlikely speculation, one thing is clear: he must have begun to work with actors on a regular footing some considerable time before 1592, by which year we know that he had established himself as a popular dramatist. Nobody – not even William Shakespeare – could have become successful in the highly-competitive world of the London theatre without professional training. So, at some time before 1592 (and most probably after the twins were christened) he left Stratford to become a learner (or 'improver') with a troupe of players, seizing opportunities to act with them and write for them whenever they considered that their new apprentice was up to it.

(Charles Dickens's hero Nicholas Nickleby was in a similar position when he joined Vincent Crummles's acting company. In the novel, the fictitious dramatic apprentice gets on at an astonishing rate; but his real-life predecessor wasted no time, either. As the established chronology proves, William Shakespeare made rapid strides in the career that he adopted at some date before 1592.)

How Shakespeare got his start is not yet known. Some scholars suggest that he arrived in London as a newly-joined member of an acting company called Strange's Men. It must be emphasised that this is only a theory, but until it has been disproved it deserves to be considered with an open mind.

Its starting-point is a tantalisingly brief statement by the writer John Aubrey (1626-97), who collected material about the lives of several eminent people, including Shakespeare. Aubrey was not always reliable. (He was responsible for transmitting the 'calf-killing' story – see Chapter 1.) However, some of his information came from William Beeston, an actor, whose father, Christopher Beeston, had been one of Shakespeare's colleagues. Christopher Beeston started his acting career with Strange's Men. He later joined the Lord Chamberlain's Men, the famous company for which Shakespeare was then acting and writing plays. It is on record that the two men were on stage together in 1595, performing in Ben Jonson's play *Every Man in his Humour*.

So there is no doubt that Christopher Beeston knew William Shakespeare professionally and could well have had reliable information about his early career leading up to his success in London – especially if (and it remains an 'if') they both began acting with Strange's Men. Unfortunately, Christopher Beeston's knowledge of Shakespeare comes to us indirectly. We cannot be sure that his son had an accurate memory of what his father told him; and we cannot be sure that John Aubrey made an accurate note of what William Beeston passed on to him.

According to Aubrey, William Beeston's father said that Shakespeare taught for a time before he became an actor. Consequently, when referring to Ben Jonson's statement that Shakespeare 'had small Latin and less Greek' (see Chapter 4), Aubrey made this comment: '. . . he [Shakespeare] understood Latin pretty well: for he had been in his younger years a schoolmaster in the country'. (By 'in the country', Aubrey meant that Shakespeare's teaching experience took place somewhere other than in London or Stratford.)

Because Aubrey gave no further information (and because he was sometimes an uncritical reporter of mere gossip) modern biographers of Shakespeare have regarded the schoolmaster theory with great suspicion. Finding nothing to confirm it, they have generally treated it as being just another of the Shakespeare myths. It has never quite gone away, however, and scholars have re-examined it from time to time. In recent years, some well-qualified researchers have given it serious attention, building a new theory on it. As they themselves recognise, their ideas fall short of proof; but their work cannot be ignored.

In bare outline, this is what they suggest. When he first left school, William Shakespeare *may* have become a tutor in the household of a wealthy Lancashire landowner called Alexander Hoghton. He *may* then have entered the service of another Lancashire magnate called

Sir Thomas Hesketh. While in Hesketh's employment, he *may* have joined Strange's Men and gone to London with them when they returned to the city after completing an acting tour in Lancashire.

They base those theories on some well-established facts. In 1579 (not long after Shakespeare left school) a Lancashire man called John Cottom became the master of Stratford school. Cottom's family owned an estate ten miles away from where Alexander Hoghton lived, and the Cottoms and the Hoghtons knew each other well. Cottom left Stratford and returned to live in his Lancashire home in 1582, the year of William Shakespeare's marriage.

In his will, Alexander Hoghton requested Sir Thomas Hesketh 'to be friendly unto Fulk Gillom and William Shakeshafte now dwelling with me and either to take them into his service or else to help them to some good master'.

Sir Thomas Hesketh was an enthusiastic supporter of the drama. He maintained his own private band of entertainers – servants of his who were acrobats, jugglers, musicians and actors.

Hesketh was on friendly terms with the greatest of all the Lancashire landowners, the Earl of Derby, and was often his guest. Derby and his son Lord Strange were patrons of the professional London players called Strange's Men. From time to time, that acting company visited Derby's great house and put on plays there.

Given those facts, the theoretical linking of William Shakespeare with Hoghton, Hesketh, and Strange's Men is not implausible. Summarised point by point, this is how the argument goes:

1. The 'William Shakeshafte' named in Alexander Hoghton's will and described as 'now dwelling with me' was in fact William Shakespeare. The name 'Shakespeare' was written in many different forms (as names often were then). The following variants are among those on record: Shakspear, Shakspere, Shackspere, Shaxberd. It is certainly not impossible that Hoghton's 'Shakeshafte' was just another version of 'Shakespeare'.

2. William Shakespeare became a tutor in Alexander Hoghton's household in the following way. When John Cottom arrived in Stratford to take up his post, the Shakespeare family's difficulties were well known in the town. Wanting to help a former pupil of the school, and knowing that he was well educated, Cottom recommended William Shakespeare to his friend Alexander Hoghton.

3. When Hoghton died, Sir Thomas Hesketh took William Shakespeare into his service, as his friend had requested. In Hesketh's household Shakespeare had plenty of opportunities to act with and to write for Hesketh's private company of players. He soon discovered that acting and writing were more to his taste than teaching.

4. Through Hesketh, Derby and Strange, William Shakespeare became known to Strange's Men on one of their visits to Lancashire. He persuaded them that his talents were worth encouraging. They took him on, and when they returned to London he went with them.

It is an attractive theory. If it could be proved, it would account very neatly for what Shakespeare was doing in 'the Lost Years'. It would vindicate John Aubrey's schoolmaster story and, most importantly, it would explain how Shakespeare obtained the professional theatre training that he must have had before 1592.

However, it has *not* been proved – yet. There are two stubborn obstacles in its way. First, there is no conclusive evidence that Alexander Hoghton's 'William Shakeshafte' was really William Shakespeare. The surname 'Shakeshafte' was not uncommon in Lancashire. In fact, several people called William Shakeshafte are known to have been living there at the relevant time, and one of them could have been the person named by Hoghton.

The date of Hoghton's will – 1581 – is the other obstacle. The wording of his request to Hesketh suggests that the 'William Shakeshafte now dwelling with me' had been in his service for some time – long enough for Hoghton to form a high opinion of him and to take special interest in his future welfare. William Shakespeare was seventeen in 1581 so, according to the Shakeshafte/Shakespeare theory, he must have become a tutor in Hoghton's household at about the age of sixteen. That is not impossible. We know of others who began to teach (as tutors or as ushers – *not* as masters) very soon after leaving grammar schools.

But, if William Shakespeare went into Hesketh's service after Hoghton's death in 1581 and then joined Strange's Men, as the theory claims, how did he come to be living in Stratford in the summer, autumn and early winter of 1582? We know that he was, because – as the records prove – that was the period in which he courted and married Anne Hathaway.

And again, even supposing that he was not in Stratford when his first child, Susanna, was born, and did not attend her christening there in May 1583, he must have been back at home with his wife during the summer of 1584. The twins were christened in Stratford church on 2 February 1585, and it is going beyond all probability to suppose that their mother had been living with her husband in Hesketh's Lancashire household nine months earlier.

As its proposers admit, the theoretical 'Lancashire connection' is very much weakened by established chronological facts. There is no doubt that William Shakespeare was sharing in family life at home in

Stratford at times when, if the theory were watertight, he would have been occupied elsewhere – first, with Hesketh's private players in Lancashire; then, with Strange's Men in Lancashire and in London.

It remains most probable that he left Stratford to begin his new life some time after the twins were christened. Exactly when, and exactly how, we do not yet know; but we do know that, in his circumstances, a fresh start had become imperative.

Financially, he had nothing to lose when he decided to leave Stratford; and he took a calculated risk in choosing an actor's life as a way out of his pressing problems. Dramatic entertainment – of many different kinds – occupied people's leisure time in those days as television does now. Joining a professional acting company offered him the chance of getting a living in a job that catered for popular taste. Indeed, it offered him the prospect of considerable reward if he had the talent to succeed and the stamina to survive.

Although the professional theatre was a London-centred industry, enthusiasm for plays and players was widespread and shared by people of all ranks. Only Puritans remained aloof. Play-going was a national pastime for which there were daily opportunities in the capital and by no means infrequent ones in the provinces.

In Stratford, as elsewhere, amateur performances were popular. The town council encouraged them and sometimes contributed to the expenses of 'shows' staged at holiday times. In 1583, local enterprise was rewarded when a man by the name of Davy Jones was paid for putting on 'a pastime at Whitsuntide'. Davy Jones was connected by marriage with both the Quineys and the Hathaways, so it is tempting to suppose that William Shakespeare may have taken part in this entertainment. Whether he joined in on that occasion or on others, the celebration of festivals by dressing-up, dancing, music and play-acting was a familiar and much-loved part of his Stratford background. There are many references to it in his plays. In *The Two Gentlemen of Verona*, for instance, Julia (disguised as a page) remembers that:

> When all our pageants of delight were played,
> Our youth got me to play the woman's part,
> And I was trimmed in Madam Julia's gown.

In *A Midsummer Night's Dream* the carpenter Peter Quince and his company of 'hempen homespuns' stage their 'interlude before the Duke and the Duchess on his wedding-day at night'. In *The Winter's Tale* Perdita, dressed for the revels, wonders at her transformation from shepherd's daughter to 'mistress o' the feast':

> Methinks I play as I have seen them do
> In Whitsun pastorals: sure this robe of mine
> Does change my disposition.

These popular seasonal entertainments, staged on temporary 'scaffolds' in the streets and inn yards or raised up on a platform in the guildhall, gave William Shakespeare an early taste for drama. Other experiences too had worked on him by the time he turned his mind to a career in 'show business'.

In 1575, the Earl of Warwick entertained Queen Elizabeth at Kenilworth Castle. For nearly three weeks of that summer the Tudor love of spectacle was sensationally gratified by expensive and elaborate 'triumphs', delighting the queen and crowds of her subjects who thronged the grounds throughout her visit. Fireworks illuminated a pageant on the lake, where a cunning contrivance displayed 'Arian on the dolphin's back' (to quote the sea-captain in *Twelfth Night*), with oars for fins and swimming to accompanying melodies. So closely do Shakespeare's references to Arian and the dolphin (in *A Midsummer Night's Dream* as well as in *Twelfth Night*) tally with contemporary descriptions of the show that it is hard to believe that Mr John Shakespeare (still in that year a respected alderman) did not take his eleven-year-old son to see the sights. They were the talk of the town, and many a Stratford citizen made the twelve-mile journey to Kenilworth.

When Shakespeare was fifteen, the craft guilds of Coventry staged performances of the famous 'Coventry cycle' of Mystery plays. It was one of the last times that these plays were put on, but their memory endured. The medieval tradition of dramatising religious and moral teaching left its mark on the 'new' theatre and, though we do not know whether he saw the Coventry plays, we do know that their echoes reverberate in his own works, especially in his Histories.

Nor was he without an academic grounding in dramatic theory and structure. Close study of the great Latin dramatists was an important part of the school curriculum; and in their weekly dramatic exercises (see Chapter 4) the boys learnt something of the actor's craft as they attempted to 'suit the action to the word, the word to the action' (*Hamlet*).

Of all the early influences that attracted Shakespeare to an actor's life by far the most important was the experience of watching professionals at work. Stratford was a regular pitch for London companies on tour. Their visits were eagerly awaited, and well-enough rewarded to ensure that they were repeated.

Each time they came they had to give their first performance to an audience of town worthies, including the bailiff. It was his duty to satisfy himself that their bill of fare contained no seditious or morally offensive material. If he approved of their programme – which might include a dumb show (miming), an interlude, a jig, or songs and dances blended into 'a gallimaufry of gambols' (*The Winter's Tale*) – he paid them a subsidy from corporation funds and licensed them to entertain the public. The players' presence in town was a time for celebration, and the streets and inn yards were packed for their performances.

The Queen's 'Interluders' came during John Shakespeare's bailiffship. He awarded them four shillings from the corporation chest and licensed them to play in public. Other companies followed and, as the Stratford account books show, satisfied his successors that they were unlikely to corrupt the morals of the town or to lure its people away from their allegiance to the crown and the church.

Throughout William Shakespeare's boyhood the London theatre was making rapid advances; and by the time he was a young married man and wondering how to earn his living, it was highly organised and sophisticated. The actors who came to Stratford in 1583/4 (three companies were there in that one year) were polished performers of plays that far surpassed the cruder material presented by earlier troupes.

Three years later, in the twelve months from December 1586, five companies played in the town. Among them were the best that London could boast. The Queen's Men (successors to the old Interluders) were there, flaunting their scarlet uniforms. They made the greatest stir and were the most handsomely rewarded, receiving twenty shillings from the corporation, quite apart from the collections they took from the crowds. The famous clown Richard Tarlton was with them. Described as 'the wonder of his time', and celebrated for 'his wondrous, plentiful, pleasant, extemporal wit', he had only to appear to

> Set all the multitude in such a laughter,
> They could not hold for scarce an hour after.

Popular idol as he was, Tarlton was just one of half-a-dozen leading actors in that company whose exploits on the London stage were talked of in Stratford, as in every other town they visited. Nor were the other touring troupes short of stars. The Queen's Men were at the top just then, but Leicester's Men and Essex's Men (two of the other companies in Stratford that year) were formidable rivals. The actors' fame went before them, and they played to enthusiastic fans who discussed their respective merits long after they had moved on.

Professionalism of such a standard could not fail to excite any young man fired by the possibility of a theatre career, and it must be assumed that William Shakespeare made himself known to some of the players on one of their Stratford visits. We are not able to state positively that he did do so; but it is nonsensical to suppose that he turned up in London without having previously convinced theatre people while they were in Stratford that he was worth a trial.

Nothing is known of the arrangements he was able to make with them. It does not seem to have been their practice to sign on new 'hired hands' while they were on tour, so any formal engagement was probably deferred until he had satisfied them of his usefulness during a probationary period in London. Certainly, he had to begin as a hired man. Membership of an acting company required capital, and he had none.

Nor do we know whether he was given his opportunity in 1583/4 or in 1586/7. At either of those times there were plenty of professional players in Stratford to take notice of an eager would-be actor and writer, greatly gifted, though as yet untried. Some of his biographers think that the earlier date is the more likely. With a wife and three children to support, and with his father's situation deteriorating, William Shakespeare could not afford to hang about. The sooner he made a new start the better. Others maintain that is was the star-studded year of 1586/7 that convinced him that his time had come.

Whichever it was, one thing is sure: he started to learn his new craft not much after 1586/7, at the latest. He was a fast worker, we know, and a quick learner; but thorough training was a prerequisite for success in the fiercely-competitive London theatre. He could not have won the reputation he had gained by 1592 without first putting in some years of hard graft.

℘ 6 ℘

'Now in London Place Him'

So, in *Henry V*, the Chorus bids the audience, reliving in 'winged thoughts' the king's triumphant return to London after his great victory at Agincourt. Shakespeare's own place in London at the time he was writing that play is known from a strictly factual – and distinctly unpoetical – source of evidence. Two other districts in which he lived and the dates of his residence in them have also been identified.

The London tax commissioners' returns show that he was resident in the parish of St Helen's, Bishopsgate in 1596/7. (By then, he had made his reputation as a leading playwright.) They show, too, that by October 1598 he had moved south of the Thames and was living in the Liberty of the Clink, Southwark. (His company, the Lord Chamberlain's Men, opened their splendid new theatre there the next year, and *Henry V* was one of the plays that gave the Globe a flying start.)

He stayed in Southwark for about four years and then moved back north of the river to lodgings in Cripplegate, a quieter district at the north-west corner of the city wall. The Liberty of the Clink and the neighbouring Liberty of Paris Garden – both outside the jurisdiction of the Lord Mayor and the city corporation – were noted for their theatres, bear-baiting gardens and brothels. Attracting crowds of pleasure-seekers, they were often noisy and sometimes riotous places.

Richard Field (Shakespeare's former Stratford companion and, later, the printer of *Venus and Adonis* and *The Rape of Lucrece*) lived in Wood Street, Cripplegate, with his French wife, Jacqueline. They were near neighbours of the Mountjoys, French Huguenots, who occupied a comfortable and spacious house at the junction of Silver and Monkswell Streets. Not far away lived two of Shakespeare's chief colleagues in the Lord Chamberlain's Men, John Heminge and Henry Condell – the former a sidesman and the latter a churchwarden in the parish of St Mary's, Aldermanbury. Cripplegate, with its respectable citizens and fine buildings, offered a writer a more peaceful environment, so it is not surprising that Shakespeare, knowing of the Mountjoys through the Fields, moved into the accommodation they had available in 1602. He was close to friends and not too far away from the Globe. For relaxation, he had the Mermaid Tavern in Bread Street. (William Johnson, the landlord, was well enough known to Shakespeare to be his trustee when he invested money in a Blackfriars property in 1613.) St Paul's Churchyard, where the booksellers had their stalls, was only a short walk away.

It is from the Belott-Mountjoy lawsuit (see Chapter 2) that we learn of Shakespeare's residence in Cripplegate. Christopher Mountjoy was a thriving man, a maker of fashionable head-dresses. (Queen Elizabeth bought one of his expensive creations.) The Mountjoys' only daughter, Mary, married their apprentice, Stephen Belott, in 1604. Later, Belott complained that Mountjoy had cheated him in the matter of Mary's dowry. William Shakespeare was required to give evidence, for he had been involved in making the match. Joan Johnson, who had been a servant in the Mountjoys' house when the marriage negotiations were in hand, was called as a witness. She testified that 'the defendant [Christopher Mountjoy] did send and persuade one Mr Shakespeare that lay in [who was living in] the house to persuade the plaintiff [Stephen Belott] to the same marriage'.

In his deposition Shakespeare agreed that he had presented Stephen Belott with arguments in favour of marrying Mary Mountjoy. He also agreed that Mountjoy had promised Belott 'a portion' but, so long after that event (he was giving his evidence in 1612), he could not remember how much Mountjoy had bound himself to pay. Nor could he remember any agreement that Mountjoy's will would contain a bequest to the Belotts.

Although Shakespeare's testimony was of little use to either Belott or Mountjoy, the papers in the case are of great interest to his biographers, fixing his residence in Cripplegate between 1602 and 1604. His relationship with the Mountjoys (simply that of ordinary good neighbourliness) reveals nothing of that 'inner life' which so many have tried to reconstruct. Nevertheless, the affair and its attendant circumstances throw some light on the manner in which he lived his London life.

In particular, his decision to move from Southwark to Cripplegate bears out what other sources tell us of his self-protective habits. Like all public entertainers, then and now, he was under pressure. Actor, manager and writer – he was all three at this period of his life – he met the demands his company made on him, but he contrived opportunities for quietness. Cripplegate offered him a domestic retreat from the hubbub of theatre life.

According to John Aubrey, Shakespeare also lived in Shoreditch for some time. Aubrey claimed to have Christopher Beeston's authority for saying that (see Chapter 5). His statement lacks the documentary support that establishes beyond doubt that Bishops-gate, Southwark and Cripplegate were Shakespeare's London addresses at successive periods. Still, Shoreditch would have been a likely district for him to find lodgings in when he first arrived in London. It was the site of the two theatres with which he was closely associated at the beginning of his career – the Theatre and the Curtain.

Aubrey added to his Shoreditch information a note that Shakespeare was known for his abstemious habits when he lived in London. (Theatre folk were notorious for their heavy drinking, and many a promising career was blighted by it.) Beeston, said Aubrey, recalled that his famous colleague 'was not a company keeper' and 'wouldn't be debauched'. He said that when Shakespeare was invited to join a drinking bout, he politely but firmly declined, excusing himself on the grounds that he was unwell. It rings true, chiming in with what we know of his residence in Cripplegate. A sociable drink and talk at the Mermaid was one thing; but 'heavy-headed revel' (*Hamlet*) was not congenial. For him, as for Octavius Caesar (*Antony and Cleopatra*):

> It's monstrous labour when I wash my brain
> And it grow fouler . . . .
> I had rather fast from all four days
> Than drink so much in one.

After Stratford (or any other town in England) the vast scale of London and the hectic pace of life there might well have distracted any young man lacking the clear-sighted plan and firm resolve with which William Shakespeare arrived. The evidence shows that he kept a steady head. It shows too that, whatever the precise details of his arrangements with the players may have been (see Chapter 5), he had made sure of a starting-point from which – unless both he and they had been much mistaken about his talents and his determination – he could realise his ambitions. Like Clopton before him (see Chapter 2) he came to London knowing exactly what he wanted. Like Clopton, too, having weighed his chances carefully, he bent all his energies to his chosen task. In the great diversity of London, all sorts and conditions of men discovered their opportunities; and for Clopton the merchant and Shakespeare the player it proved to be their 'new-found-land'.

Teeming, exciting, wondrous, wealthy, squalid, dangerous London was the seat of royal government; the legal, ecclesiastical, intellectual, cultural and commercial hub of the kingdom; a busy port and trading centre, 'the storehouse and mart' of England; a citadel. Its distinct but proximate quarters were landmarked by great edifices at once serving and symbolising its varied functions: the Palace of Westminster, the Abbey, the aristocrats' great houses, the Inns of Court, the City Wall, St Paul's, the Guildhall, the Royal Exchange, London Bridge, the Tower.

The following description of 'Paul's Walk' (the aisle of St Paul's Cathedral – then not only a place of worship but also a business centre where deals were done, servants hired, fashions displayed) captures the atmosphere of life at the heart of the city. John Earle's impressions were not published until 1628, but they match those of other observers, foreign and English alike, who described the stirring, ebullient London of Shakespeare's day. It is, wrote Earle:

. . . the land's epitome. It is more than this, the whole world's map, which you may here discern in its perfectest motion, jostling and turning. It is a heap of stones and men. The noise in it is like that of bees, a strange humming or buzz mixed of walking tongues and feet; it is a kind of still roar or loud whisper. It is the great exchange of all discourse, and no business whatsoever but is here stirring and afoot.

And there were good reasons for the self-confidence that was in the air of Shakespeare's city. The struggle with Spain – 1588 was Armada Year – fuelled a growing nationalism and a pugnacious belief that England was more than equal to that mightiest of empires. In an expanding world, there were new countries to be discovered and exploited; and in London financial resources were readily mobilised and men recruited for daring and profitable ventures. Nor were their conquests wholly material. The sciences and the arts flourished as growing wealth brought increased leisure. Medicine and astronomy emerged from their medieval wrappings. English poets challenged the giants of Greece and Rome.

But if it was a time of hope and ambition, it was also filled with conflict and contradiction. Old ways died hard, as new ideas were born. Innovation and tradition clashed in politics, economics and religion. Idealism and cynicism, brutality and compassion, wealth and poverty, beauty and ugliness went hand in hand.

The Globe and the Bear Garden were near neighbours. The spiked heads of traitors on London Bridge grinned down at crowds homeward bound from *Hamlet*. Public executions drew bigger audiences than the biggest playhouses could hold. 'Sweet Thames' ran 'softly' in Edmund Spenser's verse: in reality, it was a common highway and a sewer. The Town Ditch, once famed for its cresses, was filled with general rubbish and butchers' offal. Overcrowded and insanitary, London within the wall housed two hundred thousand people, their numbers held in check by annual visitations of the plague, and by relentless overspill that robbed the open country to the north of its rural peace.

The tensions of London life were manifest in the hostility between court and city. The Lord Mayor and his council often did not see eye to eye with the royal government. Jealously guarding their privileges, the citizens resisted every encroachment on their right to manage their own affairs in their own interests. In particular, they resented attempts to regulate their economic freedom. Their freebooting attitude to private gain caused trouble between master and man, too. Sporadic prentice riots disturbed the peace. The apprentices' anger was sometimes directed against rapacious employers, sometimes against foreigners – Hollanders, Huguenots or Jews – made scapegoats when the cry of 'Clubs' was raised, and citizens barred their doors and closed their shutters.

As for the players, they and the city authorities lived in a state of mutual hostility. Grave, money-grubbing men objected to the frivolities with which the players wasted people's time. Puritan preachers gave them godly reasons for suppressing 'the filthy play' that will 'with a blast of trumpet sooner call thither a thousand than an hour's tolling of the bell bring to the sermon a hundred'. Constantly denounced to the Queen's Privy Council for abuses, real or trumped-up, the players protected themselves by seeking court favour and the patronage of aristocratic grandees.

Yet, at times of national crisis, an exhilarating patriotic fervour forged these often warring interests into a unity against which, it was believed, no earthly power could prevail. In *King John*, ironically, it is the Bastard who speaks for all 'true-born Englishmen' and voices this stirring sentiment when, in the final scene of the play, the nobles promise fealty to the dead king's son and heir to the throne:

> This England never did, nor never shall,
> Lie at the proud foot of a conqueror,
> But when it first did help to wound itself.
> Now that these her princes are come home again,
> Come the three corners of the world in arms,
> And we shall shock them. Nought shall make us rue,
> If England to itself do rest but true.

King John (c. 1590) was one of Shakespeare's earliest plays, written when he was making his name. In *Henry V*, eight or nine years later, he delighted audiences at the Globe with another eloquent expression of the national unity to which they aspired. They applauded an imaginative presentation of the ideal, while knowing only too well how rarely it was approached. In the real world, outside the magic of the theatre, England too often 'did help to wound itself'; but a ringing declaration that things need not be so stirred a warm glow of pleasure. Mundane considerations faded during 'the two hours' traffic of our stage'. Inspired, if briefly, by a vision of what had been, Shakespeare's Londoners themselves experienced the shared resolve and patriotic pride with which their imaginary forebears welcomed home their hero-king:

> But now behold,
> In the quick forge and working-house of thought,
> How London doth pour out her citizens –
> The mayor and all his brethren in best sort,
> Like to the senators of th'antique Rome,
> With the plebeians swarming at their heels,
> Go forth and fetch their conquering Caesars in.

Among all the varied aspects of life in this crowded, turbulent, thrusting London, its theatres held a foremost place. Foreign visitors described them as superior to any then to be seen in Europe's other great cities, and commented on the high quality of the plays and on the large numbers attending the daily performances. The theatres, the acting companies and the audiences are described in Part II of this book. Here, however, we need to sketch in the situation as it was when William Shakespeare arrived in the capital.

The theatre industry was already well established. Throughout the sixties and seventies, regular performances were given at various inns noted for dramatic entertainment: the Bull in Bishopsgate Street, the Red Lion and the Boar's Head in Whitechapel, the Bell and the Cross Keys in Gracechurch Street, the Bel Savage on Ludgate Hill.

Then, in 1576 (when Shakespeare was still a schoolboy) James Burbage – 'the first builder of playhouses' – built the Theatre in Shoreditch. He had to borrow money to do it but, as he rightly foresaw 'continual great profit' from the venture, he had no difficulty in raising the capital. In the next year a second theatre, the Curtain, opened – also in Shoreditch and not far from Burbage's. The establishment of the two permanent playhouses did no harm to the innyard performances. The demand for drama was increasing and there were audiences wherever plays were staged. More theatres opened during Shakespeare's first years in London; but from the day he began there were plenty of outlets for his work if he could get its merits recognised.

There was also formidable competition for a beginner to face. Written in 1587 (before any of Shakespeare's plays had been staged) Marlowe's *Tamburlaine* took London by storm when, with Edward Alleyn in the title role, it was performed at the Rose by the Lord Admiral's Men in 1590. Part 2 of *Tamburlaine*, followed in rapid succession by *Faustus* and *The Jew of Malta*, established Marlowe at the pinnacle of success.

Marlowe was by no means the only star of the day, though he burned most brightly. He was one of a group of writers known as the University Wits whose innovations transformed the old-fashioned drama of the sixties and seventies. Traditional interludes and sprawling chronicles, staple diet of those earlier years, gave way to well-shaped, energetic plays, full of fine lines for the actors to declaim. As the group name implies, Christopher Marlowe, Robert Greene, Thomas Lodge, John Lyly, Thomas Nashe and George Peele were all university men who chose to work amid the excitements of the London stage rather than in the safety of the professions – the church, the law, schoolmastering – customarily followed by graduates.

Just before and during Shakespeare's dramatic apprenticeship they were creating the new drama. He learned much from them, especially from Marlowe, whose influence is strong in his early tragedies and histories. Marlowe's poetry and his violent death – he was killed in 1593, brawling over a tavern bill – are remembered in *As You Like It*. There is a quotation from his narrative poem *Hero and Leander* in Phebe's words:

> Dead shepherd, now I find thy saw of might,
> 'Whoever loved, that loved not at first sight?'

Touchstone refers to the circumstances of the 'dead shepherd's' killing when he exclaims that misunderstanding 'strikes a man more dead than a great reckoning in a little room'.

If he learned much from their work, Shakespeare also learned much from the lives of these brilliant but often unfortunate men. Pockets full of money today, deep in debt tomorrow, they were a byword for their roistering, feckless ways. Temperamentally, he was never much at risk of falling into dissolute habits, but he recognised that they were exploited by theatre managers, and he took care not to fall into that trap. Even those, such as Marlowe, who were closely associated with one acting company (the Admiral's Men in his case) never fully reaped the benefits of their work. Selling their plays outright, they received no other rewards. A good play by a well-known writer could fetch a tidy sum, but it was soon spent and there was no more to come until another had been written. Philip Henslowe, who controlled the Rose, conducted his business affairs with writers in a wholly unscrupulous way. We know about him from his famous *Diary*; but there is no reason to suppose that his behaviour was untypical. By dribbling out subsidies, he kept his playwrights going, binding them to him with loans and ensuring that they remained on his far from generous payroll. Little wonder that the writers were themselves driven to all sort of tricks – one of which was to sell the same play to two different companies. Feasting, starving, quarrelling, drinking and whoring, they got themselves and the theatre a bad name with the city fathers who, in any case, needed little excuse to damn it as a corrupter of morals.

When his chance came to do so, Shakespeare put himself on a very different footing. That chance did not come at once. He worked – both as an actor and as a writer – for three different companies during his earlier years in London. He then joined a company formed by the hard-headed impresario James Burbage (see Chapter 7). When Burbage's sons made their daring move from the Theatre in Shoreditch to the Globe on Bankside, Shakespeare went with them, as actor, principal dramatist ('ordinary poet' was the term used) *and* as a shareholder in the company.

Before that could happen, he had to prove his worth. Then, having done so, continue to prove it, year in and year out supplying his acting company with crowd-pulling plays. His great success and his enduring worldwide fame make it hard for us to realise just how precarious a career it was that he followed. From first to last, a cool head, hard work, technical mastery of his craft – and good fortune – were no less important than his abounding creativity.

Like his fellow dramatists (then generally referred to as 'poets') he got his living 'in the quick forge and working-house of thought' by providing entertainment for all kinds of people, high and low, rich and poor, educated and ignorant: citizens, apprentices, artisans, lawyers, gallants, courtiers – the Queen herself and, later, James I. Belonging neither to the court nor to the city, yet closely involved with and dependent on both, he was exposed to the fickleness of audiences, the rivalry of competitors, the political dangers of the times that made his occupation especially hazardous. In the inescapable conditions of their working lives he and all his colleagues were well aware of the risks that had to be run.

In 1599-1601, for example, Shakespeare's company (the Lord Chamberlain's Men), like all the other well-established professional troupes, was given a severe jolt by competition from 'the children's companies'. These were bands of boy actors, trained at the Chapel Royal, St Paul's choir and some of the London schools, who played to exclusively better-class audiences at the lawyers' Inns of Court, at the first Blackfriars Theatre, in aristocrats' houses and at the Queen's court. Their somewhat academic plays were written by dramatists who felt superior to those who wrote for 'the common stages', and the boy actors' speeches satirised the popular poets and scoffed at their audiences. In *Hamlet*, Shakespeare made his own response to these 'little eyases that cry out on the top of the question and are most tyrannically clapped for 't'. The Prince reminds them that in all likelihood they will themselves become 'common players', and he points out that 'their writers do them wrong to make them exclaim against [denounce] their own succession [their own future occupation]'.

Eventually, the adult companies saw off the competition; but they had to take the 'eyrie of children' very seriously, for their satire made 'many wearing rapiers' afraid to attend the public theatres. Some of the Globe's better-off (and higher-paying) patrons stayed away until 'the war of the theatres' died down.

Then again, there was always the danger of falling foul of moral and political censorship. For his part in a 'lewd' and 'seditious' play (*The Isle of Dogs*) Ben Jonson was sent to prison for two months in 1597. Its principal author, Thomas Nashe, bolted before he could be arrested. Others who merely acted in it were imprisoned. That one play (it was a satire on the state of England) caused the Privy Council to decree 'the final suppressing of stage plays'. They were not suppressed – the Queen and many of her courtiers and ministers were much too fond of plays to want to put a stop to them – but the episode gave players, writers and managers a nasty shock and reminded them of limits not to be crossed.

In 1601 the Lord Chamberlain's Men themselves sailed perilously close to the wind, though through no fault of their own. On 8 February the Earl of Essex launched a crazy and swiftly-terminated rising against the Queen. He thought that Londoners would support him. They did not. The day before the rising, Shakespeare's company put on a performance of *Richard II*, the subject of which is the deposition of a monarch. (It was not a subject of which Queen Elizabeth approved at any time – 'Know you not that I am Richard II?' she once angrily exclaimed.)

Not surprisingly, the government wanted to know why that particular play had been staged on that particular day. Augustine Phillips, a principal member of the company, had to do the explaining. He was questioned by a panel of three judges, presided over by the redoubtable John Popham, then Lord Chief Justice and renowned for his merciless grilling of suspects. However, Phillips managed to satisfy Popham and the others that the players had been innocent of all knowledge of the impending rising when, at the request of some of Essex's friends, they had agreed to perform *Richard II*. He explained that they had been reluctant to put it on because it was an old play and might no longer attract a big audience; but they had been paid a subsidy of forty shillings by Sir Gelly Meyrick, one of Essex's confederates. That sum, plus their takings at the theatre door, made the proposition attractive.

The judges concluded that, although Meyrick and the others wanted the play performed for its propaganda value, the players were not to blame. As far as they were concerned, it was a straightforward business deal.

They were lucky. Like Essex and several others, Meyrick was executed; but the Lord Chamberlain's Men got off scot-free. Indeed, they came out of it rather well in the end. The Queen wanted to take her mind off the whole sorry business and, at her command, they performed for her at court the night before Essex went to the block.

To a greater or lesser extent, the players came to terms with hazards of the kinds just described. They had to. By the very nature of their calling, they stayed tuned to popular taste – or went under. At once forming and following theatre fashion, they satisfied their audiences' hunger for novelty while gratifying their habitual delight in well-known themes and familiar modes of presentation. Shakespeare and his colleagues had no high-faluting notions about their job or their relationship with their customers. They 'kept to the road-way', never too much ahead of nor too much behind the hankerings of the people who paid good money to be entertained. They were always mindful that (as Samuel Johnson put it, a century-and-a-half later):

> The Drama's Laws the Drama's patrons give,
> For we that live to please, must please to live.

Those words occur in Johnson's prologue, spoken by the great actor David Garrick at the opening of the Drury Lane Theatre. Garrick's predecessor, the player-poet William Shakespeare, never forgot that he 'must please to live'. Recognised today as a universal genius, he is often – and understandably – seen in a rarefied light: idealised as 'the prophetic soul / Of the wide world dreaming on things to come' (*Sonnet 107*). It is a misguided approach to his life and work. We get closer to him by reminding ourselves that in his own day, and in his own eyes, he was the 'ordinary poet' of the Lord Chamberlain's Men and one of their actors. He was also their greatest asset because his swiftly-written plays consistently drew the crowds, and he never lost his popular touch. The enthusiasm with which audiences flocked to see *Much Ado* was typical of the response he got throughout his working life:

> let but Beatrice
> And Benedick be seen, lo in a trice
> The cockpit, galleries, boxes, all are full.

As for the perils of infringing the censorship, they were understood and avoided as far as possible. The players knew that they had to submit new plays to the scrutiny of the Master of the Revels, a royal officer, He licensed them for performance, and charged a hefty fee for doing so. Generally, if a play had been 'allowed' it could be safely put on – provided that any passages struck out by the Master of the Revels were not surreptitiously slipped back into the actors' parts. That happened; but they knew the risks. Sometimes, too, they cut corners by staging a play before it had been allowed. Like all bureaucratic departments, the Revels Office was often dilatory. Again, they were aware of what they were doing and took a chance. Their worst difficulty was that they could never be certain that an allowed play would not at some time bring moral or political controversy down on them. When that happened, it was usually the result of complaints by the city authorities. Those implacable enemies of the players lost no opportunity of making life hard for them and they could often find objectionable matter in speeches that the Master of the Revels had winked at.

Worse than any of those threats to their livelihood was the repeated menace of the plague. Every time the plague-bill (a weekly list of deaths from that terrible disease) went above a certain level the Privy Council closed the theatres at the request of the city corporation. It was a sensible measure to reduce the risk of infection; and it was also a handy weapon for the corporation to use in its vendetta against the theatres. The puritanical council lobbied tirelessly for the lowest possible level of plague deaths to trigger closure. At one time, they contended that fifty deaths a week from *all* causes for three consecutive weeks should be the limit. Such a stringent regulation would have put paid to London's theatres. With a population the size of that city there were few weeks in the year when at least fifty deaths from age, accident, murder, suicide and illnesses other than the plague were not recorded. The players countered with the not unreasonable proposal that fifty deaths in any one week from the plague alone should be the agreed signal that the sickness had become an epidemic. Until that level was reached, they argued, the theatres should be permitted to remain open. The Privy Council settled for a figure of between thirty and forty plague deaths a week, applying the lower limit when conditions – hot weather, for example – indicated that a severe outbreak of the pestilence was likely.

Once the order to close was made, the players had no choice but to go on tour. It was risky, but it was their only chance of recouping, in part at least, the loss of their daily takings. They could not possibly earn anything like what they did in London. Popular though they were in provincial towns, their street and innyard audiences there were small compared with those in the capital. There was the long trek from place to place, properties, costumes and personal belongings piled on handcarts, and accommodation to be found and paid for. It was not unknown for companies on tour to have to sell their costumes – even their precious playbooks – to keep themselves in food.

Twice during Shakespeare's working life, severe and protracted plague epidemics kept the theatres closed for months on end. Between

June 1592 and May 1594 they were hardly ever open; and only occasional performances were allowed between March 1603 and April 1604. Further interruptions occurred in 1605-1609, but the closures of that period were widely spaced-out, giving the companies time to recover.

When that first prolonged shut-down began in 1592 Shakespeare was becoming well known. An enforced silence just at that time could have been disastrous. However, he had proved his talent to some key figures in the theatre, with the result that in 1594 he was poised to take full advantage of the drastic reorganisation into which the acting companies were driven by their misfortunes.

The crucial events of 1594 are set out in Chapter 7. Before that, we must pay attention to the words of a dying playwright – Robert Greene – who, in 1592, ranted in envy and bitterness against William Shakespeare, one of the theatre's rising men.

Born in Norwich in about 1560, Greene was educated at Cambridge and then at Oxford, a double distinction of which he was always proud. If, as he claimed, his parents 'were respected for their gravity and honest life', he profited little from their good example. He soon made a reputation as an author in London; and, just as soon, became notorious for his dissolute ways. He was a prolific and popular writer. His friend Thomas Nashe described his ability to 'jack up' a pamphlet 'in a day and a night', adding that the printers were always glad 'to pay him dear for the very dregs of his wit'. He could turn his hand to any kind of writing – plays, poems, prose romances, pamphlets – and do it well; but he spent his earnings faster than he got them.

In September 1592, when he lay ill and destitute in run-down lodgings in Southwark, he realised that it was all up with him. In his own pathetic words, he was 'deeplier searched with sickness than heretofor' and he knew that 'riot and incontinence' had done for him at last. Moved to repentance, as he had so often been before, he set about writing a 'swan-like song' and managed to complete it before dying 'of dissipation' – as contemporary reports put it. 'At his dying request', his final pamphlet was published before the year ended, and it was an instant and scandalous success.

It was in two parts: *The Repentance of Robert Greene, Master of Arts* (a last flicker of his old pride in his academic status) and *Greene's Groatsworth of Wit, Bought with a Million of Repentance*. The attack on Shakespeare, part of the *Groatsworth*, has kept Greene's memory alive more than anything else he wrote.

He addressed a stern warning to Christopher Marlowe, Thomas Nashe and George Peele – 'fellow scholars about this city', he called them. Exhorting them to regard his own miserable death as a lesson, he summoned them to reform their lives. Then he told them that the players to whom they sold their work would treat them as unscrupulously as they had treated hm. He denounced the actors as 'those puppets . . . that spake from our mouths, those antics garnished in our colours'. They exploited the talents of their poets, he said, underpaid them, stole their glory, and left them to die in poverty. He cautioned his former companions to be on guard against them all, but identified one of them as being a particularly dangerous threat:

> Yes, trust them not; for there is an upstart crow, beautified with our feathers, that with his *tiger's heart wrapped in a player's hide* supposes he is as well able to bombast out a blank verse as the best of you; and, being an absolute *Johannes Factotum* [Jack-of-all-trades], is in his own conceit the only Shake-scene in a country.

That Greene's 'upstart crow' was William Shakespeare is obvious from the sneering pun on his name – 'Shake-scene'. More interestingly, the words *tiger's heart wrapped in a player's hide* are, with one word altered, lifted out of Shakespeare's play *Henry VI Part 3*, in which the Duke of York, denouncing Queen Margaret's cruelty, cries out: 'O tiger's heart wrapped in a woman's hide'. By turning Shakespeare's own words against him, Greene sharpened his attack on the man he regarded as an interloper.

It is understandable why Greene and other freelance writers felt anger against the acting companies. As explained earlier, the dramatists were open to exploitation. They got no royalties on their work and no share of the takings however often their plays were performed. Ruthless operators such as Henslowe grew rich on their writing while they slogged away in poverty. That they often added to their own misfortunes by their spendthrift ways and disorderly lives did not excuse the inherent unfairness of their situation.

But it was not fair of Greene, either, to blame Shakespeare for his misery and to rail against his success. A player himself, as well as a writer, Shakespeare had his actor's wages to keep him going, so he was not entirely dependent on the outright sums paid for each play he wrote. (Later – see Chapter 7 – he came to an even better and permanent arrangement; but by that time poor Robert Greene was no longer alive to resent it.) Nor did Shakespeare riot his way through his earnings. For neither of those advantages could he reasonably be reproached; but the author of the *Groatsworth* was in no mood to be reasonable.

What angered Greene most and aroused his bitterest scorn was the fact that Shakespeare, a mere player and not a university man, dared to aspire to authorship in competition with him and his fellow scholar-poets. That is the basis of his savage attack on the 'upstart crow'. This presumptuous creature, says Greene, like all other actors fit only to speak the words we write for them ('puppets that spake from our mouths') and to present the scenes we devise for them ('antics garnished in our colours'), is vain enough to write his own plays and set himself up as a poet ('supposes he is as well able to bombast out a blank verse as the best of you').

It used to be thought that Greene was accusing Shakespeare of plagiarism when he described him (the 'upstart crow') as being 'beautified with our feathers'; but that idea does not find much support today. There is general agreement that Greene was simply ramming home the charge that the players owed their popularity entirely to their writers. Only by wearing 'our feathers' (speaking the words we write for them), he is saying, can the 'crows' (the actors) attract attention and win applause.

The notion that Greene was denouncing his rival as a plagiarist stemmed from the now-discredited theory that Shakespeare's early years in the theatre were spent in tinkering about with other men's plays. His job, so it was believed, was to patch up once-popular work and reshape it for performance. More recent research has revealed a quite different state of affairs. It was not Shakespeare who plagiarised other people's work: they plagiarised his. The success of his early plays attracted the attention of 'pirates' whose reconstructed versions of his works appeared on stage and in print after their originals had proved popular. For example, Parts 2 and 3 of *Henry VI* were pirated in 1594 and 1595, several years after Shakespeare had made his name with them.

Greene's angry references to him are important because they confirm that Shakespeare had a very considerably body of successful work to his credit in September 1592, when the *Groatsworth* was written. The *tiger's heart* quotation proves that *Henry VI Part 3* was by then a well-known play. It must have been on stage before the end of June 1592 (when the plague closed the theatres) and written in 1591/2. Moreover, since it is the third and final part of the trilogy of plays dealing with that reign, he must have written *Henry VI Part 1* and *Henry VI Part 2* in 1591, beginning work on them perhaps as early as 1590. He wrote quickly, but they are very long plays. He was an actor as well as a playwright, so even he could hardly have completed all three parts of *Henry VI* in much less than eighteen months.

The *Groatsworth*'s reluctant testimony to Shakespeare's popularity clarifies comments made at this time by two other theatre people –

Philip Henslowe, the manager of the Rose, and Thomas Nashe, Greene's friend. Neither mentions Shakespeare by name, but Greene's outburst against the 'upstart crow' makes it certain that it was Shakespeare's remarkable ability to draw the crowds that they had in mind.

Henslowe noted in his *Diary* that a play he referred to as 'Harey the vj' played to packed houses between March and June 1592. Seen in the light of Greene's furious reaction to his rival's success, there can be no doubt that 'Harey the vj' was Shakespeare's *Henry VI* – though whether one part or all three, we do not know. Again, in August 1592, in a pamphlet called *Pierce Pennilesse* (Shakespeare later punned on that name in *Love's Labour's Lost*), Nashe says that the dead English hero 'brave Talbot (the terror of the French)' has recently been depicted on the stage 'his bones new embalmed with the tears of *ten thousand spectators at least (at several times)*'. The deeds of 'brave Talbot' figure prominently in *Henry VI Part 1*, so Nashe's reference to 'ten thousand spectators' confirms that Greene had good reason to warn him and his associates that their new rival was eclipsing them.

Just two years after the *Groatsworth* was written, Shakespeare joined the Lord Chamberlain's Men and from then on occupied a key position in the affairs of that prestigious company. (See Chapter 7.) Greene's envious description of his success – coupled with the evidence supplied by Henslowe and Nashe – makes it easy to understand how he came to be given that opportunity. He was a money-spinner – an asset to any company that could obtain his services.

It was the Henry VI plays that Greene, Henslowe and Nashe instanced when reporting his popularity, but those were by no means his only successes in the first period of his career. He also wrote two other histories (*King John* and *Richard III*); three comedies (*The Comedy of Errors*, *The Taming of the Shrew*, *The Two Gentlemen of Verona*); one tragedy (*Titus Andronicus*) – and that was just as popular as the Henrys.

Titus Andronicus was, in fact, a most significant breakthrough, rivalling in popularity Thomas Kyd's *The Spanish Tragedy* (1588/89). Kyd was a Londoner, educated at Merchant Taylors' School, where (as at Stratford School) the study of classical drama was part of the curriculum. He took the Latin dramatist Seneca as his model and cleverly adapted his characteristics to suit contemporary taste. Nashe attacked Kyd (rather as Greene attacked Shakespeare) for daring to compete with him and his fellow scholar-poets, but he could not diminish Kyd's popular standing. Audiences were enthralled by the ghosts and the bloody revenges and the resounding rhetoric of *The Spanish Tragedy*.

Then, in *Titus Andronicus*, Shakespeare struck the same note and pulled off a similar triumph. In three different and popular kinds of drama – revenge-tragedy, comedy and history – he had successfully challenged all his competitors, 'university wits' and 'London dramatists' alike. No wonder the Lord Chamberlain's Men were eager to sign him up when the time came.

Robert Greene's bombshell had an interesting sequel which tells us a lot about Shakespeare's personal reputation. The *Groatsworth* was prepared for publication by Henry Chettle, a printer and a prolific hack writer. (He churned out well over forty plays – now all forgotten – for Henslowe.) Chettle saw Greene's last work as a quick way of making money. It was; but it also brought a storm about his ears. Several of the people defamed by Greene threatened Chettle with reprisals. More importantly to us, some of Shakespeare's friends defended his character and forced Chettle to apologise.

At the beginning of 1593 Chettle published a pamphlet of his own, called *Kind-Heart's Dream*, prefacing it with a reply to his assailants. In his preface, he said that he did not care whether Marlowe was offended by the references to him in the *Groatsworth*. (When advising him to repent, Greene gave a lurid description of Marlowe's infidel opinions and dissolute habits.) He (Chettle) did not know Marlowe and he did not want to. However, Chettle continued, he was now sorry that he had assisted in the publication of Greene's scurrilous remarks about Shakespeare. When he had edited the *Groatsworth* he had no personal knowledge of him, but now he had made his acquaintance and he realised that Greene's attack on his character was entirely unwarranted.

Chettle's apology was made in handsome terms:

> I am as sorry, as if the original fault had been my fault, because myself have seen his demeanour no less civil than he excellent in the quality he professes [the calling he follows]: besides, divers of worship [several honourable gentlemen] have reported his uprightness of dealing, which argues his honesty, and his facetious [polished] grace in writing, that approves [confirms] his art.

The 'divers of worship' who testified to Shakespeare's 'uprightness of dealing' are not identified in Chettle's retraction, and it is futile to guess. It remains a fact that – in a rigidly hierarchical age – people who were his social superiors wished it to be known that they esteemed the player-poet's character.

All the other descriptions we have of Shakespeare's personality and disposition reinforce Chettle's statements. His contemporaries spoke of him as being a well-mannered, good-tempered man, open and reliable in his relationships with acquaintances, friends and colleagues, at ease in all the varied social groups into which his professional and his personal activities took him.

7

'A Fellowship in a Cry of Players'

'ALL THE world's a stage, and all the men and women merely players', declares Jacques in *As You Like It*. His metaphor is echoed by many of Shakespeare's other characters. Comments on 'the theatre of life' occur to them readily in moments of stress and at times of reflection. For the beleaguered Macbeth,

> Life's but a walking shadow; a poor player
> That struts and frets his hour upon the stage,
> And then is heard no more.

York (in *Richard II*) contrasts the London crowd's enthusiasm for Bolingbroke with its contemptuous indifference to the fallen king. He does so by describing an audience's response to two actors:

> As in a theatre the eyes of men,
> After a well-graced actor leaves the stage,
> Are idly bent on him that enters next,
> Thinking his prattle to be tedious,
> Even so, or with much more contempt, men's eyes
> Did scowl on Richard.

Discussion of the dramatic impact of these recurring analogies between the actor's life and the human lot has its proper place in Shakespearian criticism. Factual biography is more concerned with the occasional – but very direct – references to particular circumstances and events that affected Shakespeare's own professional life. In *Hamlet*, for example, allusions to conditions and prospects in the theatre throw light on the course that Shakespeare's career took between 1592 (when the theatres were closed down by the plague) and 1600 (when *Hamlet* was written).

The references to 'the war of the theatres' (see Chapter 6) is just one of several comments on theatre affairs. In Hamlet's student days, we learn, he 'was wont to take delight in the tragedians of the city'. ('The city' in the play is Wittenberg; but external evidence makes it clear that all the statements made about actors and acting in *Hamlet* apply to the London of Shakespeare's own day.) The Prince has retained a keen interest in the drama and, knowing more than a little about theatre life, he is surprised to discover that his old favourites are on tour. As he rightly says, 'their residence [at their city headquarters], both in reputation and in profit, was better both ways'.

He listens eagerly to the players' news and discusses theatre fashions with them, expressing his strong dislike of the barnstorming style of acting. That style dominated the stage during Shakespeare's early period. The plays he wrote later required actors who could, in Hamlet's words, 'hold, as 'twere, the mirror up to nature'. He also condemns the 'pitiful ambition' of stage clowns who distract the audience with laughter when 'some necessary question of the play' is being presented. (Hamlet's pronouncements on acting are discussed in Chapters 11 and 12 where the stage conventions and dramatic fashions of the day are explained.)

Nor does the Prince of Denmark overlook the economic realities of theatre life. Like his creator, he is well aware that a player-poet who could obtain 'a fellowship in a cry [company] of players' had taken a decisive step forward in his career. His knowledge of that fact comes out in an excited outburst wholly consonant with his character and interests, and dramatically matched to the situation that has arisen.

Having arranged a court performance of *The Murder of Gonzago*, which is 'something like the murder of my father', Hamlet writes 'a speech of some dozen or sixteen lines' and inserts it into the play to make sure that Claudius does not miss the point. His plan succeeds. The unnerved usurper, 'frighted with false fire', rushes out of the hall. Wildly elated, Hamlet turns to Horatio and demands:

> Would not this, sir, and a forest of feathers . . . .with two Provincial roses on my razed shoes, get me a fellowship in a cry of players, sir?

To calm him down, Horatio answers drily, 'Half a share'; but Hamlet insists that he deserves the full reward: 'A whole one, I'.

Behind that emphatic insistence on 'a fellowship' lies Shakespeare's own experience of the financial facts of a theatre career. Neither as a 'hired man' nor as a freelance writer – not even as both – could he hope to be well paid and secure. Prosperity and security went to those who had a contractual position in an acting company and a share of its profits.

By the time he wrote *Hamlet* Shakespeare had himself enjoyed for six years the benefits of a fellowship in a very successful cry of players. The steps by which he arrived at that position can be traced with the aid of public records and well-documented theatre history.

In the summer of 1592 a rapid advancement of Shakespeare's career seemed unlikely – and that for causes beyond his control. The Lord Chamberlain's company, of which he was to become a member, had not yet been formed; and, in the prevailing circumstances, neither that nor any other new venture could be envisaged. All the existing companies, even the most flourishing, were thrown on their beam ends. Like everyone else in the theatre business, Shakespeare – as yet not securely attached to any one permanent group of players – was vulnerable. True, his early plays had made him well known; but there were now no outlets for new work. Like Hamlet, he must 'eat the air, promise-crammed' and wait for things to improve – or so it seemed.

After a splendid start to the year – for him and others – 1592 turned sour just before the plague erupted. A serious prentice riot in Southwark on 11 June so alarmed the Privy Council that the theatres were ordered to close, and to stay closed until Michaelmas. The playhouses were always regarded as being fomenters of disturbance and magnets for 'tumultuous assemblies'. Strange's Men, who were then playing at the Rose, petitioned for clemency on grounds that show how much damage the players suffered when cut off from their London base. They reminded the Privy Council that the expenses of touring made it impossible for them to take all the company on the road. If they had to split up they would lose trained actors and might not be able to re-form later; in which case, they added, 'we shall not only be undone, but also unready to serve Her Majesty'. It was a despairing attempt to use the Queen's liking for court performances as an argument against her councillors' decision.

It might have worked. The players sometimes escaped from tight corners. Before the end of the month, however, their protests were silenced by the onset of the worst and longest plague epidemic that London had ever known. In 1592/3 well over twenty thousand people died. Forced out – and forced to leave their families at home in the plague-ridden city – the actors took to the road, getting what living they could.

It was a weary business, trudging from place to place along rough roads and in constant danger from footpads. All over England the various troupes went: north as far as Carlisle; south and east, to Canterbury, Dover and Southampton; west, to Barnstaple. (Some went abroad, to Holland, Denmark and Germany, where the reputation of English acting was high.) In some places they did well enough, but times were not as good as they had been. At great houses, such as the Derbys' in Lancashire and the Pembrokes' in Wiltshire, they were given barn beds and food as well as money; but between even the best of venues there were miles to tramp through a sparsely-peopled countryside. Worst of all, they carried the fear of pestilence with them, and many who would have been spectators stayed away.

Small troupes of picked men were formed from companies unable to tour at full strength. One such troupe, formed partly of Admiral's Men and partly of Strange's, was led by Edward Alleyn, the great tragedian. He and Henslowe were now partners (Alleyn married Henslowe's stepdaughter) and Alleyn toured while Henslowe looked after their joint interests in Southwark. (Henslowe's investments included the Rose, the Bear Garden and houses let to brothel-keepers.)

The two men kept in close touch, each as anxious as the other to get the actors back as soon as the plague abated. Henslowe passed on any information he had about how other companies were faring. In September 1593 he was able to send Alleyn news of Pembroke's Men: 'They are all at home [back in London and unemployed] and have been these five or six weeks, for they cannot save their charges [cover their expenses] with travel, as I hear, and were fain to pawn their apparel'.

Henslowe then asked Alleyn to assure his touring companions of the warm regard in which he held them. Telling him to couch that message in the friendliest of terms, he added a brief and revealing explanation of why it was so important. 'Commend me heartily to them', he wrote, *'for I grow poor for lack of them'*.

That frank admission makes the relationship between the proprietor and his employees quite clear. Henslowe's wealth came from his hired men. Hamlet was right to insist on getting 'a fellowship' – and a whole one at that.

There is no evidence that Shakespeare was with any of the various troupes on tour at any time in 1592-94, and there are solid reasons for believing that he was not. First, not then being a regular member of any company, he was unlikely to be asked. They took no more players on tour than they had to. Second, while it is known that he was an entirely competent actor, he was never in the star (Edward Alleyn/Richard Burbage) class. It was for his plays that his services were chiefly in demand.

Some of his biographers believe that Strange's Men sent him home to Stratford to write while the theatres were closed. He was then, so the theory goes, to rejoin them in London, armed with new plays to give them an advantage over their competitors. A neat idea; but some awkward objections stand in its way. There is no proof that Shakespeare's early association with Strange's Men was as close as all that (see Chapter 5). Nor did he work exclusively with them when he resumed his career in London. Furthermore, though he certainly did a lot of work before the theatres reopened, he was busy writing narrative poems, not plays.

Strange's Men apart, however, there are still good reasons to believe that he spent much of his time in Stratford between the summer of 1592 and the late spring of 1594. With the theatres closed, there was no point in paying for London lodgings when he could live with his family and make a worthwhile contribution to the expenses of the Henley Street household. His first years in London had not brought him anything like the income he later earned, but the money he got for his nine plays, on top of his wages as a hired man, added up to a useful sum – and, as we have seen, he was no spendthrift. He had left Stratford with little in his purse, but in 1592 he was not penniless. Certainly, he had enough in hand to tide him over, unless the theatres remained closed for a very long time.

It is worth noting here that John Shakespeare's position recovered from about this time onwards. He never again played a leading part in borough affairs, but after 1592 there is no evidence that he was in financial distress. Indeed, the grant of arms that he obtained in 1596, confirming his status as a gentleman, proves that he had been restored to prosperity. All the evidence makes it plain that the change was brought about by the exertions of his player-poet son.

On other grounds, too, it is wholly reasonable to suppose that William Shakespeare, having for the time being no material compulsion to remain in London, went home to Stratford. The place always tugged him back (see Chapter 2); and there were now three generations of Shakespeares there to welcome his presence: his father (by this time 'a merry-cheeked old man', according to a gossipy report), his mother, his sister, his three brothers, his wife and – strongest pull of all – his three children. Susanna was now nine. Judith and Hamnet were seven.

Beyond conjecture lies the undoubted fact that he got through a considerable body of work while the theatres were closed, undertaking a quite different kind of writing and making a great success of it. This achievement typifies qualities manifest throughout his working life. He was always resilient, open to new ideas, quick to perceive fresh opportunities and diligent in pursuing them. The shut-down of 1592 came just when he was winning acclaim. He not merely survived what could have been a disastrous interruption of his career, but used his enforced absence from the theatre to such good purpose that, by 1594, his reputation stood higher than before. His two long narrative poems, *Venus and Adonis* and *The Rape of Lucrece*, written while the London stages were silent, gave him an assured place among the foremost poets of the day.

It may seem surprising that he should have turned to non-dramatic writing at that particular time. With successful plays to his credit, and confident of his ability to write more, he surely had every incentive to concentrate on work that he could offer to the players as soon as they were back in business.

Plausible as that argument may seem to us, it ignores the contemporary influences that kindled his ambition to shine in *literature*. We regard their drama as the Elizabethans' supreme artistic achievement. They did not see it in that light. Plays provided popular entertainment for people of all classes, catering for courtiers, citizens and groundlings alike. The Queen did not visit the public theatres, but the actors took to her court the same plays that they presented on 'the common stages'. Audiences for whom they played at the Inns of Court and in aristocrats' houses included people who were enthusiastic patrons of the playhouses, where 'cockpit, galleries, boxes' accommodated spectators of different social classes according to their ability to pay.

Yet its own widespread and classless popularity – its accessibility to the ignorant as to the educated – denied to Elizabethan drama in its own time the intellectual esteem in which literature, especially poetry, was held. The playwrights were workers in a mass entertainment industry and, as such, debarred from the status readily accorded to the non-dramatic poets whose sonnets, verse-narratives, odes, eclogues and satires were eagerly read and discussed by people of cultivated taste. Plays were for relaxation. Their writers could not – and did not – expect to win living fame or to achieve posthumous glory.

Actors and dramatists alike were regarded as ephemeral creatures. With 'no project but to please' (see Prospero's Epilogue), their work had life only during its brief embodiment on stage. In *The Tempest*, as in many of his other plays, Shakespeare reflects on 'the baseless fabric of this vision' conjured up for the transient delight of those who pay to see it. Offering passing shows, dreams and revels that must end, the actors 'are melted into air, into thin air' when their two hours' traffic is done – and all their fine words fall silent with them.

The modesty with which the playwrights referred to their occupation was in sharp contrast to the assurance with which the poets of the day unhesitatingly proclaimed the permanence of their own art. Without fear of being scoffed at, they asserted the immortality of poetry and its makers. Moreover, they claimed that poets conferred lasting fame on those whom they honoured, whether by writing about them or by dedicating their verses to them.

Though he often referred to plays and play-acting in muted terms,

Shakespeare adopted the poet's allowed privileges when he wrote his non-dramatic verse, proudly and confidently claiming immortality for his 'eternal lines'. Thomas Thorpe, the publisher of Shakespeare's *Sonnets* in 1609, did not exaggerate when, in the dedication to that volume, he referred to 'that eternity promised by our ever-living poet'. His poems declare his enduring fame, and bestow undying memory on his subject:

> Nor shall Death brag thou wander'st in his shade,
> When in eternal lines to time thou grow'st:
> So long as men can breathe, or eyes can see,
> So long lives this, and this gives life to thee.
> *Sonnet 18*

> Not marble, nor the gilded monuments
> Of princes, shall outlive this powerful rhyme;
> But you shall live more bright in these contents
> Than unswept stone, besmear'd with sluttish time.
> *Sonnet 55*

Urged on by a deep desire for the 'fame that all hunt after in their lives' (*Love's Labour's Lost*), he was also well aware of the immediate advantages to be gained by writing poetry. The publication of *Venus and Adonis* in 1593 (it was followed by *The Rape of Lucrece* in 1594) brought him instant recognition and an assured place in the literary world. His plays had been popular, but his new reputation carried with it a status he could never win while his sole occupation was to provide scripts for the players. Cultivated people, arbiters of fashionable taste, took up the work of this brilliant newcomer. Avid readers of poetry – often themselves eager to shine as poets – they acclaimed him as an adornment of intellectual and aesthetic life.

The effect that the publication of these two poems had can be judged by Francis Meres' remarks in his book *Palladis Tamia : Wit's Treasury* (1598). Meres, a well-informed observer of literary events, set down a 'Comparative Discourse of our English Poets with the Greek, Latin and Italian Poets'. (He also commented on the playwrights of the day, and his remarks about Shakespeare's plays are discussed in Chapter 8.) He praised Shakespeare's poetry for embellishing the English language with 'rare ornaments', and he compared him with Ovid, that classical poet so loved by the Elizabethans:

> . . . the sweet, witty soul of Ovid lives in the mellifluous and honey-tongued Shakespeare, witness his *Venus and Adonis*, his *Lucrece*, his sugared Sonnets among his private friends.

Meres' description of Shakespeare's 'sugared Sonnets' as being 'among his private friends' proves that some of those poems were circulating in manuscript well before the complete collection was published by Thomas Thorpe in 1609. It was quite usual for unpublished work to become known in that way. By allowing – or asking! – influential people of recognised good taste to read the manuscripts of his poems a writer could acquire a considerable reputation long before his work appeared in print. Indeed, some work that was much talked about was never published during its writer's lifetime. If his 'private friends' were of sufficient standing, their enthusiasm was enough. They saw to it that the manuscripts were passed on and widely discussed.

Evidently, Shakespeare was content to allow his sonnets to become known by word of mouth. What arrangement – if any – he made with Thorpe for their eventual publication remains a mystery. Compared with those of *Venus and Adonis* and *The Rape of Lucrece*, the text of the 1609 *Sonnets* is poor. The many misprints indicate that he neither prepared the manuscripts for the printer nor read the proofs. Whereas he wasted no time in getting his two long narrative poems into print, he let the sonnets remain unprinted for some years. Presumably he saw no reason for haste. They lent themselves to private circulation. A fourteen-line poem or a batch of several could be passed round easily. They were being read and admired. People were talking about them and spreading his fame. So why rush to print them?

When, at last, the sonnets were published, Thorpe described them as 'never before imprinted'; and they were not reprinted in Shakespeare's lifetime. They came out in a second edition in 1640, by which year *Venus and Adonis* had gone through sixteen printings and *The Rape of Lucrece* eight. Yet, as Meres and others testified, his sonnets made a major contribution to his poetic reputation.

Even so, and for whatever reason, Shakespeare had no known involvement with the 1609 volume. He certainly did nothing to clear up the riddles posed by Thomas Thorpe's enigmatic dedication:

To The Only Begetter Of These Insuing Sonnets Mr W.H. All Happiness And That Eternity Promised By Our Ever-Living Poet Wisheth The Well-Wishing Adventurer In Setting Forth

T.T.

To this day – and after many gallons of ink have been expended in the effort – nobody has explained Thorpe's meaning satisfactorily. Who was 'Mr W.H.'? In what sense was he 'the only begetter' of the sonnets? Was he the handsome young man who is the subject of one hundred and twenty-six of the one hundred and fifty-four poems?

There are no certain answers to those questions. Many guesses – some plausible, some wildly speculative – have been made; but a factual account of Shakespeare's life is not the place to discuss them in any detail.

Though there is much we do not know about the circumstances in which Shakespeare's sonnets came to be published, the arrangements he made for *Venus and Adonis* and *The Rape of Lucrece* are well-documented. Clearly, he was eager to have those two works in print as soon as possible. Unlike the sonnets, they were not well-suited to hand-to-hand circulation in manuscript. Their length (1194 and 1855 lines respectively) made them inconvenient to read while they were in loose sheets. Until they were printed and bound they could not become widely known. He had put a great deal of work into the two poems and if he was to reap the benefit they must be got into print and publicised without delay.

He took his manuscript to one of the best printers in London – his former Stratford companion, Richard Field. The care with which they were prepared for the press and checked in proof is shown by the excellence of both texts. There are very few misprints. Shakespeare's close attention to the printing of these poems is in marked contrast to his apparent lack of interest in the printing of his plays.

Venus and Adonis was published in April 1593 and *The Rape of Lucrece* in May 1594. Exactly suited to the taste of a classically-educated readership, their literary quality was hailed by a chorus of praise that amply justified his decision to risk publication.

Their success was particularly important to his career because both works were dedicated to a well-known patron of the arts, the Earl of Southampton. By allowing himself to be publicly associated with Shakespeare in this way, Southampton had put his seal of approval on the two poems. Their failure would have mortified him by calling his judgement into question and diminishing his treasured reputation as a man of taste. Fortunately, their enthusiastic reception enhanced Southampton's literary standing. He was able to bask in reflected glory.

A noble personage accepting a dedication expected to be flattered by its writer, and Elizabethan authors were often fulsome in praise of their patrons, describing their moral and intellectual qualities in lavish terms. Neither of Shakespeare's dedications was obsequious.

In each he thanked Southampton warmly for giving his work the support of his illustrious name, and he assured him of his dutiful service and loyalty. In the *Venus and Adonis* dedication he expressed his fear that his readers might censure him 'for choosing so strong a prop to support so weak a burden'. If his poem failed, he said, 'I shall be sorry it had so noble a godfather'. In the *Lucrece* dedication he again modestly discounted his own abilities, but was confident that Southampton's favour would ensure the poem's success: 'The warrant I have of your honourable disposition, not the worth of my untutored lines, makes it assured of acceptance'.

A poet was permitted to claim immortality in his verse, but he was obliged to understate his own merits when writing a dedication, the chief purpose of which was to thank and to compliment his patron. Shakespeare's dedicatory addresses did exactly what was expected of them. They were graceful exercises in a well-established and highly-conventional mode of composition. In most elegant prose he paid his valued patron the courtesies and compliments appropriate to the occasion.

Two other points must be noted. In the *Venus and Adonis* dedication Shakespeare referred to that poem as 'the first heir of my invention'. Some of his biographers have jumped to the conclusion that he was saying that it was the first work he had written. Not so. He described *Venus and Adonis* as 'the first' because it was his first publication. The plays he had already written belonged to the players who had bought them. As yet unpublished, they had passed out of his possession and must remain silent until they were again given brief life upon the stage. His poem, on the other hand, was about to be presented to the world. Dedicated, printed and bound, it would be a permanent memorial to his gifts. It was his first published bid for a poet's enduring reputation.

That dedication also promised Southampton a further offering: 'I . . . vow to take advantage of all idle hours, till I have honoured you with some graver labour'. That 'graver labour' was *The Rape of Lucrece*, written immediately after *Venus and Adonis*. Like its predecessor, it met the taste for narrative poetry based on classical subjects, and it owed much to the influence of Ovid. In its darker theme, however, and its exploration of motive and self-conflict, it went more deeply into human nature than the earlier poem had tried to do.

All attempts to discover the details of the Southampton-Shakespeare connection have proved fruitless. We do not know how or when it began, how long it lasted, or how close it was. Henry Wriothesley, the third Earl of Southampton, was not yet twenty when Shakespeare dedicated *Venus and Adonis* to him. Already cutting a brilliant figure at court, he was also known as a patron of writers, including the scholar John Florio (his tutor in Italian) and the poet, dramatist and prose writer Thomas Nashe.

High in the Queen's favour for a time, Southampton was one of Essex's close supporters. He accompanied him on the Cadiz expedition of 1596 and he was his Master of Horse in Ireland in 1599. He also rebelled with him in 1601 and was condemned to death. That sentence was commuted to life imprisonment, from which he was freed by James I. All those events lay in the future when Shakespeare addressed him as his patron.

In 1593 and 1594 Shakespeare named him as his literary 'god-father'; and never again, as far as we know, were they linked in any way. So it seems that the connection was a brief one. It has been argued from allusions contained in *Love's Labour's Lost* (written not later than 1594) that their association was close, even if it did not last long. That play certainly contains many references to people who are known to have been members of Southampton's circle of friends and protégés. For that reason, it has been suggested that when Shakespeare wrote *Love's Labour's Lost* (and the dedication of *Lucrece*, if not the whole poem) he was living as a member of Southampton's household in Hampshire. It is no more than a guess.

People who believe that Shakespeare and Southampton were on close terms maintain that Southampton was the 'Mr W.H.' of Thorpe's dedication of the *Sonnets*. (They argue that Henry Wriothesley's initials were reversed to conceal his identity.) That guess is weakened by the fact that Southampton was an earl, not a 'Mr'. In any case, he is just one of several men confidently asserted to have been 'Mr W.H.'.

Nor is the argument that Southampton was the handsome young man addressed in the sonnets at all conclusive. There are many other theories about the true identify of that mysterious person. In any case, for all we know, 'the lovely boy' – like the 'Dark Lady' and the 'Rival Poet', who also have sonnets addressed to them – was a figment of Shakespeare's invention, a peg on which to hang the customary themes of the sonneteer.

All we can be sure of is that Southampton received dedications from William Shakespeare – a not uncommon arrangement which poets and their patrons understood perfectly well. The poet supplied compliments and offered his patron the chance of being associated with the poet's fame. The patron gave the poet publicity and status. He was also expected to produce a material reward, especially when – as in Shakespeare's literary ventures – the poet's work was well received and widely discussed. How much money, if any, Southampton gave Shakespeare is not known. The story that Rowe told is worth repeating, not because the sum it mentions is at all likely to be accurate but because the reason for the gift rings true. This is what Rowe says: 'My Lord Southampton, at one time, gave him a thousand pounds to enable him to go through a purchase which he heard he had a mind to'.

The figure is absurd. Southampton was himself hard up in 1594 ('hard up' as an aristocrat understands it, that is) and a thousand pounds was a huge sum of money. There is no doubt, however, that in that year Shakespeare raised some capital and put it to good use. Things were stirring again in London, and the 'purchase he had a mind to' was a 'fellowship' in one of the acting companies then re-forming after the long theatre shut-down.

Several attempts were made to reopen the theatres before the summer of 1594, but none lasted long. On each occasion the plague flared up again, forcing the players back to the hazards of touring or the hardships of unemployment. Some companies 'broke'; others survived in unstable coalitions.

When the worst was over, they gathered in London again and set about restoring their battered fortunes. It was a time of change and uncertainty. New companies sprang up – some soon disintegrating. The remnants of former troupes amalgamated to perform plays that had been the property of their previous companies. The survivors of a 'broken' company could often get a place in a new one by bringing their jealously-guarded playbooks with them. The title page of *Titus Andronicus* (first printed in 1594) indicates that there was a busy traffic in plays that had already proved their popularity. It states that this 'Most Lamentable Roman Tragedy' had been performed by three companies: Derby's, Pembroke's and Sussex's Men. The fact that the players were selling their plays to the printers shows that they were pushed for ready money. Once published, a play could be staged by any company that wanted to use it.

At least, however, life was returning to the London theatre. If he was to find work again as an actor, Shakespeare had to get back there. If, much more ambitiously, he was to establish himself as a regular writer for and a 'fellow' in one of the companies, now was the time to do so. The opportunity had arrived. With his previous reputation as a playwright, his new status as a poet, and some money to invest, he was well-placed to move into a key position in the reviving theatre.

There were two dominant forces in the shifting situation: the Henslowe-Alleyn combination, based at the Rose; the Burbage group, based at the Theatre. Henslowe and Alleyn between them had such complete control of the financial resources and artistic direction of their company that they had no need to offer a newcomer any share of their profits, however keen they might be to buy his plays. A hired man's wage for his acting and an outright purchase of each new play was the best to be got from them.

James Burbage and his two sons, Cuthbert and Richard, were more flexible. Successful though they had been before 1592, they had not established an acting company that equalled Henslowe's enterprises in reputation and profit. Now, back in business, they were determined to give their new company a cohesion and an identity that would enable them to challenge the Henslowe-Alleyn empire.

Between them, the Burbages had the qualities and skills required to put together such an organisation. James was an ambitious and a practical man. He had been a joiner before he turned actor (with Leicester's Men). He married into a family that had money, and his brother-in-law helped him to raise the capital to build the Theatre. Cuthbert, the elder son, shared his father's financial and managerial talents. Richard, two years younger than Cuthbert, was already hailed as an outstanding actor. By building round Richard a team of gifted players, the Burbages could tackle the Admiral's Men (Henslowe's and Alleyn's company) on level terms. If they could also secure the service of a brilliant 'ordinary poet', they could hope to outdo their great rivals. To obtain such a vital recruit they were prepared to offer good terms.

The rivalry between these two powerful groups had started in 1591, at which time Alleyn was leading a company then playing for James Burbage at the Theatre. Some of his actors were from Strange's Men and some from the Admiral's Men. Alleyn fell out with Burbage and took himself and his players off to the Rose, where he and Henslowe formed their long and profitable partnership. (James Burbage quarrelled with a lot of people. Many found him cantankerous and not always scrupulous, though Shakespeare got on with him well enough.) Richard Burbage, who was acting with the Alleyn team, remained with his father and his brother at the Theatre. There, however, lacking the resources then open to Alleyn at the Rose, he seemed unlikely to equal the reputation of that famous actor. Henslowe was buying Marlowe's plays for Alleyn, and in 1592 he was shrewd enough to stage 'Harey the vj'. Until Richard Burbage could find roles to outshine Alleyn's he would stay in his rival's shadow. That, of course, was where Shakespeare came in.

Whether the Burbages or Shakespeare made the first move that brought them together is not recorded. However, there is documentary evidence to show that what proved to be the most successful collaboration in the history of the theatre had been established well before the Christmas of 1594.

While the situation was fluid in the summer of that year the Burbages, like everyone else in the theatre business, were looking round for opportunities and picking up income whenever and wherever they could. In June, for example, they accepted a Henslowe engagement to perform at the Newington Butts theatre. (Henslowe often ran seasons at theatres other than the Rose, employing various companies to fill the openings he spotted. For all his many faults – perhaps because of them – he was a most enterprising and successful impresario.)

Meanwhile, James Burbage and his sons were putting together a cohesive and well-directed organisation capable of bidding for a leading place in the theatre. By the autumn they had secured what every acting company needed, an influential patron to be their figurehead and thus to afford them the protection of his name against their Puritan foes. Their patron was as good a guarantor of their respectability as could be hoped for – no less a person than the Lord Chamberlain himself. Henceforth they were known as the Lord Chamberlain's Men. (Later – in May 1603 – they were accorded an even more splendid title. James I became their patron and thereafter they were known as the King's Men.)

On 8 October 1594 their patron wrote to the Lord Mayor of London requesting him to permit 'my new company of players' to present a season of plays at the Cross Keys Inn. That was one of the most profitable dramatic venues within the jurisdiction of the city corporation. The Lord Chamberlain's Men were on the move.

Before the year ended their growing reputation was confirmed by an invitation to play at court. It was a much sought-after distinction, and one that carried the additional benefit of a good fee. This milestone in their progress is recorded in the account book kept by the Treasurer of the Queen's Chamber. The wording of the entry proves that the Burbages had found not only the patron they needed but the playwright as well, for it names Shakespeare as one of the three principal members of the Lord Chamberlain's Men.

The Treasurer's note refers to payment made for plays presented for the Queen's pleasure at her court at Greenwich during the Christmas festivities. He listed the three members of the company to whom he had paid the sum due: William Shakespeare, Richard Burbage, William Kempe. (Kempe was then, and for some time to come, the company's star clown, as valuable to them in comic roles as Burbage was in tragic.) All three were described as 'servants of the Lord Chamberlain', authorised as being fit and proper persons to receive money on the company's behalf; hired men would not have been so described. Those three payees were 'sharers' in the company.

At some date, then, in the course of 1594 Shakespeare got the 'fellowship' he needed; and the 'cry of players' secured for itself the 'ordinary poet' on whom its prosperity was based. He stayed with the Lord Chamberlain's-King's Men for the rest of his working life, writing exclusively for them, acting with them, taking a manager's part in all their decisions. Together, they won a commanding position in the theatre world and were still pre-eminent when, at last, he left them and returned home to Stratford.

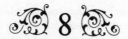

'The Great Globe Itself'

T HE newly-founded Lord Chamberlain's Men had a full programme between June 1594 and the end of that year. They were performing at the Newington Butts theatre in the summer and they had a winter season at the Cross Keys Inn. At Christmas, in addition to their Court appearances, they staged *The Comedy of Errors* for a private audience at Gray's Inn. Between those engagements they acted at James Burbage's Theatre, then their permanent base.

There was nothing unusual or unwelcome about such a crowded schedule. For the Chamberlain's Men, as for their rivals, constant activity was the condition of success. Frequent appearances at different venues brought them full purses, so they packed in as many performances as they could manage while the going was good. The authorities, alarmed by plague or riot, or angered by a subversive play, might cut the playing season short at any time.

The companies operated on a repertory system. Popular successes were revived but no play, however well received at its first performance, was given a long run. Consequently, like present-day television programmers, they used up their material fast. Their demand for new plays was insatiable. From the time he joined the Lord Chamberlain's-King's Men, Shakespeare wrote, on average, two plays a year for them (and his were not the only plays they staged). Coming on top of his acting and managerial duties for the company, that was a prodigious output.

In *Palladis Tamia* (see Chapter 7) Francis Meres named twelve of Shakespeare's plays. He did not provide a complete record of the pre-1592 plays, but the list he gave enables us to check the plays written by Shakespeare for the Lord Chamberlain's Men between 1594 and 1598. This is what Meres wrote in his 'comparative discourse':

> As Plautus and Seneca are accounted the best for comedy and tragedy among the Latins, so Shakespeare among the English is the most excellent in both kinds for the stage; for comedy, witness his *Gentlemen*

of Verona, his *Errors*, his *Love's Labour's Lost*, his *Love's Labour's Won*,
his *Midsummer Night's Dream* and his *Merchant of Venice*; for tragedy,
his *Richard II*, *Richard III*, *Henry IV*, *King John*, *Titus Andronicus* and
his *Romeo and Juliet*.

Before discussing the importance of Meres' remarks, we must note
three points. First, he classifies as tragedies four plays that we prefer
to call histories. Second, he treats the two parts of *Henry IV* as being
one single play. Third – and this is a puzzle – he lists a play which he
calls *Love's Labour's Won*. We know of no such play. It has been
argued that the play he had in mind was *All's Well That Ends Well*, but
that is not convincing. On the evidence of its theme and style, that
play (together with *Measure for Measure* and *Troilus and Cressida*)
belongs to a later period of Shakespeare's work – the period of 'the
dark comedies' or 'problem plays', as they are usually called. *All's
Well* was not written before 1602/3, so it cannot be Meres' *Love's
Labour's Won*. The best guess is that Meres was thinking of *Much Ado
About Nothing*, certainly an earlier play than *All's Well*, and one in
which love's labour is most happily won.

Even so, Meres' list is invaluable. We know that some of the plays
he names were written before 1594. Leaving those out of the
reckoning, we arrive at the following tally of Shakespeare's output for
the Lord Chamberlain's Men between that year and 1598: *Love's
Labour's Lost*, *Much Ado About Nothing* ('Love's Labour's Won'), *A
Midsummer Night's Dream*, *The Merchant of Venice*, *Richard II*, *Henry
IV Part 1*, *Henry IV Part 2*, *Romeo and Juliet*.

Those eight highly successful plays put Shakespeare and his fellows
well ahead of their rivals. By the time Meres wrote *Palladis Tamia*
they were recognised as the foremost acting company and they were
never afterwards dislodged from their commanding position. Such
difficulties as they later encountered were the common trials of the
players' lot and they came out of them in better shape than any of their
competitors.

Well over a year before Meres' book was published, however, the
Chamberlain's Men were faced with a very serious problem which
dragged on until the end of 1598. Although James Burbage had raised
money to build the Theatre back in 1576, he did not own the land on
which it stood. That belonged to Giles Allen, who leased it to Burbage
for an initial term of twenty-one years. The ground landlord received
an annual rent for the site and he and his family were entitled to free
seats 'in some one of the upper rooms'.

Some time before the first lease was due to expire (on 13 April 1597)
James Burbage started to negotiate with Allen for its renewal. Allen

was able to drive a hard bargain and Burbage agreed to pay a greatly increased ground rent. Allen then stipulated that he was to have the right to use the Theatre for his own purposes, if he so chose, only five years after the new lease came into effect. To that, Burbage could not agree. Realising that Allen was not willing to come to reasonable terms, he looked for a suitable place to which he could move his company when their lease of the Theatre site expired.

In Blackfriars, a prosperous district lying between Fleet Street and the Thames, and close to St Paul's, there was a fine building which had formerly been part of a monastery and had been used as a theatre by one of the children's companies. It had the great attraction of being within the city walls (and, therefore, easily accessible to audiences) but independent of the Lord Mayor and his corporation, for Blackfriars was then a 'liberty'. Seeing it as a splendid way out of his difficulties with Allen, James Burbage bought the former monastic refectory for £600 – a very considerable sum of money – and then spent a lot more on fitting it out as a theatre for his company's use.

The well-to-do citizens of Blackfriars raised a storm of protest. They had been used to having a 'private' theatre in the district, but they were not going to put up with a 'common playhouse' if they could help it. The Privy Council upheld their objections. Burbage had to abandon his plans. Soon afterwards, in January 1597, he died.

The theatre he had bought in Blackfriars passed into the possession of his sons, but the Lord Chamberlain's Men were still debarred from using it. Eventually, Cuthbert and Richard Burbage leased it to a children's company manager called Evans, whose 'little eyases' (see Chapter 6) were for a time such serious rivals to them. It was an ironical state of affairs. The two Burbage owned the theatre in which a children's company acted plays satirising the common players and competing with them for audiences. Not until 1608 were they able to use the Blackfriars theatre themselves. Then, indeed, they and their company (by then they were the King's Men) reaped a full harvest from James Burbage's investment (see Chapter 9).

At the time of their father's death, however, his sons and their fellow sharers in the Lord Chamberlain's Men were in an awkward and worsening position. They tried to get Allen to see reason, but he would not settle with them on terms they felt able to accept. After their lease expired in April 1597, they continued to act at the Theatre but they were at Allen's mercy. He could turn them out whenever it suited him to do so.

They made increasing use of the nearby Curtain, but it was a makeshift arrangement. The Curtain had never been as convenient or as successful as the Theatre. Its owner, Henry Laneman, was primarily a property developer and not a skilled theatre manager. As early as 1585 he and James Burbage had an arrangement whereby the Curtain was used as a stand-in or overflow for the Theatre – an 'easer', as it was called. That arrangement now provided the Chamberlain's Men with a breathing-space, but they could not hope to realise the full potential of their great assets – their management skills, acting strength and outstandingly popular plays – until they had secure possession of a first-rate theatre.

In July 1597, while they were still making do and trying to settle with Allen, the *Isle of Dogs* uproar burst out. (See Chapter 6.) The Privy Council ordered that stage plays should be finally suppressed and decreed that both the Theatre and the Curtain were to be demolished. As has been explained, that sweeping order was not put into effect. The Lord Chamberlain's Men, like the other companies, stayed in business, watching their step rather more carefully for a time. They were still hoping at this point to get the Theatre back as their permanent home, and in the autumn they agreed to very stiff conditions. Immediately, Allen confronted them with more quibbles. He told them – as Master Dumbleton the tailor tells Falstaff in *Henry IV Part 2* – that 'they should procure him better assurance . . . he liked not the security'.

After that patent evasion, they realised that they were wasting their time in trying to bargain with him. So, in the course of 1598, they gradually withdrew from the Theatre while busily making other plans. Allen believed that the Privy Council's order to demolish the Theatre had put him in an unassailable position. He owned the site and he now claimed, quite unjustifiably, that because he and the players had not agreed to a new lease, he was entitled to pull the building down and use its materials for some other and, as he put it, 'better' purpose. Foolishly, he let it be known that he intended to take possession of the Burbages' property. He greatly underestimated their determination and enterprise.

At night on 28 December 1598, Cuthbert and Richard Burbage, together with Peter Street, their expert carpenter, and a dozen skilled workmen, took the Theatre to pieces. Allen's own words – he sued them for damages and lost his case – give a vivid though one-sided account of this famous night action. Allen testified that the Burbages and their accomplices did

> riotously assemble . . . then and there pulling, breaking and throwing down the said Theatre in very outrageous, violent and riotous sort, to the great disturbance and terrifying . . . of Your Majesty's loving subjects there near inhabiting.

The work undoubtedly made a noise and surprised the neighbours – the Burbages were not so silly as to give advance notice of their operation; but it was not at all the haphazard and violent onslaught suggested by Allen's description. Under Peter Street's direction, they knew exactly what to do. The Theatre came down timber by timber and section by section, in order, each carefully marked and stacked to facilitate its re-erection. Then they ferried their former playhouse across the Thames. Thus in one night's work they brought the Theatre to an end and prepared the Globe for its beginning.

Of course, they had done a lot of planning beforehand, for there would have been little advantage in demolishing the Theatre if they had not already secured a site for its successor. As we know, Shakespeare's move from his Shoreditch lodging to Southwark took place in the autumn of 1598 (see Chapter 6), so it seems clear that he and his fellows had decided where to go three months before they took the Theatre down. They chose 28 December as the best date for the work because they knew Allen would be out of town then. They did not want to have him around, a half-demented spectator who would probably raise the Watch and would certainly try to impede Street and his workmen.

The site they had chosen for their new theatre was in Bankside, a district of Southwark, better in every way than Shoreditch. For a start, it was readily accessible, whereas Shoreditch, still part rural, was at an inconvenient distance from the most densely populated parts of the city. In bad weather, some people thought twice before making the journey, especially as they had to cross a muddy field path to reach the Theatre. Bankside was within easy reach for thousands of Londoners, coming on foot or by horse or coach (according to their means) across London Bridge, or taking a waterman's boat to that much-used landing-place, Paris Garden Stairs.

Most importantly, the Lord Chamberlain's Men were moving into the heart of London's pleasure ground. The Bankside's two 'liberties' – the Liberty of Paris Garden and the Liberty of the Clink – had long been famous, or notorious, as places of recreation free from the puritanical restraint of the city authorities. With its theatres (the Rose and the Swan were there before the Globe was built), its brothels and its Bear Garden, Bankside was the home of a thriving entertainment industry. (The memory of that vigorous life is preserved in the names on a modern street plan of the area: Bear Lane, Bear Gardens, Rose Alley, Clink Street, Paris Garden – Bankside, itself.)

By building their new theatre in the Liberty of the Clink and near to the Rose, the Chamberlain's Men were challenging Henslowe and

Alleyn on their own doorstep. In comparison with the shining new Globe, the Rose looked shabby. Expensive improvements would be needed to bring it up to the rival theatre's standards. Henslowe decided to move. North of the river and well away from his competitors, he built the Fortune in Finsbury, requiring his builder to incorporate in its design all the best features of the Globe. In 1600, he and Alleyn took the Admiral's Men off to their new home, leasing the Rose to Worcester's Men, though other companies acted there as well.

Henslowe was sensible to get away. The Globe was the finest playhouse in London – big, comfortable, replete with all the advantages an actor could wish for. (Its size, shape and technical features are described in Chapter 11.) The new theatre, its players and its plays were Bankside's outstanding attraction from the day it opened in the early autumn of 1599 to the day its thatched roof caught fire during a performance of *Henry VIII* on 29 June 1613 (see Chapter 9).

The words of a foreign visitor who was staying in London soon after the Globe opened convey something of the excitement the splendid new theatre caused. Thomas Platter, a doctor from Basle, was taken to see *Julius Caesar* and he described how

> After dinner on 21 September, at about 2 o'clock, I went over the river with my companions, and in the straw-thatched house saw the Tragedy of the first Emperor Julius Caesar, with at least 15 characters, acted very well. At the end of the play two of the actors in men's clothes and 2 in women's clothes performed a dance, as is their custom, wonderfully well together.

The money to build the Globe was raised by the leading members of the Lord Chamberlain's Men – the 'sharers', as they were called. They thus became 'housekeepers' or 'householders' in the theatre itself, while also being sharers in the acting company that used it. (How important a factor that was in the development of the Chamberlain's Men is explained in detail in Chapter 12.) As housekeepers, they were entitled to a share of the daily takings at the theatre as a first charge on the company's profits.

Once the theatre was open, heavy running costs had to be met (site rent, of course, was due whether the building was in use or not): the expenses of repair and maintenance increased the more popular it became; money was needed to buy plays and get them licensed; properties and costumes had to be provided; actors, musicians, carpenters, doorkeepers and tire (costume) keepers had to be paid.

The housekeepers and the sharers were responsible for all outgoings and they took the profits generated by the employment of those human and material resources.

London from Bankside (1647)
part of Wenceslaus Hollar's famous 'Long View'
the labels for the Globe and the Beargarden – also called the Hope – were transposed

Because they risked a great deal of money – and stood to make a lot if their venture prospered – the details of their agreement were most carefully worked out by their lawyers. The Lord Chamberlain's Men ratified their articles of association well before the Globe opened. The following main provisions are set out in a complicated document dated 21 February 1599.

The two Burbages, who had inherited the Theatre from their father and who contributed most to the building of the Globe, took a half share in the theatre between them. The remaining half was divided between five other housekeepers: William Shakespeare, John Heminge, Augustine Phillips, Thomas Pope and William Kempe. Shakespeare's share thus amounted to one-fifth of one-half. In other words, he was a ten per cent housekeeper in the Globe.

As we know, he was already a sharer in the acting company when that new agreement was signed, but the size of his pre-Globe holding is not known. It was large enough to bring him a considerable income on top of his actor's wage and the money the company paid him for each new play he wrote. Just how well he had been doing financially since becoming a sharer in 1594 can be judged by the benefits he was able to provide for his family after that year. (Details of his Stratford activities during his first years with the Chamberlain's Men are given in the last section of this chapter.)

For Shakespeare, as for his fellows, the Globe proved to be a very profitable investment. It was a much more lucrative playhouse than the Theatre had ever been. He continued to act, though his stage appearances gradually became less frequent. He continued to supply his players with scripts that drew the crowds and, as a manager, he was heavily involved in the company's artistic direction and business affairs. Later, when they decided to open another theatre that was even more profitable than the Globe (see Chapter 9), they ran the two enterprises in tandem. It was characteristic of Shakespeare and of the men he worked with so closely that they saw no reason to abandon the still-vigorous Globe just because the Blackfriars Theatre proved to be a resounding success.

Few of his biographers can resist the temptation to guess how much Shakespeare earned, but it is not a game worth spending much time on. Even if we could arrive at a convincing figure we would still be left with the near-impossible task of describing his earnings in meaningful terms by present-day reckoning. Estimates of his annual income vary from two hundred to a thousand pounds – the former certainly much too low, and the latter probably much too high. Any calculation must at once be qualified by pointing out that his income undoubtedly fluctuated from year to year. Good years were followed by others spoilt by adverse and unforeseeable conditions. When the theatres were closed, neither he nor anybody else in his or in any other company could earn anything.

The best way of looking at it is this: when he retired he owned a valuable property in London; one large house, one substantial house, and two smaller houses in Stratford; an extensive estate of land and tithe holdings in and around that town. In addition to those very considerable assets, he retained his sharer's rights in London's major theatre company. Though he was no longer active in the management of the King's Men, he continued to participate in their profits. If he chose, he could sell his share and get a great deal of money for it.

So, to the question 'How much did he earn?' the only sensible answer is: 'A lot'!

In Chapter 7 it was mentioned that Shakespeare was a competent actor rather than a star, but the importance of his training and long experience as a player must not be underestimated. It contributed greatly to his success as a playwright. He knew, as only a practised actor can, what would 'go' on stage. He gave his players lines that worked, exits and entrances they were comfortable with. As many a present-day actor testifies, his scripts are the work of a writer steeped in the theatre – one who knew what it was like to get out there on the stage and hold the spectators' attention.

For the first twenty years of his career he was a regular performer, and we know the names of some of the plays in which he acted. When Ben Jonson published his own plays in a collected edition in 1613 he listed Shakespeare as having been one of the 'principal comedians' when *Every Man in his Humour* was staged in 1598. (Christopher Beeston was in the cast, too – see Chapter 6.) Jonson also included Shakespeare in the list of 'tragedians' acting in *Sejanus* in 1603. It is worth remembering that *Every Man* was popular, whereas *Sejanus* flopped. Shakespeare had firsthand experience of the ups and downs of acting – and it was far from pleasant to encounter the uninhibited expression of an audience's disapproval in those days. He shared in the applause for *Every Man* with his regular acting colleagues, Richard Burbage, John Heminge and Henry Condell; and together they received the jeers that sent *Sejanus* packing.

Rowe's *Life* (see Chapter 1) claimed that it was Shakespeare who gave Jonson his chance to write for the Lord Chamberlain's Men. Jonson, he said,

> offered one of his plays to the players in order to have it acted, and the persons into whose hands it was put, after having turned it carelessly and superciliously over, were just upon returning it to him with an ill-natured answer that it would be of no service to their company, when Shakespeare luckily cast his eye upon it and found something so well in it as to engage him to read it through and afterwards to recommend [it].

It is a pity that Rowe did not say where he got that story. Without supporting evidence, its truth cannot be relied on. It sounds likely. Jonson had kind memories of Shakespeare (see Chapter 10). The quick professional glance, as described by Rowe, that detected merit in the rejected manuscript, is as typical of Shakespeare's working habits as the subsequent readiness to read it through and to encourage its author is typical of his good nature.

When his fellow actors and sharers Heminge and Condell edited the First Folio in 1623 they placed Shakespeare's name first in their list of 'The Names of the Principal Actors in all these Plays'. It was fitting to give him pride of place in a memorial tribute, but the phrase 'in *all* these plays' was perhaps not intended to be taken literally. Not all the actors in their list acted in every one of the plays. However, we can be quite sure that Heminge and Condell were recording it as a fact that Shakespeare appeared on stage in many of – perhaps most of – his own plays. They were in the best possible position to know. They had worked with him for many years.

A persistent thread runs through many of the stories that have been told about his acting: the suggestion that he specialised in oldish, rather grave and dignified roles. For example, one story says that he was Adam, the faithful servant in *As You Like It*. Another describes him as having excelled as the murdered King of Denmark's ghost in *Hamlet*. Strong support for that tradition is provided in a book called *The Scourge of Folly*, published in 1610. It included some anonymous lines of verse addressed to Shakespeare:

> Some say (good Will) – which I, in sport, do sing –
> Hadst thou not played some kingly parts in sport,
> Thou hadst been a companion for a king,
> And been a king among the meaner sort.

The meaning of the last line is disputed, but the statement that Shakespeare 'played some kingly parts' confirms the other stories. Whoever the writer was, he was Shakespeare's contemporary and could have seen him on the stage or, at least, have heard theatre talk about his roles. If it does nothing else, the verse suggests yet another layer of meaning in Hamlet's ambiguous remark on hearing that the players had arrived in Elsinore: 'He that plays the king shall be welcome; his majesty shall have tribute of me'.

Another contemporary story about Shakespeare and his fellow actors was recorded in 1602 in a diary kept by John Manningham, a law student at the Middle Temple. Manningham got the story from another student named Edward Curle.

According to Curle (as Manningham reported) Richard Burbage and Shakespeare had been acting together in *Richard III*, with Burbage in the title role. After the performance, Shakespeare overheard a conversation between Burbage and a pretty woman who had taken a fancy to that fine actor. They arranged to meet at her house, and Burbage told her that he would tap on the door three times and then say, 'It is I, Richard the Third'.

At once, so the diary records, Shakespeare followed her to her house and got there before Burbage had left the theatre. He used Burbage's signal to gain admission and though she was surprised to see him instead of Burbage, 'he did not want wit or eloquence to win her over'. They were 'mutually happy' when Burbage tapped at the door and announced that 'Richard the Third' had arrived. To which message, Shakespeare 'with some relish returned word that William the Conqueror preceded Richard the Third'.

It would be unwise to build theories about Shakespeare's character on the evidence of that story. It is, after all, merely an amusing anecdote; but it does demonstrate the interest that theatre fans took in the real or supposed lives led by their favourite players. Curle and Manningham were two educated and fashionable young men who delighted in a scandalous piece of gossip about Burbage and Shakespeare, leading lights of the much-admired Lord Chamberlain's Men.

During their first four years at the Globe (from 1599 to 1603) they established their predominance over all the other adult companies and fought off the competition of the child actors (see Chapter 6). Their ascendancy was signalled not only by packed houses at the Globe but also by more Court appearances than any of their rivals. They played for the Queen every Christmas – twice in 1599-1600, twice in 1600/1, three times in 1601/2.

Well paid and prestigious private commissions also came their way. In March 1600, for example, their patron employed them to entertain Ludovick Vereiken, an important diplomat who was negotiating with Elizabeth and her ministers on behalf of the Duke of Burgundy. The occasion is described in a contemporary account of the diplomat's reception: ' . . . upon Thursday my Lord Chamberlain feasted him, and made him very great [made much of him] and a delicate dinner, and there in the afternoon his players acted, before Vereiken, *Sir John Old Castell* [*Oldcastle*], to his great contentment'.

'Sir John Oldcastle' is the character we know as Falstaff, so the play they acted for the Lord Chamberlain and his guest was either Part 1 or Part 2 of *Henry IV*. Originally, Shakespeare had called Falstaff 'Oldcastle', a choice of name that caused him and his company some trouble. Sir John Oldcastle (later created Lord Cobham) was an historical person, an extreme Protestant, who had been a friend of Prince Hal's before he became Henry V. He then intrigued against the king and was executed in 1417. Many people in Shakespeare's day regarded him as having been an early Protestant martyr. (He had a place of honour in Foxe's *Book of Martyrs*.) Others saw him as having been a narrow-minded Puritan killjoy, and thought that he deserved to die for conspiring against the hero-king. Whatever the truth of it, he was not at all like Shakespeare's famous and immensely popular comic character.

Oldcastle's descendants, the Cobhams, were outraged by

Shakespeare's use of their ancestor's name. They regarded the character of the fat, debauched knight as an insult to their family honour; and the enthusiasm with which theatre-goers received him fuelled their resentment. The Lord Chamberlain's Men saw no point in offending the Cobhams, so 'Sir John Oldcastle' became 'Sir John Falstaff'.

Shakespeare did his best to cool things down by including some mollifying words in the Epilogue spoken at the end of *Henry IV Part 2*. There, he promised that Falstaff would appear again in his next play, and he emphasised that the character bore no resemblance whatever to Oldcastle and had never been intended to represent him:

> If you be not too much cloyed with fat meat, our humble author will continue the story with Sir John in it, and make you merry with fair Katherine of France: where, for anything I know, Falstaff shall die of a sweat, unless already a' be killed with your hard opinions; for Oldcastle died a martyr, and this is not the man.

As it turned out, Shakespeare had second thoughts about including Falstaff in *Henry V*, and decided against it. There was no room for his complex and comic anarchy in that celebration of heroic deeds. Falstaff's fans had to be contented with Mistress Quickly's moving description of his death and his companions' laments for the broken-hearted knight.

In spite of Shakespeare's attempts to remove Oldcastle's name from *Henry IV*, the association lingered on. Part 2 of the play was published in 1600 and in that text one of Falstaff's speeches is marked *Old* – for 'Oldcastle'. Either the printer was working from an uncorrected manuscript, or – more likely – his memory slipped back to the character's original name. Nor could Shakespeare remove every trace of 'Oldcastle' from the text. In Part 1 Prince Hal addresses Falstaff as 'my old lad of the castle'. The pun on his name was also a jest at his obesity, but the point was lost when the fat knight ceased to be 'Oldcastle'.

The Oldcastle affair was a nuisance, but it did the Chamberlain's Men no serious harm. By changing the character's name (at Queen Elizabeth's own command, it was rumoured) they demonstrated their good intentions, and they were much too popular to be penalised for having offended the Cobhams. Most of their admirers cared little for Oldcastle's memory and less for his descendants' hurt pride. The Lord Admiral's Men tried to cash in on the publicity by staging a play which purported to recount 'The True and Honourable History of the Life of Sir John Oldcastle, the Good Lord Cobham'. As an attempt to take audiences away from Shakespeare it was a resounding failure.

Even if the Queen did intervene to soothe the Cobhams' hurt feelings, she shared the general enthusiasm for Shakespeare's plays, which by now were so well known that people were referring to them and quoting from them (not always accurately!) in their talk and correspondence. His words and characters were entering daily life. For instance, Lady Southampton wrote in a letter to her husband:

> All the news I can send you that I think will make you merry is that I read in a letter from London that Sir John Falstaff is by his dame, Mistress Pintpot [one of Falstaff's nicknames for Mistress Quickly] made father of a boy that's all head and very little body [a clear reference to Falstaff's diminutive page].

Sir Charles Percy, writing from a manor house in Gloucestershire, was obviously remembering *Henry IV Part 2* when he said, 'If I stay here long, you will find me so dull that I shall be taken as a Justice Shallow'. John Marston, a younger man than Shakespeare and beginning to make his name as a dramatist in 1600, said that playgoers were so bewitched by the Chamberlain's poet that they were trying to talk like people in his plays. Just listen, he complained, 'from their mouths doth flow/Nought but pure Juliet and Romeo'.

The Queen's delight in Falstaff was said to have led directly to one of Shakespeare's triumphs. 'She was so well pleased with that admirable character of Falstaff . . . that she commanded him to continue it for one play more and to show him in love'. He obeyed and wrote *The Merry Wives of Windsor*, working so fast that no more than a fortnight elapsed between the day the royal command was received and the first performance of the play in the Queen's presence. Perhaps! It is a pleasing story, but its author, John Dennis, who adapted Shakespeare's play in 1702, gave no supporting evidence for it. There is no doubt, however, that *The Merry Wives* followed quickly after *Henry IV Part 2*. Its title page when it was printed in 1602 announced that the play had been acted 'before her Majesty' so, if she did not command him to write it, she very soon commanded him to present it at Court.

These were golden years for the Chamberlain's Men. The scripts they were getting from their 'resident dramatist' were so very much better than any their rivals could buy. With all his money and all his experience, Henslowe could not find a dramatist to compete with Shakespeare; and Alleyn, with all his talent, could not obtain parts to challenge those that were being written for Burbage.

In their first four triumphant years at the Globe Shakespeare's company had his previous smash hits to draw on and he supplied them with a stream of new and equally successful plays. For six of the plays listed by Meres in 1598, they could still count on having full houses: *Romeo and Juliet, Much Ado* ('Love's Labour's Won'), *A Midsummer Night's Dream, The Merchant of Venice*, the two part of *Henry IV*. Between that date and 1601 he added: *Henry V, Julius Caesar, The Merry Wives of Windsor, As You Like It, Twelfth Night* and *Hamlet*. After *Hamlet* and before the Queen's death in 1603 he wrote *All's Well that Ends Well* and *Troilus and Cressida* for them. No company in London had a stock of playbooks to equal theirs. (No acting company anywhere in the world has again enjoyed exclusive possession of and the right to exploit a dramatic property of such value.)

Shakespeare's working life had another ten years to run when Queen Elizabeth died on 24 March 1603, but for him and his company – as for all England – her death was a turning-point. The new regime brought about many changes, not least in the entertainment business. In altered conditions, success went to those who were quick to recognise and respond to movements in fashionable taste. Shakespeare and his colleagues (now the King's Men) were always innovators and they flourished exceedingly in James I's reign.

Critics point to the darker mood of the plays he wrote in the Queen's last years – *Hamlet, All's Well* and *Troilus and Cressida* – as prefiguring his 'tragic period', which spanned the first five years of the new reign. Such matters are not the concern of an objective biography. It may be pointed out, however, that his supposed preoccupation with life's ills coincided with a period when his material fortunes were prospering exceedingly. Of course, there is no reason at all why a successful man may not be sad. Equally, it cannot be assumed that the writing of tragedies must be the expression of personal unhappiness or of an unrelieved awareness of world sorrow. There are no known facts in Shakespeare's life which can be used to 'explain' why he concentrated on tragic themes between 1603 and 1608.

Certainly, there are marked differences of mood and technique between his Elizabethan and his Jacobean plays, but he and his company were operating in different circumstances after James I became king. For that reason alone – and without needing to speculate about an emotional or spiritual crisis – we can recognise that 1603 brought one period of his career to an end. It also marked the beginning of the most successful years of his working life.

Before describing the achievement of the King's Men at the Globe and at the Blackfriars theatre (see Chapter 9) we must bring our account of Stratford events up to date. Though he lived in London for most of the year, it would be a great mistake to think of him as being – or as feeling himself to be – cut off from his family and his birthplace. Closely involved in every aspect of his theatre company's work, supplying his fellow actors with two new plays each year, and acting himself, he yet found time and energy for Stratford matters, some of which were complicated and expensive. When he was unable to attend to his affairs there in person, he had trusted agents on whom he relied. Even so, the evidence bears out John Aubrey's statement that Shakespeare 'was wont to go to his native country once a year'.

In all material respects his life was uninterruptedly successful from 1594 onwards, but in the summer of 1596 fate dealt him a cruel blow. Hamnet, his only son, died. Neither the date nor the cause of his death is known. His burial took place on 11 August and was entered in the register of Holy Trinity Church: 'Hamnet, filius William Shakespeare'. He was eleven years and six months old.

Nothing remains to tell us of his parents' grief. Neither William nor Anne Shakespeare left any records of their sorrows or of their joys. Finding it impossible to believe that the plays do not reflect his deeply-felt bereavement, commentators search through them for its traces. Some conjecture that in *The Winter's Tale* Polixenes' expression of delight in his young son's companionship recalls Shakespeare's poignant memories of time spent with his own boy. It may be so, but how can we know? *The Winter's Tale* was written fifteen years after Hamnet's death. The plays that came immediately after that sad event are exuberant in comedy.

What we do know is that his son's death deprived him of a male heir to inherit his estate and to bear the Shakespeare name. His careful custodianship of his family's worldly interests implies that he had his full share of the dynastic ambitions common in his day. That implication is borne out by the fact that he encouraged his father to proceed with his application for a grant of arms. Ironically, that hereditary honour was conferred just two months after Hamnet's death. In due course it descended from John to William Shakespeare. In the fullness of time it would have passed from him to his own son had he outlived his father.

John Shakespeare had applied for a grant of arms twenty years earlier, shortly before his financial problems became acute. As he could not then afford to pay the hefty fee, he did not proceed. Now, however, the money was available.

The grant itself has been lost, but two drafts and their accompanying notes explain the reasons given for granting the application. Garter King-of-Arms (the principal herald) made some vague references to Shakespeares who had served Henry VII. He then moved to more solid matters. The applicant, he noted, had been a justice of the peace, bailiff of Stratford and a Queen's officer. He had married the daughter of a gentleman and he was now 'possessed of lands and tenements of good wealth and substance'.

His credentials were acceptable and the fee was paid. Garter King-of-Arms pronounced that 'it shall be lawful for the said John Shakespeare gentleman and for his children, issue and posterity to bear and make demonstration of that same Blazon or Achievement [coat of Arms] . . . without let or hindrance . . . '.

The Shakespeare coat of arms is instantly recognisable even by those who have little knowledge of heraldic devices, for it has been reproduced in many books and stamped on innumerable souvenirs. The spear prominent on the shield and in the crest (each forming part of the whole coat of arms) attracts immediate attention – and was meant to. Heraldry delights in punning symbols. Carved on William Shakespeare's monument in Stratford church, his arms take a fitting place among the other formal manifestations of bygone honours. Where Clopton memorials proclaim a family's glory, why should not his?

What is missing from the monument is the motto *Non Sanz Droict* ('Not without right') which the herald's clerk wrote above the shield and the crest on the draft grant. Unlike a coat of arms a motto is not hereditary nor, in England, does it form an integral part of the 'Achievement'. It is adopted at choice and is usually suggested by the applicant for the grant or introduced by a later bearer of the arms. Though the Shakespeares did not use their motto, it is tempting to suppose that William himself suggested it. 'Not without right' is a quietly-worded but firm assertion that seems in character. He neither overvalued nor despised worldly honours. Just about the time his father's tenure of the arms descended to him he was writing the jokes for his comic gravediggers in *Hamlet*:

First Clown   There is no ancient gentlemen but gardeners, ditchers, and grave-makers; they hold up Adam's profession.
Second Clown Was he a gentleman?
First Clown   A' was the first that ever bore arms.
Second Clown Why, he had none.
First Clown   What, art a heathen? How dost thou understand the Scripture? The Scripture says Adam digged; could he dig without arms?

Today, some people feel that Shakespeare's wish to establish his father (and, therefore, himself) as a gentleman was snobbish. The social ambition belittles him in their eyes. It really is a waste of time to make so much of the matter. By the values of his day, he was no more snobbish in encouraging his father to obtain a grant of arms than in buying a large and impressive house for his family to live in. John Shakespeare had married an Arden, so there was 'gentle blood' in the family. As they saw it, the Shakespeares were not making a brash attempt to break into 'society'. They were obtaining official recognition of a status to which their Arden connection and John Shakespeare's former civic dignities fully entitled them.

It is interesting to remember that both John Heminge and Edward Alleyn applied for and obtained the right to use a coat of arms. William Shakespeare was not the only actor who reckoned that a 'household coat' (Bolingbroke: *Richard II*) would be a comfortable garment to wear in retirement.

Seven months after the grant of arms he bought New Place, the mansion that Sir Hugh Clopton had built many years earlier. Referred to by Clopton as 'my Great House', it stood at the corner where Chapel Lane joins Chapel Street. New Place was demolished in 1759 by a foolish and bad-tempered parson called Francis Gastrell who was quarrelling with the corporation about the rates. (The year before, he had cut down the great mulberry tree that had been growing in New Place garden since Shakespeare's time.) Fortunately, from various descriptions and one excellent drawing we know pretty well what it looked like. The five-gabled front faced onto a courtyard separating the house from Chapel Street, entrance from which was afforded by a fine gateway. The house had three storeys. It was sixty feet wide and seventy feet deep, the windows on its south (Chapel Lane) side overlooking the Guild Chapel, the guildhall and the school. It had ample room for family, guests and servants, and it stood in extensive gardens.

The deed of transfer (dated 4 May 1597) states that Shakespeare paid 'sixty pounds in silver' for New Place, together with all its outbuildings and 'two barns and two gardens'. There is some reason to believe that he paid more than that. Transfer documents did not always state the correct sum – the lower the purchase price was declared to be, the lower the fees and taxes due on the transaction. But whatever the exact cost may have been, the purchase of New Place was a large venture requiring considerable resources. Without needing to borrow, he bought a mansion and the land that went with it, paying cash down and finding the money out of his current income.

New Place had been occupied by several different owners and tenants since Clopton's day, some of whom had neglected its fabric. Shakespeare repaired it thoroughly and made extensive alterations – 'he modelled it to his own mind' – before moving his family into their new home. It took time, but we know that they were living there early in 1598. On 4 February of that year Stratford corporation took an inventory of the quantity of malt held by each household. Shakespeare was listed as having laid in a good store for brewing the family beer in New Place.

New Place
George Vertue's sketch shows it as it was in 1737

From then on, he maintained his wife and two daughters in comfort in their fine Stratford house while sustaining the expenses of his own lodgings in London and the cost of his journeys to and from his home. His father and mother remained in the Henley Street house, with plenty of space round them now that Anne and the children had moved out. However, it was a short walk from John Shakespeare's house to William's and there was a good deal of coming and going between the two.

While his wife and children were settling in at New Place in January 1598, Shakespeare was back in London. His Stratford friend Richard Quiney was there, too, much occupied with Stratford corporation business. While he was there Quiney received a letter from Abraham Sturley (see Chapter 4). Sturley's letter shows that Shakespeare's friends and acquaintances in Stratford continued to regard him as their own 'countryman'. The famous London playwright was to them first and foremost a Stratfordian, and one who was naturally on the look-out to increase his possessions and his status in his native town.

The purpose of Sturley's letter was to give Richard Quiney the news that Shakespeare was interested in buying some more property and to suggest that Quiney should discuss the matter with him. Sturley's information had come from Richard's father, Adrian Quiney, who had undoubtedly got it from his old friend and former colleague John Shakespeare. Those two aging men remained on close terms all their lives. There was little they did not know about each other and about their children's and their grandchildren's doings.

Prompted by old Adrian, Sturley at once passed on the information and pressed Richard Quiney to open the subject with Shakespeare. The letter, dated 24 January 1598, provides a vivid glimpse of the tightly-knit Stratford community to which Shakespeare always belonged.

> It seemeth to him [your father] that our countryman Mr Shakespeare is willing to disburse some money upon some odd yardland or other [any suitable plot of land] at Shottery or near about us; he thinketh it a very fit pattern [a very appropriate plan] to move him to deal in the matter of our tithes.

Several interesting points emerge from that letter. First, though Shakespeare had recently been spending a lot of money (the fee for the grant of arms, the cost of buying, repairing and altering New Place), in the opinion of those who knew him well he was in a position to spend more, and he would if he liked the proposition.

Second, Sturley considered it proper to refer to him as '*Mr Shakespeare*'. In London he was a player, but in Stratford he was recognised as having a social position of some dignity. His father was now a gentleman 'of coat armour' and William was himself the master of New Place. He was entitled to a respectful form of address.

Third, Adrian Quiney had been told that Shakespeare was particularly interested in buying land at Shottery – his wife's birthplace. Both he and Anne knew that district well and could judge the value of any 'odd yardland' on offer there. Moreover, it would have pleased them to acquire property near where Anne's father had farmed and she had grown up. We know from the will of her father's old shepherd, Thomas Whittington, that she kept up her Shottery connections, though it was sixteen years since she had lived there. Whittington (he died in March 1601) requested that a sum of money he had deposited with 'Anne Shaxspere, wife unto Mr Wyllyam Shaxspere' be paid over to his executor and used for the benefit of 'the poor people of Stratford'.

A fourth point that arises is Adrian Quiney's belief that this might well be the time to persuade Shakespeare to join Sturley and Richard

Quiney in buying tithes. Investing in tithes was potentially very profitable and it carried social prestige. A tithe owner was entitled to receive an annual tax (tithe) from landowners and their tenants who were subject to that ancient form of levy. Originally a source of income for the church, the tithes payable on many estates were still in ecclesiastical ownership. Others had been bought by lay investors, and any that came up for sale were keenly sought after.

As it happened, Shakespeare did not then proceed with the ideas put forward. Throughout 1598 he and the other sharers in the Chamberlain's Men were very busy with their plans to leave the Theatre and move to Bankside. Later, he made substantial purchases of land and tithes in and around Stratford.

In the October of 1598, when Shakespeare had moved into his lodgings in Southwark, Richard Quiney was again in London on corporation business, staying at the Bell Inn near St Paul's. He was trying to persuade the Privy Council to improve the terms of the town's charter and to reduce its taxes. Kept hanging about for a decision, he found his money running out and he turned to his 'loving good friend and countryman Mr. Wm. Shakespeare' for the loan of £30 to clear the debts he had incurred in London. For some reason Quiney did not send the letter in which he made this request. Probably he went to see Shakespeare instead. The letter was found among Quiney's papers at his death in 1602 (see Chapter 4).

There is no record that the loan was made, but in the November of 1598 both Sturley and Adrian Quiney knew that Richard was negotiating with Shakespeare. News travelled remarkably fast between London and Stratford! In the end, Quiney's mission was successful and his out-of-pocket expenses were refunded by the Privy Council.

People who cherish romantic notions about the life style of creative geniuses are reluctant to accept the blunt fact that mundane affairs took up a lot of Shakespeare's time. While he was writing his immortal plays, he was also up to his neck in company business and family matters. In 1599, for example, the year of *Henry V* and *Julius Caesar*, John Shakespeare's long-delayed lawsuit with Walford got under way (see Chapter 5). William's consent and support were needed.

In that year, too, Shakespeare's sister Joan married William Hart, a hatter. It was a far from brilliant match, but she was thirty and past the time when she could pick and choose. There were complications at once. Shakespeare's brother-in-law was sued for debt in 1600 and again in the following year. Without more information than the records provide, it is hard to know how culpable he was. People went to law very readily in those days – and about issues we might think trivial. Shakespeare himself took a Stratford man, Philip Rogers, to the Court of Record (where small debt cases were decided by the bailiff) for a few pence outstanding on the sale of malt and a subsequent loan. Readers who like to keep 'The Bard of Avon' up on a pedestal will not be pleased to know that this matter was in hand while Shakespeare was busy with *Othello*!

Family business required a lot of attention in 1601. John Shakespeare died in the September. As he did not leave a will, the Henley Street house passed to his eldest son, William, but his widow continued to live there (see Chapter 3). Joan and William Hart and the first-born of their four children moved in with her, a satisfactory arrangement all round.

In May 1602 Shakespeare consolidated his Stratford estate with further investments. He bought one hundred and seven acres of good farmland in Old Stratford, an agricultural district to the north of the town. It was a big venture for which he had to find £320 in cash. Unable to be in Stratford himself, he got his brother Gilbert, then aged thirty-five, to act as his agent. In the September he bought a house for his gardener to live in, a cottage standing in a nice plot of land off Chapel Lane. From his earliest occupancy of New Place its big garden had been one of the major interests of his Stratford life.

The build-up of his Stratford properties is the more remarkable because he had no male heir. Nor was it probable that he would. In 1602 Anne was in her late forties and most unlikely to bear more children. Their daughters – Susanna was nineteen and Judith was seventeen – were of marriageable age and it seemed that their husbands, when they had them, would in due course be the principal beneficiaries of their father's wealth. Shakespeare's own awareness of this and the steps he took to lessen its disadvantages are discussed in Chapter 10.

He made his biggest investment in 1605, a date that falls outside the chronological framework of this chapter (1594-1603). However, since it completed the careful Stratford moves to which he had devoted so much time, effort and money since becoming a sharer in the Chamberlain's Men, it can fitly be included here.

When the Quineys and Sturley had suggested an investment in tithes he was not ready, but in July 1605 the successes of the King's Men were already such that he was able to find a very large sum of money for that purpose. He spent £440 in acquiring an interest in the tithes of three hamlets near Stratford and in Stratford parish itself. He took the advice of his excellent lawyer and friend, Francis Collins. He also had the trusty Anthony Nash of Welcombe (one of the hamlets in which he was buying tithes) to witness documents and generally keep an eye on things. The legal and financial arrangements were complicated, but the investment was a sound one. It brought him £60 a year, after all charges had been met. That, it will be remembered, was the declared purchase price of New Place.

Eight years afterwards, Shakespeare decided that, in the words of his own magician, the time had come to 'break my staff' and 'drown my book'. By then, he had prepared for himself a more attractive and more secure place of retirement than Prospero's Milan seems likely to prove.

9

'These our Servants'

O N the feast of Candlemas (2 February) 1603 the Lord Chamberlain's Men played before the Queen's Majesty for the last time. Elizabeth died on 24 March, in the forty-fifth year of her reign.

Few of her subjects could remember a time when she had not reigned. She was as much a part of their lives as the English weather, and regarded in much the same way – as an unpredictable force of nature that, taking the rough with the smooth, brought them more good than ill. They were used to her; and while she lived she protected them from the terrors of 'base and bloody insurrection' (*Henry IV Part 2*). People of William Shakespeare's generation (when he was born, Elizabeth had already been Queen for eight years) had no wish to experience the civil strife of their grandfathers' days or the shifting allegiances imposed on their fathers when they were young men.

As the Queen aged and tired, fears grew that a childless monarch's death would be followed by a disputed succession. Those fears proved groundless. Elizabeth named James VI of Scotland as her successor. Her secretary of state, Robert Cecil, saw to it that power was transferred smoothly. King James made a stately progress through England and was received with welcoming ceremonies in every town through which he passed on his way to be crowned in London.

King James I – for that, of course, was how the first Stuart King of England was known in his new realm – started his English reign with much goodwill in every quarter. The war with Spain had dragged on until people were weary of it, so his peace policy was welcome. Besides, it was a change to have a king again. The new reign promised novelty, not least because of the new monarch's view that money was for spending. Elizabeth's careful – some said, parsimonious – attitude to expenditure was replaced by James's liberal – some said, spendthrift – use of a royal exchequer far larger than he had been accustomed to in his poorer northern kingdom. In particular, James and his Queen (Anne of Denmark) were eager for the pleasures that the players could provide. Such delights had not been readily accessible in the extreme puritanical climate of the capital they had left, where gloomy Presbyterian divines were quick to denounce harmless entertainment.

Only ten days after setting up his Court in London, James granted to the Lord Chamberlain's Men a licence or patent declaring that they were from then on to be known as the King's own servants and assuring them of his royal protection whenever and wherever they exercised their profession:

> We . . . do licence and authorise these our Servants, Laurence Fletcher, William Shakespeare, Richard Burbage, Augustine Phillips, John Heminge, Henry Condell, William Sly, Robert Armin, Richard Cowley and the rest of their Associates freely to use and exercise the Art and Faculty of playing Comedies, Tragedies, Histories . . . like as they have already studied or hereafter shall use or study as well for the Recreation of our loving Subjects as for our Solace and Pleasure when we shall think good to see them.

To move with such speed in that matter he must have considered it important, for he had plenty of other things to attend to. He must also have been implementing a decision taken some time previously. Always enthusiastic about the theatre, he had kept himself informed about the London companies, and on his month-long journey to his new capital, accompanied by Elizabeth's former courtiers and officials, he had sounded out opinions about the merits of the various troupes of players.

The supremacy of Shakespeare's company was quite plainly recognised by King James's action in the May of 1603. By then – and after repeated previous attempts by the authorities to reduce their numbers – the adult acting companies of London had been whittled down to three 'privileged companies': the Lord Chamberlain's Men, the Lord Admiral's Men and the Earl of Worcester's Men. By the King's command, the Chamberlain's became the King's Men. The other companies also received royal patronage, but not from the monarch himself. They had to make do with lesser members of his family. The Admiral's became Prince Henry's Men and Worcester's became Queen Anne's Men – valued titles, of course, but not the first prize.

The company sharers named in King James's patent as his servants were made Grooms of the Chamber. This was an unpaid and minor position in the royal household, but it was an official rank. On suitable occasions, they wore the royal livery (hence the grant to each of four-and-a-half yards of scarlet-red cloth) and, as His Majesty's Servants, they were not likely to be harassed by their Puritan enemies.

Most of those named in the royal patent had been sharers when the

Lord Chamberlain's Men came into being and most of them were to appear again in the list of principal actors which Heminge and Condell included in the First Folio in 1623. It was a characteristic of Chamberlain's-King's Men to stay together. In the other companies there were frequent changes of membership, but Shakespeare and his colleagues worked so harmoniously and successfully that it was most unusual for anyone to find reason to leave. He himself stayed with the company for twenty years and when he ceased to be an active working member he kept up his connections with it.

Two of those named in the King's patent were recent additions to the list of sharers. Laurence Fletcher had been an actor ('comedian to his Majesty') at James's Scottish Court so he was, in a sense, a 'King's Man' already. His place of honour in the list was his reward for having done his best to cheer his royal master in less palmy days. His name did not appear in any of the company's acting lists, nor did Heminge and Condell include it in their Folio list. However, if he was not a foremost member of the company, he got on with the others well enough. Augustine Phillips, a founder member, left a small legacy to 'my Fellow, Laurence Fletcher'.

Robert Armin, on the other hand, was a very active King's Man, a key player, in fact. He had been trained by the great Richard Tarlton (see Chapter 5) but had gone on to develop his own distinctive style of comic acting. He was a quiet, subtle performer who blended humour with a wistful melancholy. Shakespeare wrote the parts of Touchstone in *As You Like It*, Feste in *Twelfth Night* and the Fool in *King Lear* for him. An author as well as an actor, Armin referred in one of his books to his 'constableship' and said that he had been 'writ down an ass in his time'. Those remarks must mean that he had taken over Will Kempe's former role of Dogberry in *Much Ado*.

Kempe, one of the original Chamberlain's Men, sold his share and left the company soon after the Globe was opened. In 1600 he danced his way from London to Norwich and wrote a book about his astonishing experience. He then travelled in Germany and Italy and was said to have 'danced the morris over the Alps'. Having had enough of adventure, he rejoined the Chamberlain's Men in 1601, but he did not settle with them. In 1602 he borrowed money off Henslowe and joined Worcester's Men. Nothing is known about him after that, except that he died in 1608.

Will Kempe was the only 'Fellow' of the Chamberlain's Men whose membership of the company was broken in an unhappy way. He had been their chief 'comedian', and his past services were remembered by Heminge and Condell when they compiled their First Folio list; but after 1599 he was never again on close terms with his old colleagues. It seems that he resented attempts to persuade him to restrain his exuberant style of comic acting. Shakespeare and Burbage got tired of his habitual determination to steal the limelight (see Chapter 7 and *Hamlet*, Act III Sc.2) and were angered by his obstinate refusal to adapt his great talents to changing tastes. If – as has been argued – the time came when the Lord Chamberlain's Men had to choose between retaining Kempe's services or Shakespeare's, they did not have to think long before deciding. They could get another comic actor, but they could not get another William Shakespeare.

The benefits of King James's patronage were great. Shakespeare and his colleagues had enjoyed Queen Elizabeth's favour, but on an entirely unofficial footing, to be bestowed or withdrawn as it pleased her. True, she had smiled upon them and they had reason to remember her with gratitude; but she had never accorded them any kind of special status. Successful though they had been in her time, they had remained common players. Now, as soon as James arrived in London, they became the King's own players, with a ranking (however minor) among the officers of the royal household. It was a huge step towards security and the respectability that goes with it.

Financially, too, they did very well out of the new régime. Queen Elizabeth had paid £10 for a Court performance. King James paid twice that. He also made much more frequent use of the company 'for his solace and pleasure' than she had done. On average, the Lord Chamberlain's Men performed at Court three times each year between 1594 and 1603. Between 1603 and 1613 the King's Men averaged thirteen Court performances a year. That was more than all their rivals, adult and children's companies, combined. The King's Men were indisputably the leaders of their profession.

In some ways, the new reign began inauspiciously. There was a bad outbreak of the plague, and the public theatres were closed when James arrived in London. He was crowned in July but, compared with the festivities that had been planned – triumphal arches and 'shows' all along the processional route – it was a quiet occasion, with the public kept at a distance. That, in fact, was no great disadvantage, in James's eyes. Unlike Queen Elizabeth, he was uneasy and distrustful when his 'loving subjects' got close to him, and he had nothing of her ability to win their hearts. This royal preference for keeping the crowds at a distance inevitably influenced social attitudes. The advance of the 'private' theatres and the gradual separation of audiences by social class brought about changes in theatre fashions during the later years of Shakespeare's career. As we shall see, he and his company soon recognised the need to adapt to new conditions.

The King and Queen were eager to see the plays that had been popular before they arrived in England. Consequently, the revenue that His Majesty's Servants were losing because the theatres were closed was in great part made up by command performances, either at his London palaces or at great houses in the country. When James held Court out of London, they were sent for to beguile his leisure. From October to December, for example, he was at Wilton House, the Wiltshire home of the Herberts, Earls of Pembroke. He summoned his players to be there on 2 December and paid them £30 for their trouble. At Christmas, when James was back in London, they played for him twice at Hampton Court, receiving a larger than usual fee to which was added a bonus to compensate them for the continuing closure of the Globe. At Candlemas and on Shrove Tuesday they gave Court performances at Whitehall.

As the plague eased off, the theatres got back into their stride and the King's Men were busy indeed, what with Globe and Court productions and their State duties. The processional pageantry for James's coronation (postponed from the previous July) took place in March 1604. Then, in August, resplendent in their royal uniforms, they attended upon the newly-appointed Spanish ambassador at Somerset House, where James had lodged him. It was sixteen years since England and Spain had last had diplomatic relations, so no expense was spared to impress the envoy with the warmth of his welcome and with the splendour of his host. For eighteen days, in their official capacity as Grooms of the Chamber, Shakespeare and his fellows made themselves useful and pleasant – and received a handsome payment for their services.

By the winter of 1604, when the Queen's brother was on a visit, James and Anne had seen most of the King's Men's current repertory and had caught up with many of their past successes. Sir Walter Cope, the Chamberlain of the Exchequer and responsible for arranging Court shows, told Robert Cecil of his problems in finding fresh entertainments. Fortunately, as he explained, Richard Burbage was able to help him out:

> Burbage is come and says there is no new play that the queen hath not seen, but they have revived an old one, called *Love's Labour's Lost*, which for wit and mirth, he says, will please her exceedingly.

It was just as well that the King's Men had a back list of successes to draw on, for they were in great demand. They were enjoying royal favour and public acclaim such as no theatre company had previously known. Because of his several different functions, Shakespeare was carrying a bigger workload than anybody else. The unrivalled popularity of his plays was the company's chief asset so, from now on, his acting commitments were reduced to give him more time for writing. After 1603, he seldom acted in plays by other dramatists. His stage appearances were gradually restricted to small parts in his own plays. This sensible conservation of his energies can be traced in the acting lists. As we have seen, he took a part in Jonson's *Sejanus* in the winter of 1603, but he did not act in his *Volpone*, which the King's Men staged in 1605, nor in that fine comedy, *The Alchemist*, in 1610.

Now, too, when the company toured, he went home to Stratford to write. It was to everybody's advantage that he should have a new play ready for rehearsal when they reassembled in London to prepare for the opening of the next theatre season. In the first five years of James's reign, Shakespeare wrote seven plays for his company. Though not equalling his previous rate of two new plays every twelve months, his output between 1603 and 1608 included *Othello*, *King Lear*, *Macbeth* and *Antony and Cleopatra*. Evidently, his creative energies were undiminished. He began this astonishingly successful period with *Measure for Measure* (performed at Court on 26 December 1604) and ended it with *Coriolanus* (1606/7) and *Timon of Athens* (1607/8).

The completion of *Timon* coincided with a turning-point in the history of the King's Men. While Shakespeare was writing that play, he and his fellow sharers were planning a new venture, comparable in its risks and in its potential rewards with the building of the Globe. On 9 August 1608 they took over the Blackfriars Theatre – the most exclusive playhouse in London – and made it their main house, while continuing to keep their Bankside audiences happy.

Before discussing the details of that momentous development, it must be emphasised that the history of Shakespeare's company and the history of his life are inseparable. Nobody else was as active in every aspect of its work as he was. For twenty years he had a decisive voice in everything it did. Put it in present-day terms: he was a member of the board of directors of, and a principal shareholder in, the leading theatre company of the day. With his fellow directors, he was responsible for its business and artistic management, its day-to-day running and its long-term planning; but because he was involved in every department, his responsibilities were wider than theirs.

Attention is so often – and so understandably – focussed on his creative work that we are in danger of forgetting that company business occupied much of his time and energy on every working day. Critical and interpretative studies – 'Shakespeare's tragic vision', 'Shakespeare's view of history', 'Shakespeare and love's healing power', and so forth – may offer valuable insights; but the student enquiring about Shakespeare's life will learn more by concentrating on him as a man of the theatre. We cannot resist speculations about the mind that conceived *King Lear*, but we should remind ourselves that it was often busy with mundane considerations, such as the wages of hired men or the need to replace worn-out benches at the Globe. When we are tempted to interpret Timon's frenzied outbursts as autobiography, it is sensible to recall that while Shakespeare was writing them, he and his colleagues were coolly deliberating whether to take over the lease of the Blackfriars Theatre and calculating the terms on which it would be prudent to accept the risk.

For twenty years, Shakespeare and three other men – Richard Burbage, John Heminge and Henry Condell – controlled the company, jointly taking every major decision and stamping the organisation with the imprint of their collective personality. Their shared counsel and mutual trust transformed a business association into an enduring brotherhood. Whenever, as in 1598 and 1608, drastic action was required, they made a shrewd appraisal of the situation and then, confident of their judgement and of each other, boldly seized their opportunities. Their habitual response when adversity threatened is aptly described in Hotspur's words: 'out of this nettle, danger, we pluck this flower, safety', (*Henry IV Part 2*). Unlike Hotspur, however, they were realists.

As we saw in Chapter 8, when James Burbage realised that he was not going to get a renewed lease of the Theatre site on reasonable terms, he bought the Blackfriars Theatre and spent a lot of money to prepare it for the Chamberlain's Men. When he died in 1597 its ownership passed to his sons, but the strenuous opposition of the Blackfriars residents to having a company of common players in their well-to-do district prevented them from using it. Left with a costly property on their hands, the Burbages leased the theatre to Henry Evans, whose company of boy actors, the Children of the Queen's Revels, staged many successful plays there. The people of Blackfriars did not object to a children's company and a 'private' theatre with its better-class audiences. It was the thought of a common stage and common players and a mixed and rowdy following they could not stomach.

Among the many successes that 'the little eyases' put on was a play called *Poetaster* by Ben Jonson, in which leading members of the Chamberlain's Men were ridiculed. That attack was answered when Shakespeare's company staged *Satiromastix* (by Thomas Dekker) at the Globe; but the fact that they felt it necessary to take up the challenge showed that they were rattled, while the references in *Hamlet* to 'the war of the theatres' (see Chapter 6) were an admission that the competition was costing them money.

What made it the more annoying, of course, was that the Burbages owned the theatre from which these satirical shafts were being launched by rivals who were capturing part of their audience. Admittedly, the Burbages were getting rent from Evans, but they were still out of pocket. Successful productions at the Blackfriars playhouse were attracting well-to-do spectators away from the Globe. Richard Burbage was particularly incensed for he, unlike his brother Cuthbert, was under personal attack. Cuthbert was not an actor. He was a money man and a manager so, though he disliked competition from a theatre of which he was part owner, he was not a target for the jibes that in Richard's case added insult to financial injury.

Altogether, James Burbage's investment in Blackfriars was turning out badly for the Chamberlain's-King's Men. It was the one unfortunate development in their hitherto wholly successful history. The sharers were faced with a problem that they very much wanted to solve as soon as they could find a way.

Their particular difficulty with Evans and his boy actors was symptomatic of a general predicament confronting the adult acting companies in the common playhouses. Competition from the children's troupes was nothing new. It had persisted throughout Shakespeare's career, but as a nuisance rather than as a serious threat to the livelihood of the common players. From 1603 onwards, things were changing. The socially mixed audiences of Elizabeth's reign were splitting into two quite distinct groups.

The Globe had flourished in a period when a typical audience at a public theatre contained representatives of every social class and of many different occupations – aristocrats, knights, country squires visiting the city, merchants, lawyers, students, artisans, apprentices, half-pay soldiers waiting for employment, sailors between voyages, shopkeepers, prostitutes. According to their means, they paid for standing room or seats in different parts of the theatre – 'cockpit, galleries, boxes' – but they were all there together, members of the same audience watching plays that catered for a wide range of tastes and satisfied all.

It cost more to see a play at a private theatre, and only the better-off could afford the price of admission. For many years, the gentry and the professional classes divided their favours between the two kinds of playhouses. They were just as likely to seek pleasure at the Globe as at the Blackfriars. From the beginning of James's reign, however, the greater comfort and the more elegant surroundings of the private theatres began to tell. The better-class patrons developed a fastidious distaste for the proximity of the 'groundlings', preferring the socially superior company and the more sophisticated entertainment (concerts and masques, as well as plays) on offer at the Blackfriars, the Phoenix and, later, the Salisbury Court. The masses continued to enjoy themselves at the larger, more plebeian and rowdier public theatres, such as the Red Bull, the Fortune and the Globe.

By 1608 the King's Men were still not seriously damaged by these new developments. They were unquestionably the premier adult company. Their Court performances were very lucrative and attendances at the Globe were keeping up remarkably well. Their humbler patrons were as enthusiastic as ever. As for the better-off, they continued to come to the Globe for Shakespeare's plays. If they wanted to see them – and they did – that was the only theatre at which they could. As can be gathered from Shakespeare's investments in Stratford at this time (see Chapter 8), he and his fellow sharers were doing well, despite the competition from the private theatres.

But, if there was no immediate crisis, the King's Men took the opposition very seriously. They understood what was happening and they were well aware that the problem would not go away. Through their Court connections they had close contacts with the kind of people who preferred the private theatres and they recognised that it would not be possible to win them back. Shakespeare and his partners were much too experienced to indulge in easy optimism. They had an unrivalled knowledge of the London theatre and they did not make the mistake of underestimating their rivals. They noted it as a fact that Ben Jonson's repeated successes at the Blackfriars Theatre were winning him a formidable reputation in literary circles. Plays by a rising pair of dramatists, Francis Beaumont and John Fletcher, were also being much discussed, and the King's Men did not dismiss this as a passing fad. They recognised that Beaumont and Fletcher were in tune with the new tastes. Their sophisticated plays appealed to growing numbers of people who felt less and less inclined to rub shoulders with the common folk who crowded into the public playhouses. Neither Shakespeare nor his partners pretended otherwise.

It was wholly in character that they made such a hard-headed appraisal of the way things were going. Since forming the Chamberlain's Men in 1594, they had always kept a step or two ahead of their rivals, and their readiness to take calculated risks had won them a commanding position which they had no intention of surrendering. Faced now with a new kind of opposition, they decided to take on their opponents at their own game. The question was, how? The private theatres were the preserve of the children's companies – society's spoilt pets – and no company of common players had ever been able to break into that exclusive world.

However, they had some strong cards in their hand if they got the chance to play them. Blackfriars, the most fashionable of all the private theatres, belonged to two of the company sharers. If Henry Evans could be persuaded to surrender his lease, control would pass to the Burbage brothers. Moreover, they and their associates were no longer merely a troupe of common players. They were Grooms of the Chamber, officers of the royal household. They wore the King's livery on state occasions and he had made it abundantly clear that they enjoyed his favour. If they were ever able to move in, the residents of Blackfriars would not find it easy to object to the presence of His Majesty's Servants.

Fortunately for the King's Men, Evans and his company got into serious trouble. Society's favourites though they were, they incurred the severe displeasure of the authorities for staging impertinent and satirical plays, meddling in matters that were none of their business. In 1605, for example, *Eastward Ho!*, a comedy by George Chapman, Ben Jonson and John Marston, angered the King by making jokes about the Scots. As a result, the boy actors lost the Queen's patronage. They were no longer allowed to call themselves the Children of the Queen's Revels, but were known simply as the Children of the Blackfriars.

Worse was to come. In 1608, Chapman committed another indiscretion. He wrote, and the Blackfriars Children acted, a play called *The Conspiracy and Tragedy of Charles Duke of Byron*. It dealt with recent French politics and it so enraged the ambassador of that country that King James ordered the suppression of the Children of the Blackfriars. He swore they should never act again, even if they had to beg their bread.

Evans now had no use for the theatre and he told the Burbages that he would surrender the lease if they could come to terms. That was in March 1608. On 9 August, after long and complicated bargaining, the Blackfriars Theatre was taken over by a syndicate of the King's Men: Cuthbert and Richard Burbage, William Shakespeare, John Heminge, Henry Condell and William Sly.

It was a daring venture. Not only were they going to compete in a sector of the entertainment industry from which companies such as theirs had previously been excluded, but they intended to keep the Globe on as well. They had to meet the running costs of two theatres, in one of which they must cater for the tastes of a different kind of audience from that with which they were so completely in tune. Furthermore, the stage and auditorium of their new theatre necessitated adjustments to their repertory, their production methods and their style of acting. At the Globe, in broad daylight, they entertained a mass audience with plays in which big themes, expressed in mighty lines and vigorously declaimed, stirred the spectators in every part of that large playhouse. At the Blackfriars, a smaller, indoors theatre lit by candles, a quieter and more intimate delivery suited the taste of a sophisticated audience, eager for novel themes, complex plots, masques, musical interludes and spectacular illusions contrived by the manipulation of stage machinery.

Formidable though it was, the challenge was one that Shakespeare and his company were well prepared to meet. From their early Chamberlain's days, they had been used to playing in the halls of great houses, at the Inns of Court and in royal palaces, where the stage, the seating arrangements and the social background of the audiences were foretastes of private theatre conditions. If they could please those patrons in those surroundings – as they so often had – they might reasonably expect to please their Blackfriars audiences.

Typically, they planned well ahead and left as little to chance as possible. They had been keeping a close eye on Blackfriars plays and production methods for some time. For example, in 1604 they adapted a Blackfriars success (John Marston's *The Malcontent*) to suit it for staging at the Globe. Well before Evans at last surrendered his lease, they knew what they would need to do if they ever managed to get possession of the theatre James Burbage had bought for their use.

Once the lease was signed their immediate job was to acquire plays suitable for Blackfriars. The departing Children had taken their playbooks with them, hoping somehow to find a way round the King's ban. (They did; and under new direction and in a different theatre went along quite merrily. In fact, just two years after James had decreed their suppression they were again allowed to call themselves the Children of the Queen's Revels!) Though the Globe play chest contained some scripts that could be adapted, it would have been a fatal mistake to present their new and trendy clients with a diet of old plays.

Ironically, a severe visitation of 'the sickness' now occurred and gave them time to carry out plans they had been making while the negotiations with Evans were going on. Both 1608 and 1609 were plague years and there was little acting at the Globe or Blackfriars, or any other London theatre, between July 1608 and mid-December 1609.

Financially, the King's Men lost less than the other companies. They were handsomely paid for twelve Court performances in 1608 and for thirteen in 1609. In between, most of the company toured, while the four principal partners completed their arrangements to secure a steady flow of new plays for the Blackfriars Theatre. Their

Globe repertory could look after itself for the time being. With about a hundred plays in stock, a quarter of which were by Shakespeare, they were not going to run short of popular work to offer an audience that liked to have its old favourites brought back. As for the Blackfriars repertory, they had agreed on the way to solve that problem. They selected three dramatists who seemed most capable of writing plays for the King's Men to act in that theatre and they put them on their payroll.

Such a practical plan was typical of them. They were all deeply experienced and wise in the theatre world. Richard Burbage was one of the two best actors in London. Many considered him the best. Heminge and Condell were eminent in their profession, too. William Shakespeare – actor, manager and playwright – was master of every theatre skill and unrivalled in his judgement. If those men could not pick a winner, then nobody could. They chose one certainty and they backed a couple of promising youngsters, whose remarkable success quite soon proved how well Shakespeare and his colleagues knew their business.

The certainty was Ben Jonson. As we have seen already, he had not always been successful; but in 1608 he was riding high. He had written six successful masques for James's Court. A brilliant architect, Inigo Jones, devised and designed those spectacular shows and Jonson supplied the literary and dramatic elements. The reputation his masques won for him was enhanced by four plays written for the Children of the Blackfriars. He was just the man to exploit the facilities of that stage, with its lights and its machinery, and to gratify the tastes of its elegant patrons, who were already his fans.

Besides, he had written plays for the Chamberlain's-King's Men in earlier days (though nothing after 1605) and Shakespeare was on good terms with him. Ben Jonson managed to quarrel with many people, but never with Shakespeare, so it was not difficult to persuade him that he could do well by selling his future work to the new Blackfriars management. With one exception, all the rest of his plays were written for Shakespeare's company; and he provided them with a splendid early success in their new house with *The Alchemist* in 1610.

They took a bit of a gamble with Francis Beaumont and John Fletcher, but it paid off handsomely. These young men shared the tastes of an audience drawn from the gentry and the professional classes. They had a snobbish appeal for people who preferred exclusive surroundings and sophisticated plays, and felt more comfortable when their entertainers were 'well-bred'.

That alone would not have been decisive. The King's Men were not in the market for plays written by well-born dunderheads. By 1608, however, Beaumont and Fletcher had collaborated in several Blackfriars plays, and though they had not as yet been very successful, the talent was there. Shakespeare recommended them and his company bought their work, a decision that was triumphantly vindicated in 1609 when their play *Philaster* was a smash hit. After that, all but two or three of their plays were written for the King's Men, to the great advantage of the dramatists and of the company.

The way in which Shakespeare and his partners were able to bring out the best in their young playwrights is illustrated by the history of one of their plays, *The Knight of the Burning Pestle*. It had not succeeded when first acted by the Children of the Blackfriars in 1607. Unvalued in consequence, the playbook remained at the theatre when the Children left. Soon after the King's Men took over, they encouraged Beaumont and Fletcher to revise the script. In its new form, and with the help of the most skilful direction and the best acting in London, it was an immediate and lasting success.

Not that all the advantages were on one side. If the King's Men had much to teach their new dramatists, they also had much to learn from them. Shakespeare was as ready to experiment as he had always been. The writing of his last years shows how willing he was to pick up useful lessons, especially from John Fletcher. He adapted his plotting and his style of writing to suit new tastes, concentrating all his creative energies and innovative skills on writing 'Romances' or 'Tragi-comedies'. (Both those terms are used to describe the plays he wrote in his final years, though sometimes they are quite simply called 'The Last Plays'.) A little hesitant at first, he was soon master of this newly-fashionable kind of drama, his touch as sure as it had ever been when he wrote his comedies, histories and tragedies.

Necessary as it was in 1608 for the King's Men to buy in new plays by other writers, it was very important to them that Shakespeare should supply fresh work for their new house. His prestige was immense, and his fellow sharers had every reason to hope that he could repeat at Blackfriars the successes that had established their fame and made their fortunes. It was also a matter of professional pride for him and for them that their new theatre should be able to boast as its distinctive attraction the performance of plays by the writer who had been supreme for so long.

Even before the negotiations with Evans had been completed, Shakespeare had demonstrated that he had no intention of allowing new men and new fashions to push him to one side. Always a close observer of the theatre world, he saw how the tide was running and he knew that he must swim with it. The determination with which he accepted the challenge was characteristic. He had always been resolute – always keenly aware that, as Ulysses reminds Achilles in *Troilus and Cressida*:

> Perseverance, dear my lord,
> Keeps honour bright. To have done is to hang
> Quite out of fashion, like a rusty mail
> In monumental mockery.

So, in the early months of 1608, he wrote *Pericles*. It was not one of his best plays (though it held the stage for many a year) but it was a well-timed experiment in the romance or tragi-comic mode, gratifying the appetite for surprise and discovery. A sensational plot unfolded a strange story of separation and journeyings, culminating in a happy outcome snatched – however improbably – from apparent disaster.

Then, soon after the 1608/9 plague subsided and the theatres reopened, Shakespeare supplied the King's Men with the first of three new plays in the popular fashion. *Cymbeline*, a big improvement on *Pericles*, was written in 1609/10. It was followed in rapid succession by *The Winter's Tale* and *The Tempest*, both written in 1611. Those two plays delighted their modish, trend-setting audiences and almost immediately received the stamp of royal approval. His Majesty's Servants were commanded to bring them to Court in the November. In the winter of 1612/13 both plays were again performed at Court during the glittering festivities held to celebrate the marriage of James's daughter Elizabeth to the Elector Palatine of Bohemia. (The playbill for the celebrations shows that Shakespeare's earlier plays were still in demand. *Much Ado*, *Henry IV Parts 1 and 2*, *Julius Caesar* and *Othello* were performed as well as his latest successes.)

There was no doubt of his continuing ability to write money-spinners. His new plays satisfied the most fashionable audiences in London and, as contemporary comments reveal, they pleased Globe audiences, too. The popularity of his work had never been confined to any one social class and now, at the end of his career, he still knew how to entertain courtiers and groundlings alike. Different acting scripts of the tragi-comedies were prepared to suit the requirements of the two different stages, a simple enough job for the dramatist and the actors. The King's Men were trained to be versatile and this was not the first time they had acted in different versions of the same play.

Still frequently acted and greatly admired, Shakespeare's last plays (*Cymbeline*, *The Winter's Tale* and *The Tempest*) attract worldwide attention today. Though many volumes of critical studies have been devoted to them already, scholarly interest in them shows no sign of flagging. It is not surprising. They are dramatic masterpieces. In a factual account of his life, however, the emphasis must be placed on the sheer professionalism with which he responded to the challenge he faced in 1608. Only three years separated *Pericles* from *The Tempest*, but in that time he advanced from experimenting with a new form of drama to mastering it. It was the mark of a supreme craftsman, deeply experienced in every department of the theatre.

At all periods of his career, and in the post-1608 years in particular, there is more to be learnt about 'the real Shakespeare' by studying his role in the company organisation than by hunting for personal revelations in his dramas. Apart from being its chief dramatist and sharing responsibility for the company's policies, finances and administration, he was also what would nowadays be called its principal artistic director. In that capacity, and in consultation with Burbage and the other actor-managers in the fellowship, he was responsible for deciding what new plays to buy and then for getting them into production. He attended rehearsals and he took part in conferences between writers and actors. Nobody worked more closely with the production team than he, for nobody had more experience of what would 'go' on stage and what would not. Better than anyone else, he knew how to sort out problems and how to make the most of a play, how to improve a halting speech and how to tighten a lagging scene.

So it came about that, in getting other writers' plays onto the Blackfriars stage, he soon had a new range of dramatic technicalities at his own command. With all his experience and his consummate sense of the theatre he was not likely to be a slow learner, especially when he had so much at stake.

Shakespearian critics have always been fascinated by the plays he wrote as his career was coming to its end. In them, they argue, he must have uttered his farewell messages and expressed his wisest views about human life. They search them, singly and as a group, for their 'meaning' – and, as is to be expected, the plays 'mean' different things to different people. For example, Edward Dowden's view (in 1875) was that they express the serenity that Shakespeare had attained after his tragic period. In 1608-11, said Dowden, he was 'On the Heights', joyfully contemplating life and recollecting past emotions in tranquillity. Thirty years later, Lytton Strachey received a very different message. According to his reading of the plays, Shakespeare was 'bored with people, bored with real life, bored, in fact, with everything except poetry and poetic speeches'.

Late twentieth-century critics have little patience with either of those views. They dismiss Dowden's as sheer sentimentality and Strachey's as contentious nonsense. Their theory is that the plays express a deep sense of our human need for mutual understanding and forgiveness – for 'reconciliation'. Reviewing Sir Peter Hall's productions of *Cymbeline*, *The Winter's Tale* and *The Tempest* at the National Theatre in 1988, Michael Billington, a leading dramatic critic, heard in them 'Shakespeare's own intimations of mortality'. For him, as for most of his contemporaries, 'The Last Plays' have a common and quasi-religious theme.

Subjective interpretations are not facts; and they should not be treated as if they were. They may – often do – enlarge our appreciation by suggesting new ways of looking at the plays, but they do not deal in verifiable truths. Who knows what Shakespeare's final work may 'mean' to the critics of fifty – even of five – years hence? It may be that current views will seem as misguided to them as Dowden's and Strachey's seem to us. Our only reliable information about Shakespeare in 1608-11 is provided by the record of his and his company's activities in the theatre. As the following summary shows, the known facts have a lot to tell us about what he and his colleagues were thinking and doing in those years.

His own reputation and prosperity were inextricably bound in with the fortunes of the King's Men. It was vital for him and for his fellows that their Blackfriars venture paid off. Having arranged to buy in plays by successful and potentially successful writers, the company was still in urgent need of his work. If he could top the bill at the Blackfriars as he had done at the Globe, their success was assured. That was why he studied current hits closely and then wrote three plays in the new fashion. All three were successful; *The Winter's Tale* and *The Tempest* outstandingly so. The old master had proved himself more than equal to his new task.

Many examples could be given to show how careful he was to ensure that these plays would satisfy fashionable tastes and suit the company's new theatre, but just three must suffice, one taken from each play. In *Cymbeline*, the scene in Imogen's bedchamber was planned to take full advantage of the artificial lighting and illusions of the Blackfriars stage. In *The Winter's Tale*, the dance of the twelve satyrs was suggested by flamboyant features of Jonson's brilliant Court entertainment *Oberon*. In *The Tempest*, the popular ingredients of music, dance and magic were brought together in what Prospero calls 'some vanity of mine art' – the spectacular masque he conjures up for the delight of the young lovers.

The facts speak for themselves. Nobody familiar with the developments of 1608-11 can be in any doubt that, first and last,

William Shakespeare was a working playwright, intent on giving his audiences what they wanted.

The King's Men opened their first season at the Blackfriars Theatre in mid-December 1609, and it was very soon clear that their enterprise was a success. They used their new theatre as their winter house and played at the Globe in the summer. For two reasons, their Blackfriars income far exceeded what the Globe brought them. First, they were able to charge a great deal more for entrance; and second, because it was an indoors theatre, bad weather did not keep people away. By 1612 it was estimated that they were taking a thousand pounds more for a winter season at their new theatre than they had previously taken at the Globe.

Though Blackfriars became their principal house, the Globe remained profitable. Indeed, it was still so important to them that when it was burnt down in 1613 they at once rebuilt it. What happened was this. On St Peter's Day (29 June) during a performance of *Henry VIII* cannon were discharged to mark the monarch's ceremonial entry on stage. A piece of burning wadding from one of the guns lodged in the thatch over the stage and speedily set fire to the building. A contemporary account described how

> it kindled inwardly, and ran round like a train [of gunpowder], consuming within an hour the whole house to the very grounds. This was the fatal period [end] of that virtuous fabric, wherein yet nothing did perish but wood and straw, and a few forsaken cloaks; only one man had his breeches set on fire, that would perhaps have broiled him, if he had not by the benefit of a provident wit [by quick thinking] put it out with bottled ale.

Less than a year later, a new Globe – with tiles above the stage instead of thatch – rose from the ashes of the old. The King's Men never wasted time.

We do not know whether Shakespeare was in London when the Globe was destroyed. He was then in his fiftieth year and after the success of the Blackfriars enterprise was assured he had been spending most of his time in Stratford. He kept his links with the company. He was still a sharer and his friendship with his colleagues was unbroken. He was still doing some writing for them, too, though *The Tempest* was the last play of which he was sole author.

John Fletcher had succeeded him as the King's Men's principal dramatist, and in 1613 Shakespeare joined forces with him to write *Henry VIII* and *The Two Noble Kinsmen*. (A lost play, *Cardenio*, is thought to have been theirs, too.) The big speeches were Shakespeare's work. It was a practical and successful arrangement.

With their fine acting roles and spectacular scenes, both plays were popular.

Fletcher stayed with the King's Men for the rest of his life. He was a good team man, a quality that the company had always valued. A master of the tricky art of collaboration, he wrote plays with Francis Beaumont and Philip Massinger as well as with William Shakespeare. In 1634, when he and his most illustrious partner were both dead, *The Two Noble Kinsmen* was published. The title page of that first edition provides a fitting conclusion to the history of Shakespeare's career as a public entertainer:

The Two Noble Kinsmen

Presented at the Blackfriars Theatre by the King's Majesty's Servants, with great applause. Written by the memorable Worthies of their time: Mr John Fletcher and Mr William Shakespeare, Gent.

10

'I, William Shakespeare'

S HAKESPEARE'S withdrawal from the theatre was a gradual process. It could hardly have been otherwise. All the circumstances – his long service as a principal member of the company, his continuing financial stake in it, the personal ties that bound 'the fellowship' together – made a sudden break unthinkable, even if he had wished for it. By 1612, however, they were playing to full houses at the Blackfriars Theatre, and the Globe was still profitable. By then, too, he had supplied the company with new and extremely successful plays to add to a repertory already richly stocked with his past work. It was clear, also, that John Fletcher would serve them well if he took over as their chief dramatist. From then on, satisfied that his absence would not damage the King's Men, Shakespeare felt able to spend most of his time in Stratford.

He kept up his London connections. He was there in the May of 1612 (the Belott-Mountjoy suit: see Chapters 2 and 6). In the following year he was writing for his company again, collaborating with Fletcher (see Chapter 9). There is no record that he was with his colleagues when they performed his plays during the royal wedding celebrations in the winter of 1612/13 but, if he was not, they soon had the opportunity of giving him a first-hand account of the proceedings. In March 1613, soon after the festivities ended, he was in London again and he certainly spent some time with John Heminge, if with no other member of the company.

On this visit, Shakespeare was busy with a private transaction. He took possession of a substantial property, called the Blackfriars Gatehouse, on 10 March. It cost him a lot of money – £140 – half of which he paid in cash. He had no intention of living there. The house was bought purely as an investment and at once let to a good tenant. Before returning to Stratford, Shakespeare appointed three London trustees to manage the property for him. One was his trusted friend John Heminge. Another was William Johnson, well known to Shakespeare as landlord of the Mermaid Inn. The third trustee was John Jackson, a wealthy man who – like Shakespeare and Ben Jonson

– had been a regular member of a celebrated 'company of wits' whose lively conversation had made the Mermaid famous as a meeting-place for playwrights, actors, poets and fashionable young men about town.

The Blackfriars investment was a carefully considered step, an important part of Shakespeare's plans for the consolidation of his estate. In the last years of his father's life he had made himself responsible for his parents' welfare. Now, father and mother both gone, and his duty to them as their eldest son lovingly discharged, he was intent on safeguarding the interests of his own children.

A well-known passage in Rowe's *Life* paints an idyllic picture of Shakespeare's closing years:

> The latter part of his life was spent, as all men of good sense will wish theirs to be, in ease, retirement, and the conversation of their friends. He had the good fortune to gather an estate equal to his occasion [meeting all his needs] and, in that, to his wish.

There is a good deal of truth in the description. Shakespeare was now a gentleman of ample means, a tithe-holder and a landowner, on easy terms with local dignitaries, secure and respected in his native place. He owned a fine house, and he was at home again with his family, enjoying the company of friends and neighbours he had known since youth.

After years of extremely hard work and much stress, he had time for his leisure interests, chief among which was gardening – a fact that will surprise no-one who has visited the gardens at New Place. Though Shakespeare's house has gone, his famous Knott Garden and Great Garden remain, in design and planting looking much as they did when he made them. It is said that the mulberry tree now growing in the Great Garden was rooted as a cutting from the one he planted. A pleasing thought.

We know that his gardening skill was recognised in his lifetime and remembered afterwards. Fifteen years after his death, a keen gardener sent one of his men to Stratford to obtain budding shoots from 'Mr Shakespeare's vines'. It was as stock that they were valued, not because they had been planted by a literary genius. (People took a different view in 1758, when his great mulberry tree was wantonly felled. By then, the developing Shakespeare industry had created a market for the hundreds of 'relics' into which it was carved.)

For Shakespeare, however, gardening was much more than a leisure activity. It was an art that had always engaged his imagination. His plays and poems abound in garden and orchard images, figuratively embodying emotions and ideas. In gardening he habitually found symbols to represent the subtle interplay of nature and nurture in human affairs; and his own expert knowledge of its theory and techniques provided the details on which those images were based.

This characteristic feature of his writing is well illustrated by the dialogue between Perdita and Polixenes in Act IV, Sc.4 of *The Winter's Tale*. They have different views about the ethics of human intervention in the operations of 'great creating nature', and they support their opinions with detailed references to gardening principles and methods. While this animated but good-tempered discussion takes place, the audience is aware of circumstances that are driving these two people towards bitter and dangerous, but not yet open, conflict. In consequence, their disagreement about the use of plant-breeding techniques is seen to symbolise their deeper and real confrontation. An impending and violent clash is foreshadowed in the language of a well-informed debate about gardening.

Shakespeare's love of gardens had for years and very often supplied him with images that his dramatic art required. Now, the creative spirit no longer given to writing plays found its expression in the designing and planting of his New Place grounds.

He had time for entertaining guests, too. Ben Jonson is reputed to have stayed with the Shakespeares. Another visitor was the poet and dramatist Michael Drayton; though he, a Warwickshire man, did not have far to come. On at least one occasion, official hospitality was provided at New Place for a guest of the corporation. In 1614 the preacher who had come to Stratford to sermonise the bailiff and the council – there were three visiting preachers every year – was entertained by Mr Shakespeare and his wife. To help with his refreshment, the corporation contributed a quart of claret and a quart of sack – strong white wine, usually 'burnt' (heated) and drunk with lumps of sugar. Like John and Mary Shakespeare before them, William and Anne Shakespeare occupied an eminent position in the social hierarchy of the town; but unlike his father, William took no part in council business. Having spent his working life in the public gaze, he valued his privacy.

However, as a propertied man with many financial interests, he was not able to spend all his days at ease, as Rowe pictured him. The day-to-day administration of his holdings in property, land and tithes could be left to his agents but, from time to time, consultations were necessary and decisions were required. Farming methods and traditional ways of managing agricultural estates were changing, and much arable land was being enclosed and converted to sheep pasture. There were enterprising men about – 'sharp dealers' is another description –

who were quick to seize their opportunities and skilful in using the law
to their advantage.

In 1614, for example, a long-running and complicated dispute was
set on foot with a proposal to enclose common fields at Welcombe,
where Shakespeare had his most lucrative tithe holdings. His interests
and those of the other tithe holders were likely to be damaged if the
scheme went through. The Town Clerk of Stratford, Thomas Greene,
persuaded the council to oppose the development. He was a distant
kinsman to Shakespeare (he generally referred to him as 'my cousin
Shakespeare') and he was personally affected by the proposed
enclosure, having investments of his own in the Welcombe tithes.
Consequently, he tried his best to enlist Shakespeare's help in
vigorous opposition to the plan; but he was not successful. As
Greene's diary records, his 'cousin' calmly maintained that nothing
would come of the proposal.

Shakespeare's confidence was justified. In the end, and after a great
deal of to-do, the corporation's case against enclosure was upheld in
the courts. Shakespeare was dead before this issue was settled but,
while the controversy was at its height, he had quietly negotiated with
the promoters of the enclosure scheme. He obtained from them a
legally-binding assurance that they would compensate him or his heirs
for any loss they might cause him. Characteristically, he had looked
after Greene's interests as well as his own, persuading them to
indemnify him too. However, that excitable and over-anxious man
refused to be comforted. He continued to agitate, while Shakespeare
turned his mind to other matters that were claiming his attention.

In these last years of his life, he was much occupied with making plans
for his daughters' future. 'Devouring Time' had inflicted on him
family griefs and lasting anxieties. The death of his only son had
dulled the brightness of his worldly achievements and diminished his
expectations. With no male heir to inherit his very considerable
estate, he must be watchful in safeguarding Susanna's and Judith's
inheritance should their husbands prove greedy or feckless.

He had many material and social advantages; and he also had the
heavy responsibilities of what was an increasingly lonely position. Not
Hamnet only, but many others, too, who should have been gathered
round him, were dead. Before the winter of 1613 ended, of the eight
children of John and Mary Shakespeare only William and his sister
Joan were still alive. Two daughters of the Henley Street household
(the first Joan and Margaret) had died in infancy. The third (Anne)
had not lived to see her seventh birthday. One son, Gilbert, who had
been for some years a haberdasher in London and was later William's

trusty agent in Stratford, died unmarried in 1612. He was forty-six. Another son, Richard, also unmarried and a Stratford dweller all his short life, died twelve months after Gilbert, aged only thirty-nine.

It must be likely that his brothers' deaths, occurring when they did, played some part in William Shakespeare's determination to concentrate on his Stratford affairs; but we have no direct knowledge of how he was affected by those two bereavements, one so closely following the other. However, the recorded circumstances of an earlier and similar loss testify to the strength of his family affections and speak clearly of his grief at partings so cruelly enforced.

Edmund, the youngest of John and Mary Shakespeare's children, was born in 1580, when their times were troubled. He was sixteen years and one month younger than William, but he seems to have grown close to him. It is known that he followed his eldest brother's calling, though we have no details of his acting career.

Nor can we be quite sure that an entry in the register of St Giles's Church, Cripplegate, refers to him. Dated 12 August 1607, it records the burial of 'Edward, son of Edward Shackspeere, Player: base-born [illegitimate]'. The surname 'Shakespeare' was spelt in many different ways, so the clerk's spelling ('Shackspeere') affords no proof that the dead child's father was not Edmund Shakespeare. However, the Christian name 'Edward' (instead of 'Edmund') *may* mean that the entry refers to another player called Shakespeare. That seems unlikely, especially when it is remembered that William Shakespeare himself had lodgings in Cripplegate (see Chapter 6). It would have been practical to arrange for his young brother to live in the same London district.

If – as is most probable – Edmund Shakespeare was the father referred to in the Cripplegate register, he did not long survive his own little base-born son. On the last day of that same year – it was bitterly cold and the Thames was frozen – he was buried in the Church of St Mary Overy (St Mary 'Over the River') in Southwark. Aged only twenty-seven, he was tolled to his resting-place 'with a forenoon knell of the great bell' – so the sexton recorded in his note of the funeral expenses.

The obscure player was honoured with ceremony and accorded a dignified 'bringing home of bell and burial'. At the funeral of such as the world accounted him, a churchyard interment and a lesser knell would usually have sufficed; but for Edmund Shakespeare, his brother William bought a grave inside the church and the solemn tolling of the great bell. He arranged, too, for Edmund to be buried in the 'forenoon', though funerals usually took place later in the day. Only in the morning could William Shakespeare and his fellow actors be present to take their last leave of his youngest brother. At two o'clock in the afternoon the trumpets would sound at the nearby Globe Theatre and the play would begin.

Three major pieces of legal and financial business occupied Shakespeare between 1613 and 1616. Two of those – buying the Blackfriars house and protecting his Welcombe tithes – have been described. Before turning to the third, the making of his will, we must bring the story of his daughters' lives up to date.

Since Hamnet's death in 1596, Susanna and Judith had carried all their parents' hopes; and in the social framework of the day, the realisation of those hopes depended on a good marriage for each of them. To further that desired outcome, it was their mother's task to train them in the arts of household management. It was their father's to endow them well and to do everything possible to safeguard their material interests after marriage. Not easy: a married woman's property was at her husband's command unless special provisions were made.

In passing, we may note that somebody taught Susanna to read and write. Probably not her father: he was away in London for much of the time when she was young. Judith, on the other hand, seems not to have been literate; but girls rarely were.

It is not in the nature of things for children to be wholly amenable to their parents' wishes, even when domestic discipline is as strict as it was in those days. Susanna caused the Shakespeares less anxiety than Judith did, but in 1606 she gave them a jolt. Just before her twenty-third birthday she committed a serious breach of the law.

For some reason, she neglected to receive Easter Communion at Holy Trinity Church. It was a bad time to be careless about religious duties. Scared by the Gunpowder Plot in the previous November, the government had tightened the laws to punish non-communicants. Susanna had made herself liable to pay heavy fines. Twenty other Stratfordians committed the same offence that Easter. Some were known Papists. Others, like the Shakespeares' old friends, the Sadlers, were neither devout Anglicans nor zealous Catholics. They were certainly not willing to make martyrs of themselves. Hamnet Sadler put up the old excuse that he and his wife had not taken the sacrament on Easter Sunday because they were not then in a fitting spiritual frame of mind to do so. Given time 'to clear their consciences', they did their duty later and escaped punishment. In the end, Susanna also took communion, and the case against her was dismissed.

That episode has been used to argue that she was a Roman Catholic at heart; but her reluctance to be ordered about probably influenced her more than religious convictions. After her failure to take communion she was summoned to appear in the vicar's court to explain herself. She ignored the order, preferring to conform quietly when she no longer dared to disobey than to make excuses in public. In any case, the Papist theory collapses in view of what happened soon afterwards. In 1607 Susanna married Dr John Hall, a man well known for his strong Protestant beliefs.

'John Hall, gentleman, and Susanna Shakespeare' were joined together in holy matrimony on 5 June. It was a marriage answering the best hopes of Susanna's parents. Eight years older than his bride, their son-in-law was a serious-minded man whose upright character impressed everyone. He was comfortably placed in the world, having inherited property (and a coat of arms) from his father, a doctor who lived in Bedforshire.

John Hall had begun to practise medicine in Stratford in 1600 and had rapidly won a reputation as a skilful and devoted doctor. In some ways he was much ahead of his time. He was interested in the psychology of sickness (he did not use that term, of course) and he treated each patient as an individual person, to be studied and understood. He was unusual, too, in recognising that the unhealthy diet of those days (a lot of salt meat and few fresh vegetables) caused scurvy, and that many of the illnesses he was called upon to treat were, in fact, symptoms of scurvy. He dosed his patients with his own 'scorbutic beer', a concoction of plant and vegetable juices. The results were excellent. Inevitably, he was not wholly free from the quackery of the time. As his famous *Casebook* shows, he made use of traditional 'medicines' – dried windpipes of cockerels, spiders' webs and peacock dung, for example. Even so, like the good physician Cerimon in his father-in-law's play *Pericles*, he relied chiefly on 'blessed infusions' and on his own deep knowledge of

the disturbances
That Nature works, and of her cures.

He had another of Cerimon's qualities, too. John Hall was 'not thirsty after tottering honour'. He twice refused to take office as a burgess of Stratford. Elected a third time, he reluctantly agreed to serve; but he was fined several times for missing council meeings to attend to his patients. Eventually, he was allowed to resign. In 1626 he rejected a greater distinction than any the corporation could confer. In Charles I's 'coronation honours' the well-known Stratford physician was offered a knighthood. He paid a large fine for the privilege of refusing it.

In addition to his professional duties and his family life, the affairs of Holy Trinity Church took up a lot of his time. He was a church-warden, a generous contributor to church finances, and the loyal champion of a vicar who was too much of a Puritan for the liking of the town council. Hall gave up part of his own income to augment the vicar's stipend, accusing the councillors of failing to increase it because they were spending the money on 'feasting and private means'.

John Hall's battles on behalf of the vicar, like his rejection of honours, occurred after his father-in-law's death, but his strong Protestant convictions were well known when he married Susanna. It has been conjectured that in that one respect the marriage may not have pleased Shakespeare, no friend of Puritans. That surmise is not borne out by the known facts. Hall was no fanatic. He was an educated man with wide interests, 'broad-minded' enough to court and marry a young woman whose father's career was spent in the playhouse. All the evidence suggests that Shakespeare had a high regard for his son-in-law. The two men went to London together to negotiate when the Welcombe tithes affair began. Thomas Greene, who was there on the same business, called on them the day after they arrived. As he noted in his diary, he found that Shakespeare and Hall were in complete agreement. Two years after that, Shakespeare's confidence in Susanna's husband was affirmed when he made him one of his executors. Everything we know points to mutual respect and trust.

John Hall's big house (now known as Hall's Croft) was less than five minutes' walk away from Susanna's old home, and it was there that they lived for the first nine years of their marriage. (In 1616 they moved into New Place and shared it with Shakespeare's widow until her death). Their daughter Elizabeth was born in 1608. She was their only child; and she was the only grandchild that Shakespeare lived to see. Judith's children were not born until after he died. If Susanna's marriage caused him any disappointment, it was the Halls' failure to produce a son. As we shall see, when he made his will he was still hoping that they might provide him with a male heir.

Susanna's lively mind and pleasant ways were remarked on by her contemporaries. She had inherited her father's disposition, they said. Like him, too, she was practical and decisive. Her firm character saw her through a severe test in 1613, when she faced up to and overcame a crisis in her personal life. She discovered that a young man called John Lane had been spreading vile slanders about her. Lane was well known in Stratford. His father owned Alveston Manor, two miles away, and his family was connected by marriage with the Greenes and other prominent townspeople. Lane was also a notorious drinker, and

Susanna was not the first victim of his intoxicated babblings. On this occasion, he was given a lesson. Supported by unimpeachable witnesses to her good character, Susanna brought an action of slander against him in the ecclesiastical court at Worcester. Lane was too scared to appear. The court declared its complete belief in her probity and excommunicated the slanderer.

It was a nasty business and would be best forgotten but that it demonstrates Susanna's strength of mind. Unfounded as Lane's gossip was, she could not afford to ignore it. She and her husband lived in a tight-knit society in which rumour spread quickly. To have treated Lane with contemptuous indifference would neither have silenced him nor repaired the damage he had done. It took courage to proceed as she did, taking her case to the higher and more authoritative ecclesisastical court at Worcester rather than to the vicar's court in Stratford. Her decisive action saved her good name and affirmed the integrity of her marriage.

Susanna lived to be sixty-six, a good age in those days, and was spared further calumny. Two later events of special note in her life's story provide ironical comments on the events of 1613. Thirteen years after Lane was busy 'stuffing the ears of men with false reports' about Susanna, her daughter married his first cousin, Thomas Nash. Seventeen years after that, the woman whose moral character Lane had so grievously maligned entertained the Queen of England as her guest at New Place. As Feste says, 'The whirligig of time brings in his revenges'.

About Judith's personality we know less. Compared with Susanna, she is a shadowy figure. What we do know is that, unlike her sister, she made an unfortunate marriage. She was thirty-one when she and Thomas Quiney became man and wife in Holy Trinity Church on 10 February 1616; and is not clear why she left it so late to marry. There should have been little difficulty in finding a husband for the daughter of a prosperous man.

When she finally made her choice – or when it was made for her – it seemed a fitting one. The Quiney and the Shakespeare families had long been on the friendliest terms. Each in their generations, fathers and sons had been good companions: Adrian Quiney and John Shakespeare; Richard Quiney and William Shakespeare. How suitable, then, for Richard's son to marry William's daughter. There was no awkward disparity of wealth or social standing. Adrian Quiney and his son Richard had been bailiffs of Stratford; and all the men of the family knew how to make money – except, as it turned out, Thomas.

As became a Quiney, he was given a good education; but after leaving school he showed none of the family resourcefulness. Having tried his hand in the wine trade, he opened a tavern in the High Street and he was living there when he married Judith. Helped by their parents, the newly-wed couple soon moved into a larger establishment – inauspiciously known as The Cage – where Thomas sold tobacco as well as ale and wine.

From the start, things went badly for them. They were married in Lent and should, therefore, have obtained a licence from the Bishop of Worcester. That, Thomas neglected to do; and the assistant vicar conducted the ceremony without it, though he should have known better. Their marriage was legal, but they were in breach of church regulations, and for that offence they were summoned to the bishop's court. Characteristically, Thomas Quiney failed to show up and was sentenced to a brief period of excommunication. The court record does not state whether Judith was there or not. Nor does it say whether she was punished.

Much worse trouble than that clouded their lives in their first weeks of marriage. In the previous summer, a Stratford woman named Margaret Wheeler had been made pregnant by Thomas Quiney, a secret he had kept from his own family and from his bride's. A month after he married Judith, Margaret Wheeler and her baby died in childbirth. They were buried on 15 March.

Tongues had been wagging before that pitiable event. Afterwards, it was impossible to hush up a scandal touching the Quineys and the Shakespeares, two of Stratford's best-known families. The town was buzzing with talk, and the vicar's court was bound to act. It had jurisdiction over a wide range of offences: non-attendance at church, Sabbath-breaking, drunkenness, swearing, malicious gossip, and so on, (see Chapter 2). Moreover, it was expressly enjoined to examine and punish those guilty of sexual misdemeanours. (Hence its irreverent nickname, 'The Bawdy Court'.) Thomas Quiney's flagrantly immoral conduct could not be ignored.

On 26 March he appeared before the court in Holy Trinity Church, with the public present and the vicar of Stratford as his judge. He confessed his guilt and he was sentenced to endure 'open shame'. He was ordered to perform public penance at service time on three successive Sundays, in the presence of the whole congregation, and clad in a white sheet symbolising his remorse. It was the most severe penalty the court could inflict.

In the end, and in return for a contribution to Stratford's poor box, Thomas Quiney was permitted to do penance in a private chapel in a nearby hamlet, where few people could witness his disgrace; but his mitigated punishment did little to spare his wife, her family and his own from humiliation. The court's denunciation of his base conduct was on public record, and its sentence had been pronounced in the parish church crowded with their fellow townsfolk.

Shakespeare was deeply distressed by the revelation of Quiney's callousness and duplicity. In poor health since the beginning of the year, he was further weakened by the shock and by his anxiety for Judith. Even so, physically infirm though he was, he took prompt action to offset the ill consequences of a bad situation. As soon as he was convinced of her husband's untrustworthy nature, he revised his will to safeguard Judith's interests. The legal formalities were completed on 25 March, the day before Quiney made his open confession in court.

Shakespeare's will has been the subject of much comment. Last wishes, even those of obscure people, have a particular and solemn interest. As John of Gaunt says (*Richard II* Act II.Sc.1):

> the tongues of dying men
> Enforce attention like deep harmony.

Small wonder, then, that the last known utterance of the world's greatest playwright has been scrutinised so minutely; and small wonder, too, that it has so often given rise to needless conjectures and speculative 'interpretations'.

In fact, the will is a plain enough document, strictly formal in character and conventional in its wording. It presents few problems when the following matters are given due consideration: the circumstances in which it was made; the strictly legal style of its language; the overriding purpose it was designed to serve; the careful provisions it made to fulfil that purpose. Each of those is now described in turn.

In the January of 1616 Shakespeare sent for his lawyer, Francis Collins, to discuss his will and to make a first draft. Few people in those days made wills before receiving some kind of warning that they were not likely to live much longer. Just how ill Shakespeare was that winter we do not know. Far from well, certainly; and feeling old and tired. He had worked extremely hard, and at a punishing pace, for many years; and though he was not yet fifty-two – not even elderly by our reckoning – he had by then outlived all his brothers.

The will, a three-page document, was written by Collins' clerk at the dictation of Shakespeare and the lawyer. That was the custom. Seventeenth-century gentlemen did not write out their wills themselves; and busy lawyers employed clerks to do their donkey work. All the subsequent alterations were inserted by the clerk at Shakespeare's and Collins' instructions; and there was no fair copy. It was not legally required. Shakespeare's will, like many others, eventually went for probate with all its crossings-out and insertions. (It was taken to the probate office in London on 22 June 1616 by Dr John Hall, who then swore to administer Shakespeare's estate according to the dead man's wishes.)

All the most important provisions of the will (they are described later) were written down at the first drafting; but Shakespeare added one item after Judith's wedding on 10 February when he made a generous bequest to the newly-married couple. It was intended for their joint benefit, but it named his son-in-law as the legatee. Soon after that, however, rumours about Quiney reached him. His will was as yet unwitnessed and unsigned, and he decided not to give legal force to the bequest until Judith's husband could prove his integrity.

By the middle of March, it was no longer possible to hope that the rumours were false. Given the circumstances of Margaret Wheeler's death, Quiney could not deny his guilt. Shakespeare sent for Collins again and altered the terms of the legacy. The words 'to my son-in-law' were struck out and replaced by 'to my daughter Judith'. All the legal formalities were completed on 25 March, the day before Quiney appeared in court.

By then, Shakespeare was a very sick man, barely able to write his signature at the foot of each sheet of his will. Indeed, some handwriting experts are convinced that the lawyer's clerk had to guide his hand as he painfully formed the letters. Others go further, and argue that the clerk wrote the signatures himself, imitating Shakespeare's handwriting. It would have been legal then, provided it was done in the presence of witnesses – and there were five of those: Collins, the lawyer; Julius Shawe of Henley Street; Hamnet Sadler, so long Shakespeare's friend; Robert Whatcote, godfather to Hamnet Sadler and a chief witness for Susanna when she cleared her good name; John Robinson, one of the Halls' trusted servants.

Such were the circumstances in which Shakespeare's will was drawn up in January and February 1616 and put into its final form on 25 March.

As befits a legal document, its tone is impersonal; though, as we shall see, unspoken last messages are implicit in minor bequests to relatives and friends. Shakespeare knew precisely what he wanted to do. He was intent only on devising a will that would stand up in law and dispose of his estate according to his wishes. Together, he and

Collins framed his instructions in precise, dry language and dictated them to the clerk.

Failure to recognise that Shakespeare's will as a typical legal document of its time has caused a lot of misunderstanding. Finding in it no great literary merit, some writers have complained of its 'dullness' – as if they had expected him to express his last wishes in a blank verse drama or a sonnet sequence. Others have searched it for significant nuances of meaning, which it neither does nor was intended to contain. Others have mistaken its legal formulas for personal statements of Shakespeare's own convictions. For example, much more has been read into the opening declaration than its nature warrants. (It is quoted here with modernised spelling and punctuation.)

In the name of God, Amen. I, William Shakespeare of Stratford-upon-Avon in the County of Warwick, Gentlemen, in perfect health and memory, God be praised, do make and ordain this my last will and testament in the manner and form following. That is to say, first I commend my soul into the hands of God my Creator, hoping and assuredly believing through the merits of Jesus Christ my Saviour to be partaker of life everlasting; and my body to the Earth whereof it is made.

That eloquent declaration has often been cited as proof that Shakespeare was a devout Christian and a convinced Protestant. He may have been; but those words do not *prove* anything about his religious beliefs. The declaration follows a standard pattern, then in general use. (Note, for example, the conventional affirmation of being 'in perfect health' – which Shakespeare most certainly was not.) It was customary to preface a will with a profession of faith, expressed in a fine flourish of suitable language. After that, the real business began, and the style changed abruptly: 'Item. I give and bequeath . . .'.

Lawyer Collins knew what the form was; and either he or his clerk could supply the expected preamble without any prompting from the testator. How truly those pious words represented Shakespeare's beliefs we simply do not know; and it is most unlikely that he and his lawyer would have felt it necessary to discuss them. Each assumed that the accepted formulas would be used as the opening words of the will – and so they were.

Before leaving the subject, we may note that, whatever his attitude to religion may have been, Shakespeare's charitable disposition is evident in one briefly-worded item in his will: 'I give and bequeath unto the poor of Stratford ten pounds'. That was an unusually generous gift, five times as much as was generally reckoned to be the 'proper' sum – 'the done thing'. Richer men than Shakespeare considered they had amply discharged their obligations to charity if they left two pounds to relieve the hardship of the poor people of their town.

All Shakespeare's individual bequests (to which we shall shortly turn) were secondary to the one great purpose he had in mind. He desired above all things to ensure that his estate was kept together after his death; and that it was handed down, generation after generation, to those who would be his 'right heirs for ever'.

To that end, and having no son, he decreed that his elder daughter, Susanna, should be the first inheritor of his land and property. On her death, it must pass to her son, if by then she had a male heir. If Susanna died without a son the estate must go to her daughter Elizabeth. When Elizabeth died, *her* son must inherit it; and *his* son after him. If however, Elizabeth died without a son, the estate must pass from her to the senior male descendant of Shakespeare's younger daughter, Judith.

Thus he tried to ensure that the fruits of his life's work would descend intact to a succession of specified persons, none of whom would possess the estate absolutely. Each, in turn, would hold it in trust for life and, at death, pass it on entire to an appointed heir. By creating an 'entail' (as it is called) he was adopting the legal device commonly used by propertied people when planning for the welfare of their posterity.

Some of his biographers have expressed regret that, nearing his end, Shakespeare was so much occupied with mundane matters; and his strongly-felt dynastic ambition has been deplored as 'the last infirmity of a noble mind'. Those are sentimental attitudes. Wills are made to dispose of possessions and to settle the material affairs of a lifetime; and Shakespeare's decision to entail his estate was – as he and his contemporaries saw it – the practical expression of his natural concern for his descendants. His own worldly task nearly done, he turned his thoughts to people as yet unborn, of whom he knew no more than that they would bear his surname and hold him in memory as their benefactor.

Given the facts already set out, the provisions of Shakespeare's will require little explanation. His gift to the poor has been mentioned. Other bequests were made to the following people: his daughters Judith and Susanna; his son-in-law John Hall; his granddaughter Elizabeth; his sister Joan and her family; his godson William Walker; various acquaintances and friends in Stratford and in London. Finally, there was a gift for his wife, about which so much has been written that it must be discussed in some detail after the other legacies have been described.

For Judith he made handsome provision, hedging it round with legal defences. What the law could do to protect a married woman's property was done. The bequest of one hundred pounds that had previously stood in her husband's name was transferred to her. In addition, she was to have a further fifty pounds, provided she made no claim to the ownership of the Chapel Lane cottage. (It must be remembered that fifty pounds was a generous valuation of the cottage's worth. Judith's grandfather had once bought two Stratford houses for that amount of money – see Chapter 5.)

A further one hundred and fifty pounds was to go to Judith three years after Shakespeare's death, but only if her husband settled land on her to that value. If he did not, Shakespeare's executors (John and Susanna Hall) were to retain control of the capital and pay Judith the interest on it for the rest of her life. When she died, any children of hers then living were to share the money. Thomas Quiney was not to get his hands on it. As we shall see, Quiney's later conduct proved that Shakespeare was neither over-cautious nor vindictive in the measures he took to protect Judith's inheritance.

As a personal memento of her father, Judith got 'my broad silver gilt bowl'. He had intended to leave all his plate to her, but when he learnt the truth about her husband he changed his mind and left it to his granddaughter instead. In the Hall family's possession it would be safe from Quiney's shifty ways.

The bulk of his estate went to Susanna but, as described earlier, he created an entail and left it to her:

> . . . for and during the term of her natural life, and after her decease to the first son of her body lawfully ensuing, and to the heirs male of the body of the said first son . . ..

If, as has been said, Susanna had no son, then her daughter Elizabeth was to inherit the estate. After her, the will made provision for 'first, second, third, fourth, fifth, sixth and seventh sons', and then on again 'for default of such issue' to the 'heirs male of my daughter Judith'. (It all came to nothing. No male heir ever inherited the estate of William Shakespeare.)

It was a fine inheritance that Susanna was to have for life: New Place; the family house in Henley Street and the one next door to it; the cottage in Chapel Lane; the Blackfriars Gatehouse; land in Old Stratford and tithes at Welcombe. Nor did Shakespeare forget her husband – the son-in-law on whom he could rely. Having created the entail and made individual bequests, he left all his other possessions to him and to Susanna jointly and for their own use. The wording is legal, but the feeling comes through:

> All the rest of my goods, chattels, leases, plate, jewels and household stuff whatsoever . . . I give, devise and bequeath to my son-in-law John Hall, Gentleman, and my daughter Susanna, his wife, whom I ordain and make executors of this my last will and testament.

The 'leases' mentioned there included his theatre shares. It is not clear whether they were sold just before or soon after his death, nor for how much, but their cash value was a very considerable addition to the Halls' personal legacy.

When John Hall took the will to London for probate he took with him an inventory of Shakespeare's 'goods, chattels . . . and household stuff'. It listed among all his other personal possessions the books and papers he left behind him. Unfortunately, that document has been lost, so we know nothing of the contents of his library. The absence of a list that would have told us so much about him has been keenly felt by all Shakespeare students; and the more so because a later reference to 'a study of books' at New Place reminds us painfully of what has been lost. (The manuscripts of his plays were not kept with the other papers at New Place. They did not belong to Shakespeare and they were with their owners, the King's Men, in London.)

To Joan Hart, his married sister – and apart from him the sole survivor of John and Mary Shakespeare's eight children – he left twenty pounds. He also stipulated that she was to enjoy a life-tenancy of the family house in Henley Street, in which she had been living since their father's death. Their widowed mother had then shared it with Joan, her husband and their children for the rest of her life. (See Chapter 3.) A token rent of twelve pence a year was all that Joan was to pay. It was valuable gift, in remembrance of shared lives. They had grown up there together.

Shakespeare left Joan's three sons, William, Thomas and Michael Hart, five pounds each; and Joan was also to have – as a gift for her husband – all Shakespeare's 'wearing apparel'. Clothes were a major item of household expenditure in those days, and his wardrobe included the costly garments appropriate to his rank as a gentleman. What William Hart did not choose to wear could be sold for a good sum. Unhappily, he did not live to benefit from his brother-in-law's kind thought. He died a week before Shakespeare.

Then there were personal bequests for friends and for people with whom he had business dealings. In Shakespeare's life those categories often overlapped. He had always been frank and easy in his relationships, and the list of those he remembered in his will included local gentry, professional men and townsfolk.

He left his sword to Thomas Combe, nephew of old John Combe

who had died in 1613 reputed to be the richest man in Stratford. John Combe was widely disliked, but Shakespeare (he bought land in Old Stratford from him) got on well with him. His esteem for the Combe family is clear from the nature of his gift to Thomas. A gentleman's sword was customarily left to his eldest son. Shakespeare's would have gone to Hamnet, had he lived.

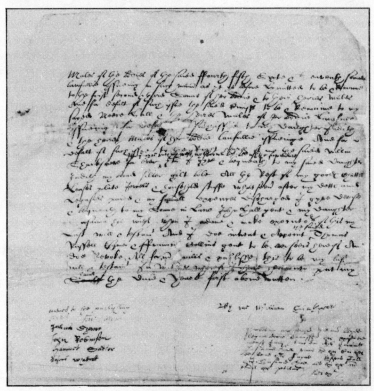

'By me William Shakespeare'
the last sheet of the will

The lawyer ('Francis Collins, Gentleman') received a legacy in settlement of his fee; and five pounds went to 'Thomas Russell Esquire' who had agreed to act with Collins as an overseer of the will. 'Anthony Nash, Gentleman' and his brother Thomas, both of whom had been helpful to Shakespeare in land and tithe business, were left money to buy mourning rings to wear in his memory. So was William Reynolds, a local landowner. So, too, was the Stratford baker, Hamnet Sadler, oldest of Shakespeare's friends, and witness of his will. Shakespeare's gift of twenty shillings to his little godson William Walker was to be paid 'in gold'. He was too young to be given money for a ring, but the gold piece could be kept as a memento.

The list of those to whom Shakespeare left money to buy tokens of remembrance ended with bequests to the three friends who had been with him in the great fellowship of the Chamberlain's and the King's Men:

> . . . to my fellows, John Heminge, Richard Burbage and Henry Condell, twenty-six shillings and eight pence a-piece to buy them rings.

Burbage did not wear his mourning ring for long. He died three years after his old colleague and companion. Heminge and Condell lived on to edit the First Folio, that most splendid and enduring of monuments to genius, in order, as they said: 'to keep the memory of so worthy a friend and fellow alive, as was our Shakespeare'.

In addition to the personal bequests already mentioned, Shakespeare left a special gift to his wife. The nature of that gift has attracted a lot of comment, and it has given rise to some over-confident pronouncements about their marriage. The evidence is by no means conclusive, however. This is a matter about which it is wise to be cautious. The facts do not warrant positive judgements; and those who consider them carefully recognise that they can be interpreted in different ways.

The bequest to Anne was an afterthought, squeezed into the space between two lines near the end of the will:

> Item. I give unto my wife my second best bed with the furniture.

Many believe that in its substance and in its wording that bequest shows – and was intended to show – that he had no love for her. They see it as a deliberate slight. Having made no financial provision for his widow, Shakespeare left her a paltry and contemptuous souvenir of their thirty-four years of married life.

Is that the truth of the matter? If so, it was a malicious, wounding and underhand action, quite out of keeping with all we know of him. In the opinion of his contemporaries his disposition was 'most generous and free from all contriving' (as Laertes says of Hamlet's) and the facts available to us support their judgement of him. Given that evidence, it seems most improbable that the bequest was a calculated insult. Nothing in the record of Shakespeare's life suggests that, even supposing he had no affection for his wife, he would have chosen to make their unhappiness a matter of public knowledge.

As we shall see, a very different interpretation is possible – and on good grounds. There are reasons for believing that, so far from being a cold-hearted snub, his bequest to Anne was an expression of his regard for her.

True, he did not make provision for her to inherit money or land, but it was not necessary for him to so. The law guaranteed her 'portion': one-third of his estate for life. It has been argued that the widow's portion did not apply unless it was specified in the will; but that depended on local custom. Had it been so in Warwickshire, and had Anne Shakespeare been disinherited by its omission, she could have contested the will. In fact, she lived at New Place for the rest of her life, in possession of ample means and cared for by her daughter and son-in-law. When Shakespeare made his will he knew that Anne's future was safe.

Again, it is true that the bequest was not made until after the rest of the will had been written; but there is a simple explanation for that. Because he knew that she would have her widow's portion, he had not needed to mention her. Then, realising that other named and substantial beneficiaries had received remembrances, he directed that she was to have a valuable gift; and the clerk duly inserted that provision. (Beds and their 'furniture' – curtains and bedding – were much prized as inheritances.) But why the second best bed? Why not the best bed? The answer is that the best bed was kept in the guest room. Shakespeare left Anne the bed that they had shared. He could not have given her a more personal or a more loving memento of their life together.

Finally, it is often said that his bequest to her is worded coldly: 'I give unto my wife . . . '. True feeling would surely have been expressed in some affectionate phrase or other – 'my beloved wife', perhaps. That is special pleading. In none of the bequests are any terms of endearment used. There are no affectionate phrases. The language is uniformly factual, objective – dry. Impersonal in tone throughout, the document contains no direct expression of Shakespeare's feelings for the people who were in his thoughts when he made his last will and testament.

He died on his birthday – 23 April. The exact cause of his death is not known; nor do we know whether his son-in-law attended him. Dr John Hall's surviving *Casebook* records Susanna's and Elizabeth's illnesses and the cures he applied, so it may be that in the missing *Casebook* (and we know there was another) he noted the details of Shakespeare's end. Nearly fifty years later, a Stratford vicar set down in his diary a story he had been told when he first arrived in the town:

> Shakespeare, Drayton and Ben Jonson had a merry meeting, and it seems drank too hard, for Shakespeare died of a fever there contracted.

If the story is true, then Shakespeare had time – and cause – to remember the words he had given to Constable Dogberry years before: 'If a merry meeting may be wished, God prohibit it'! But it seems an unlikely tale. The worrying events of the February and March of 1616 would not have put him in the mood for 'a merry meeting', even with two old friends. In any case, he had never been a hard drinker. His illness was probably brought on by the lingering effects of a winter chill and the nagging anxieties of the Quiney affair. Together, they fatally undermined a constitution on which years of arduous labour had left their mark.

On 25 April he was buried in the chancel of Holy Trinity Church, an honoured last resting place. Four lines of doggerel verse (quoted here with modernised spelling and punctuation) were carved on his gravestone:

> Good friend, for Jesus' sake forbear
> To dig the dust enclosed here.
> Blest be the man that spares these stones,
> And cursed be he that moves my bones.

The tradition is that Shakespeare composed that 'curse' himself, using language that would be readily understood by the sort of people, (sextons and gravediggers) who, in the distant future, might be tempted 'to move his bones' – that is, to open his grave and remove his remains to make room for another burial. It was quite common for graves to be disturbed for that purpose. It happened in the overcrowded churchyards; and Shakespeare's chancel grave might well be coveted by the relatives of a rich person, looking for a suitably distinguished burial place for a family corpse. If there were no Shakespeares still alive to protect his grave, then his verse might save it. It may be doggerel, but it is perfectly plain and forceful. Like Hamlet, Shakespeare had seen gravediggers at work, and he had no intention of allowing some 'rude knave to knock him about the sconce [skull] with a dirty shovel'.

His grave – now a place of pilgrimage – has remained undisturbed; and the verse may have contributed to its safety in the years before it became unthinkable to lay sacrilegious hands on it. In a letter written in 1693, a Warwickshire man called Dowdall said that 'not one for fear of the curse dare touch his gravestone, though his wife and daughters did earnestly desire to be laid in the same grave with him'.

A little before Anne died in August 1623, the family set up a elaborate monument to Shakespeare on the north chancel wall, about five feet away from his grave. Its centre piece is a half-length figure of the dead man, placed in a round-arched niche. Beneath the 'bust' (as it is generally called) two inscriptions recite his praises. The first is in Latin, as was suitable for a gentleman's memorial. It salutes him as a

Nestor (for wisdom), as a Socrates (for genius) and as a Virgil (for poetry). The earth, it says, covers him; the people mourn him; the gods now have him with them in Olympus. Neatly-worded, it is a typical product of the classical education of the day, and it was probably composed by Dr John Hall.

For the benefit of those who cannot read Latin, the second inscription is in English. (It allows for the possibility that some who see it may not be able to read that language either: 'Stay Passenger . . . Read If Thou Canst'.) In rhyming and rather awkward lines, it bids the passer-by to reflect on Shakespeare's greatness.

The tablet then records the date of his death and states that it occurred in the fifty-third year of his life. That is accurate. He died on his fifty-second birthday, so he had just entered his fifty-third year when 'he paid his score'.

Interestingly, both inscriptions are wholly taken up with Shakespeare's literary eminence. The references generally made (whether deserved or not) to the remarkable piety and uncommon virtues of the dead are omitted. Whoever composed the inscriptions for Shakespeare considered it more important to celebrate him as a writer than to pay him the conventional moral tributes. Clearly, his family agreed, for the memorial was executed in accordance with their wishes. Hall supervised the arrangements in consultation with Shakespeare's widow and daughters.

Consequently, we must suppose that his family accepted the effigy as being at least a recognisable likeness of Shakespeare. Dressed in a doublet and gown, he is standing with his hands resting on a cushion, which seems to represent a desk. He holds a pen in his right hand, and there is a sheet of paper under his left. The sculptor tried, not very successfully, to depict the writer at work. He has a prominent forehead, a bald pate, short side hair, a neat moustache and beard.

Today, it is generally agreed to be a poor and lifeless piece of work, even allowing for the fact that such 'portraiture' is often stiff and conventional. The eyes are particularly disappointing; their vacancy takes all expression out of the face. Yet Hall commissioned the work from a well-known tomb maker. Gerard Johnson – his workshop was near the Globe – made church monuments for several noble families; and old John Combe's very expensive tomb in Stratford church was his work. There are two particular points of interest about the Shakespeare figure. The sculptor is believed to have worked the features from a death mask. If so, that would account for the unnaturally smooth, unlined appearance of the well-rounded face. It is also believed that the auburn colouring of the hair, beard and moustache is authentic.

With all its faults, the church bust is not ludicrous; and that is more than can be said for the portrait used as the frontispiece of the First

153

Folio. The Folio portrait was the the work of a young man called Martin Droeshout. (Although his surname was Flemish, he was a Londoner.) Droeshout was only fifteen when Shakespeare died and twenty-two when he engraved the portrait, working – it is said – from a line drawing of Shakespeare as a young man. The printers commissioned him to do the job because he did not charge much for his work.

However little he was paid, it was too much for this wretchedly unskilful 'portrait'. The forehead is mountainous. The left eye is lower in the face and much bigger than the right; and both are egg-like and void of all intelligence. The huge head is perched precariously on shoulders too narrow to support it. Indeed, that mighty dome appears to have become separated from the misshapen body, for the neck is completely hidden by a ridiculous ruff looking rather like a horse-collar. (No wonder Ben Jonson's introductory verses advised Shakespeare's reader to 'look / Not on his picture, but his book'.)

As time went on, several artists attempted to portray Shakespeare in a more pleasing light. It was not difficult to improve on the work of Gerard Johnson and Martin Droeshout; but even the best of the later portraits could be no more than imaginative impressions of what his appearance may have been. There was not much to go on – just the unsatisfactory bust, the dreadful Folio frontispiece, and John Aubrey's encouraging but vague statement that Shakespeare 'was a handsome, well-shaped man'. The famous 'Chandos' portrait (reproduced on the cover of this book) has long been considered the best. Until very recently, however, it was believed to have been painted after Shakespeare's death. Now that experts have attributed it to the artist John Taylor and dated it 1610, or thereabouts, we know that it is, in fact, an authentic likeness of the living man. (See the notes inside the front cover.)

Not long after Shakespeare's monument was erected in Stratford church, the devoted labours of his old friends John Heminge and Henry Condell were brought to a triumphant conclusion. Late in 1623, the printing of the First Folio was completed. Then, at last, all 'the comedies, histories and tragedies' of William Shakespeare were collected together and published in one volume – the greatest memorial to literary genius that the world has ever seen. The importance of the First Folio to scholars is discussed in Chapter 14. Here, it is its influence on Shakespeare's reputation that concerns us. More than any other single event, its publication established his colossal stature in people's minds – and for ever. By making his plays available 'to the great variety of readers', Heminge and Condell believed that they were ensuring Shakespeare's immortality. They were right. Since 1623 his works have never been out of print. Rapidly in his own land, gradually throughout the world, they became recognised as one of the supreme artistic achievements of all time – an international heritage. 'Read him, therefore', his first editors commanded, 'Read him, therefore; and again, and again'. And nowhere in the world have their words gone unheeded.

Shakespeare's estate, so carefully kept together by the terms of his will, survived intact for less than sixty years after his death. He had four grandchildren: Elizabeth Hall, Susanna's daughter; Shakespeare, Richard and Thomas Quiney, Judith's sons. They all died childless. Elizabeth was the last survivor. When she died in 1670, the direct line of descent from William Shakespeare came to an end. The entail was broken, and the possessions he had left to his 'right heirs for ever' were dispersed.

Of the New Place household, Anne was the first to go. She died on 6 August 1623, aged sixty-seven. She was buried in a grave alongside her husband's. Her son-in-law composed her epitaph in a neat Latin verse, extolling her as a good mother, and as one who had lived and died in Christian faith and in certain hope of resurrection.

John Hall's own death occurred on 26 November 1635, during a plague epidemic. The good physician, then aged sixty, attended his patients with characteristic devotion and was worn out by his exertions. His grave is close to Shakespeare's. The church burial register describes him (in Latin) as 'John Hall, most skilled doctor' – a well-deserved tribute.

Susanna survived her husband for fourteen years. Her widowhood was cheered by the company of her daughter and her husband, Thomas Nash, who lived in the big house adjoining New Place. Susanna's calm existence was disturbed by two out-of-the-way events, each of a very different nature.

In 1637, a man called Baldwin Brooks claimed that John Hall's estate owed him money, and he sent bailiffs to force their way into New Place. Never one to be intimidated, Susanna took legal action against Brooks and his men, declaring that they had broken down the study door and seized 'divers books' and other valuables. What the outcome was is not known; nor is it known whether any of those books had once been Shakespeare's.

Six years after that, during the Civil War, Charles I's Queen (Henrietta Maria) arrived in Stratford with troops to join up with Prince Rupert and his forces. New Place was chosen to provide accommodation for her, and the Queen was Susanna's guest for two nights. It was a doubly suitable choice. Shakespeare's daughter had a large and comfortable house; and her royal visitor was a great admirer of her father's plays, many of which she had seen performed at Court by his old company. Charles I shared his wife's enthusiasm for Shakespeare's works and often declared that the First Folio was his favourite book.

Susanna died on 11 July 1649, aged sixty-six. The inscription on her gravestone reads: 'Here lieth the body of Susanna, wife to John Hall, gent.: the daughter of William Shakespeare, gent.'. Those words are followed by a lively character-sketch which, if it was not composed by one or both of them, certainly reflects what her daughter and son-in-law thought of her:

> Witty above her sex, but that's not all,
> Wise to salvation was good Mistress Hall,
> Something of Shakespeare was in that, but this
> Wholly of him with whom she's now in bliss . . .'.

Elizabeth, the only child of John and Susanna Hall, married Thomas Nash in 1626. It was a good match from a wordly point of view. He was a wealthy man. It was also a happy marriage, despite the difference in their ages. She was eighteen and he was thirty-three when they married. Thomas was the son of Anthony Nash, the landowner at Welcombe to whom Elizabeth's grandfather had left money for a mourning ring. He was also first cousin to John Lane who had slandered Susanna, but quite unlike him in character; and quite unlike him, too, in his opinion of her. He left his mother-in-law a handsome legacy in token of his regard for her.

Thomas Nash died in 1647. He was buried near Shakespeare, and the Arms of the three families – Nash, Hall and Shakespeare – united by his marriage to Elizabeth were carved on his stone. His childless widow soon married again. Her second husband was John – later, Sir John – Bernard (or Barnard, as it is often spelt), Lord of the Manor of Abington, in Northamptonshire. It was his second marriage, too. He had a large family by his first wife, but his union with Elizabeth was childless. For some years, Sir John and his wife divided their time between New Place and the Abington Manor house, but they gradually withdrew from their Stratford home. It was at Abington that Elizabeth, Lady Bernard died, just a day or two short of her sixty-second birthday. Neither there nor in Stratford was any monument raised to the memory of Shakespeare's granddaughter, his last direct descendant.

Shakespeare's other daughter, Judith, was seventy-seven when she died in 1662. Thomas Quiney had died in 1655, so at least she had the last seven years of her life free from anxiety about her weak and selfish husband. Quiney's behaviour after their marriage had amply confirmed Shakespeare's forebodings. Frequently in trouble, he was fined for swearing and for encouraging excessive drinking on his premises; and he was denounced for selling watered-down wine. Thanks to his family's high standing, he was given the chance to make good as the corporation's chamberlain, but his two-year term of office was unsatisfactory. He had nothing of his father's and grandfather's ability and integrity. On one occasion his own relatives had to act quickly to prevent him from cheating his wife and children by selling a lease that was their joint property. Judith would have had a hard time indeed if her father had not left her an income of her own for life.

Thomas and Judith Quiney had three sons, none of whom lived long. Their first-born (christened Shakespeare) died an infant in 1617. Richard and Thomas, their second and third sons, both died in 1639, aged twenty-one and nineteen respectively.

Though Shakespeare's direct line perished, descendants of his sister Joan survived. She lived until 1646, outlasting her husband and her brother by thirty years. She outlived three of her four children too. Her daughter Mary was only four when she died in 1607. Joan's eldest son, William, became an actor and joined his uncle's old company in London. He died unmarried, aged thirty-nine. Her youngest child, Michael, was only ten when he died; but Joan's second son, Thomas, lived to be sixty-five. He married and had two sons, thus establishing a Hart family line that has endured. To this day, there are Harts in England and in Australia who can trace their ancestry back, through Joan, to John and Mary Shakespeare of Henley Street, Stratford.

When the entail was broken on the death of Shakespeare's grand-daughter in 1670, the Henley Street property passed into the Harts' ownership. By the will of Elizabeth, Lady Bernard, her kinsmen Thomas and George Hart inherited the house in which William Shakespeare was born. It remained in the possession of the Hart family until 1806, when it was sold. Forty-one years later, it came on the market again and was then bought by public subscription. Ever since, it has been in the care of Trustees (now known as the Trustees and Guardians of Shakespeare's Birthplace). Gradually and lovingly, it has been restored. The Birthplace Trust has also acquired the site and gardens of New Place and the land that Shakespeare owned in Old Stratford. In part, at least, the estate he so greatly desired to keep together has been reunified.

The Trust now safeguards, too, places which Shakespeare did not own, but which figured largely in his life's story: the house at Shottery where Anne Hathaway was living when he courted her; his mother's girlhood home at Wilmcote; the Stratford house in which John and Susanna Hall began their married life.

The last words may be left to Ben Jonson, whose opinion of Shakespeare was expressed very frankly. He regarded him as a fellow writer and saw no need to stand in awe of him. Fourteen years or so after his great contemporary's death, he recorded his views in a notebook, making some characteristically testy remarks about what he saw as the habitual fault in Shakespeare's work. He gave too free rein to his teeming imagination, Jonson said, and too seldom disciplined his over-fluent style. He ought to have corrected and revised his hastily-written manuscripts before handing them over to the players. Even so, Jonson was in no doubt about the quality of his work:

> . . . he redeemed his vices with his virtues. There was ever more in him to be praised than pardoned.

Jonson saw himself as a writer in the classical tradition – as one who knew 'the rules' and observed them. Hence his objections to Shakespeare's 'lack of restraint'. He felt it his duty to voice his criticism of the artist he had always seen as his chief rival. That done, however, he was quick to express his deep affection for the greatly-gifted man he had known so well and for whose personality and character he had a warm-hearted admiration:

> . . . for I loved the man and do honour his memory (on this side idolatry) as much as any. He was indeed honest, and of an open and free nature: had an excellent *Phantsie* [imagination]; brave notions, and gentle expressions.

The choleric Ben Jonson knew and worked with many people in the theatre. Of them all, it was William Shakespeare alone with whom he had a true and lasting friendship. The candid remarks in his notebook, critical though some of them are, in no way tarnish the sincerity of his dedication of the memorial verses in the First Folio:

> To the memory of my beloved,
> The Author
> Mr William Shakespeare:
> And
> what he hath left us.

And succeeding generations have agreed with Ben Jonson's affirmation that William Shakespeare has made us all his 'right heirs for ever'.

Part II
HIS STAGE

theatres, actors, audiences
and play scripts

11

The Theatres
and their Stages

FOR NEARLY thirty years after Shakespeare's death the London playhouses and the acting companies went on much as they had done during the last period of his career. The 'public' and the 'private' theatres remained as popular as ever, and though their audiences were becoming increasingly differentiated (see Chapter 9), between them they still provided the population of the capital with one of its favourite sources of relaxation. If Shakespeare could have returned to attend a performance at the Globe or at the Blackfriars Theatre in which his nephew William Hart was appearing, or to be present at Court when his old company was entertaining Charles I and his Queen, he would not have found any great changes in the theatre, the stage, or the style of acting. The play might have been new to him; though it might quite likely have been one that he had seen – quite likely, indeed, one that he had written.

A return visit in 1660, however, would have been a wholly different experience. Then, he would have taken his seat in a new theatre, for none of those that he had known was still in use; and he would have seen a greatly changed stage, a different style of acting and a new kind of audience. If, by chance, the players had been acting one his plays he would have had difficulty in recognising it. In all probability its title would have been changed; and it would certainly have been extensively rewritten.

The theatre world that Shakespeare had known came to an abrupt end in 1642, when the outbreak of the Civil War put a stop to all professional acting. London was controlled by Parliament; and Parliament decreed that this was no time for 'public sports'. The order was given that 'public stage plays shall cease and be forborne'. At last, the Puritans were able to do what they had always wanted. The playhouses, public and private alike – the Globe, the Blackfriars and all the others – were closed; and they remained closed for eighteen years, Indeed, the famous theatres of Shakespeare's day never reopened.

As soon as the monarchy was restored in 1660 the new king,

Charles II, allowed professional acting to start again. The long closure of the theatres had profound effects, however, and conditions were now very different from those in which Shakespeare had worked. Theatre-going was no longer among the chief leisure activities of Londoners, and just two theatres sufficed to meet the diminished demand for plays. Audiences were drawn from a narrower social range. Many of the better-off citizens were puritanically hostile to stage entertainments. The poorer ones could not afford the prices charged and, in any case, they did not share the tastes of the educated people who were now the actors' regular patrons. Gone were the days when 'penny stinkards' and 'gallants' alike flocked to the playhouses in the afternoon.

The new playgoers followed the fashions set by a Court that had spent years in exile in France; and the new dramatists had to cater for those tastes. In the Restoration theatre there was little understanding of or enthusiasm for the pre-1642 conventions and artistic values of the 'native' English drama.

The 1660 theatres had physical features that dictated fundamental changes in the ways in which plays were presented and acted. Whereas the Globe and the other public theatres had been round or hexagonal, the new ones were oblong. They could not accommodate the huge 'platform' stage on which Shakespeare and his fellow actors performed. They were much smaller, too, and seats had to be provided where the acting space used to be. Memories of playing 'in the round' (or, at least, with spectators on three sides) remained, and the new theatres retained a shrunk-down version of the 'apron' stage that jutted out into the auditorium of the Blackfriars. Even so, post-1660 actors were withdrawn into a more confined arena and were in far less intimate contact with their audience. In presenting action within a 'picture-frame' the Restoration stage resembled the 'modern' stage (as developed in the eighteenth and nineteenth centuries) much more than it resembled any of the stages for which Shakespeare had written.

In the new theatres, too, stage lighting became a major contributor to dramatic effects; and painted 'wings' and 'flats', drawn across the picture-frame stage as required, represented changes of location. Stage designers exploited these resources to the full, aiming at 'realism' when creating their illusions, either of ordinary life settings or of exotic backgrounds. Audiences expected to be entertained by these and other conjuring tricks, considering them an important part of their enjoyment of the play.

The combined effect of all these developments revolutionised production and acting. Shakespeare's plays (like those of his contemporaries) were crippled when performed on a stage that had jettisoned the essential features of his. The shaping spirit that guided his writing and directed his actors died when spectacle elbowed language aside, when continuity and flexibility of action were no longer paramount, and when the intimate communication of actors with audience was diluted.

Just how far removed from Shakespeare's theatre that of 1660 was can be judged from a few examples of how his plays fared on stage in Restoration (and in much later) times.

The licences granted to the two acting companies established at the beginning of Charles II's reign expressly permitted them to 'reform' and 'make fit' Shakespeare's plays; and they made full use of that permission. They pillaged his works, rewriting and cutting freely to get them onto their stage. What they did to his art is made clear by the comments of that intelligent and enthusiastic playgoer Samuel Pepys. In his *Diary* he recorded the experience of seeing *Hamlet* acted 'with scenes' – the action chopped up, and the stage effects more prominent than the dramatist's words. He thought that a re-hashed version of *Measure for Measure* (it was called *The Law Against Lovers!*) was 'a good play and well acted'; but the fact that he was particularly impressed by its 'dancing and singing' indicates how little it resembled the play that Shakespeare wrote. Having seen *A Midsummer Night's Dream* for the first time, he resolved never to repeat the experience, 'for it is the most insipid, ridiculous play that ever I saw'.

The mangled productions of Shakespeare's plays that Pepys attended were typical of the treatment his work got then, and for a long time afterwards. To give just one example of later mishandling, *King Lear*, as Shakespeare wrote it, was not restored to the stage until 1838. From 1681 onwards it had been acted in Nahum Tate's absurd version. Tate 'reformed' that great tragedy and 'made it fit' for presentation by altering it out of recognition. He rewrote the plot and gave the play a happy ending. The Fool disappeared from the cast. Edgar rescued his sweetheart Cordelia from the gallows. Then, with the blessing of a repentant and mellowed Lear, they were married.

Somehow, Shakespeare's reputation survived the botching of his plays: the garbled texts and the misconceived staging. They never ceased to be performed; and they never lacked readers to acclaim their greatness as works of literature. Many influential critics argued that they were more suited to be read than to be performed. In 1811, for example, Charles Lamb (an authority on the plays of Shakespeare's contemporaries as well) maintained that 'the plays of Shakespeare are less calculated for performance on stage than those of almost any other dramatist whatever'. Lamb's experiences of the plays on stage fell far short of the expectations he had formed when reading them. Contrasting the *King Lear* he had seen in the theatre with the play he had come to know so well in his study, he concluded that it was unactable. (Burbage and the rest of the King's Men would have thought him very foolish!)

Nowadays, we have little use for any view of Shakespeare that does not begin with the recognition that he was a *dramatist* – that he wrote for the theatre, not for the study; to be acted, not read. For us, his reputation stands securely on the success of his plays – as he wrote them – on our stage. But then, we live at a time when actors and directors assume that Shakespeare knew his business. They approach him as a practical and immensely skilful playwright whose dramas will succeed on the modern stage if we take the trouble to learn how he expected things to be done – and then do them in his way. That approach has ensured that his plays are as much a part of our living theatre as they were of his; but it is an approach that was not available until the principles and methods of his stagecraft had been rediscovered.

It was not until long after his death that his plays were considered 'difficult' to appreciate or 'intractable' to perform. Before 1660, they were known to be superbly well written for performance. For many years after that, however, because they were staged in a manner wholly alien to the nature of his dramatic art the life was drained out of them. Actors penned behind a proscenium arch, confined within a 'picture-frame', were in a completely different relationship with their audience. No longer could players and spectators actively share in the unfolding of the dramatic action. Gone, too, the essential mobility and the flexibility of voice and gesture. Shakespeare's plays perished on a frozen stage.

The most important achievement of Shakespearian studies in this century has been to discover the main features of the stages for which he wrote. Actors and directors have been equipped with a new understanding of his stagecraft and they have applied it to their productions. In so doing, they have removed the barriers that were for so long placed between the plays and their audiences, and we can now enjoy his work on stage as his own spectators did.

Research goes on; and it is important that it should. Every addition to our knowledge is valuable in itself, and many can be put to practical use. Even so, as the twentieth-century theatre has proved, it is not necessary to know *everything* about Shakespeare's own theatres and stages to perform his plays in all their abundant vitality. We do not need exact replicas of the Globe or the Blackfriars or the Cross Keys innyard in order to see his plays acted as he intended them to be. For many years now, actors of Shakespeare in theatres of many different shapes and sizes, permanent and temporary, (and in many different countries) have been demonstrating how right Ben Jonson was when he said that 'He was not of an age, but for all time'.

Professional acting was well established in London before James Burbage built the first public playhouse in 1576. Plays were popular with people of all social classes, so the actors had to perform in various kinds of places and conditions. They played at Court, in the halls of aristocrats' houses, in the lawyers' 'colleges' (the Inns of Court), in bear- and bull-baiting arenas and in inn yards. Each of those locations contributed something to the design of theatres and stages when the permanent playhouses were built.

Two other factors greatly influenced the development of the theatre throughout Shakespeare's career. The first of these was the inveterate hostility of the Puritan city authorities, who regarded playgoing as a sinful waste of time and playhouses as centres of immorality and riot. They imposed irksome and damaging restrictions on the players, though they were unable to suppress them because acting enjoyed royal and aristocratic support and was immensely popular with most Londoners. To escape persecution, theatres were sited outside the Lord Mayor's jurisdiction: in the suburbs north of the city limits; in the 'Liberties' of the Clink and of Paris Garden on Bankside, south of the river; in Blackfriars, which was also a 'Liberty', though within the city.

Then there was the competition that the 'public' theatres (or 'common playhouses') encountered from the 'private' theatres. The terms did not have the meaning we might expect, and it is important to be clear about this. The private theatres, like the public theatres, were commercial enterprises. The main differences between them were these: the private theatres were roofed over, so the spectators were protected from bad weather; their seats were more comfortable; they were smaller than the public theatres and charged much more; they were artificially lit; they offered music and masques as well as plays.

To sum up: the term 'private theatre' was used to describe a roofed-in playhouse that provided a better-off and 'single-class' audience with more sophisticated entertainment and in more comfortable surroundings than was expected by the socially mixed audience at a public theatre.

Another difference between the two kinds of theatres was that until 1608/9 the private theatres were the exclusive preserve of the children's acting companies – see Chapters 8 and 9 for the story of how Shakespeare's company entered the private theatre world . (The origins of the acting companies – children's and adults' – are described in Chapter 12. Here, it is the physical features of the theatres themselves and of their stages with which we are concerned.)

It is important to remember, too, that throughout Shakespeare's career he and his fellow actors were accustomed to performing in a variety of places and on different stages. There was indeed 'a Shakespearian stage', having its own characteristic features which profoundly influenced the construction of the dramas he and the other playwrights wrote for that stage. Even so, the plays and the actors who performed them had to be readily adaptable to meet varied conditions.

James Burbage built the Theatre in 1576 because he foresaw that there was great profit to be had from a permanent playhouse. He was right, and other enterprising men followed his example. The immediate advantage that Burbage had in mind was that everyone who saw a performance would be a paying customer. At innyard plays the hat was passed round, and spectators who dodged the collectors enjoyed a free show. At the Theatre and the playhouses built later, everyone had to pay at the door to get in.

A permanent playhouse also gave the actors a much better chance of attracting regular audiences. People knew that the Chamberlain's Men were at the Globe and the Admiral's men were at the Rose, so the companies and their theatres became associated in the public's mind. A following – a company loyalty – could be established. Nevertheless, the actors still had to be prepared to move around. A season at their own playhouse might be followed by 'guest appearances' in other theatres. (Henslowe often booked companies in for short seasons at the Rose and at Newington Butts. See Chapters 7 and 8). They might end an afternoon performance at their own theatre by packing up and by taking themselves off to Court or to some aristocratic house to give a candle-lit performance in a great hall for a fee. The actors of Shakespeare's day were nothing if not versatile.

A brief account of the principal acting centres in use in Shakespeare's London – public theatres, private theatres, innyards, great halls – indicates how flourishing and varied his theatre world was.

Here, first, is a list of the public theatres, arranged in the chronological order in which they were built.

> 1576. *The Theatre*. In Shoreditch. Built by James Burbage. Used by Leicester's Men and then by the Chamberlain's Men. Pulled down in 1598. Its timbers used in building the Globe. (See Chapter 8.)

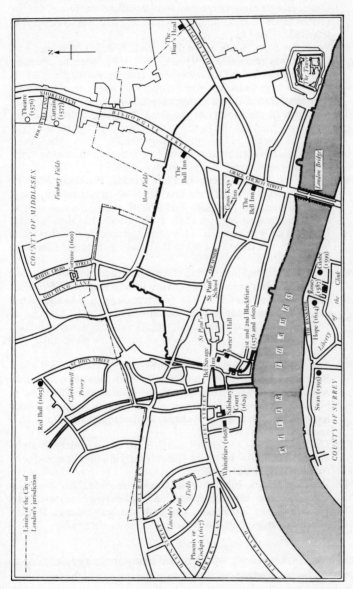

A plan of London (c. 1630)
showing the playhouses in use after 1574

1577. *The Curtain*. In Shoreditch, near to the Theatre. Built by Henry Laneman. Used by various companies, including the Chamberlain's Men. Often used as an 'overflow' playhouse, and for various kinds of entertainment as well as plays. Survived until at least 1627. (See Chapter 8.)

1580. *Newington Butts*. South of the river. Lord Strange's Men used it in 1592. It was controlled by Henslowe in 1594, when he arranged short seasons for the Chamberlain's and the Admiral's Men. It seems to have been litle used after 1595, and it was always an occasional (rather than a regular) playhouse.

1587. *The Rose*. In the Liberty of the Clink, Bankside. Built by Philip Henslowe. First used by Lord Strange's Men. Principal home of the Lord Admiral's Men until competition from the Lord Chamberlain's Men at the nearby Globe caused them to move to the Fortune – see Chapter 8. Pulled down in 1606.

1595. *The Swan*. In the Liberty of Paris Garden, Bankside. Built by Francis Langley. Used for other kinds of entertainment, too – prize-fighting, for example. The Chamberlain's Men used it in 1596; Pembroke's Men in 1597; Lady Elizabeth's Men in 1611. Johannes de Witt's sketch of the Swan (see later in this chapter) is our principal evidence of what the inside of a public playhouse looked like.

1598/9. *The Globe*. In the Liberty of the Clink, Bankside. Built by Cuthbert and Richard Burbage, partly from the Theatre's timbers. The home of the Chamberlain's-King's Men. Burnt down in 1613 and rebuilt the following year. The headquarters, until 1608/9, of Shakespeare's 'great fellowship'; and after that its 'summer house'. The finest and the most famous of all the public playhouses. (See Chapters 8 and 9.)

1600. *The Fortune*. In the northern suburbs, outside the city boundary. Built by Philip Henslowe and Edward Alleyn to be the home of the Admiral's Men when they quitted the Rose. The contract for its building survived in Henslowe's papers. Built of wood on a brick foundation, it was square in shape. Badly damaged by fire in 1621 and rebuilt in brick in 1623.

1605. *The Red Bull*. In Clerkenwell, north of the city boundary. Built by Aaron Holland. In use by the Queen's Men in 1609. Famous for its 'roaring' barnstorming plays.

1614. *The Hope*. In the Liberty of the Clink, Bankside. Built by Philip Henslowe and Edward Alleyn. A dual-purpose venture: part playhouse, part 'gamehouse' (for bull- and bear-baiting). It had a removable stage. Not much used as a theatre after 1620.

Throughout Shakespeare's working life many more people went to the public playhouses than to the private theatres, which were fewer in number and smaller in size. Individually, however, they were more profitable. They charged much more for admission and they took better-off patrons away from the public theatres.

The stiffest competition came from the Blackfriars Theatre, where those 'little eyases', the children of the Chapel Royal, were a thorn in the flesh of the adult companies. The story of 'the war of the theatres' and of the final triumph of the King's Men at Blackfriars has been told in Chapters 8 and 9. Here, we may note that the dispossessed Chapel Children re-formed and started up again in another private theatre (Whitefriars) and later moved to Porter's Hall. Neither of those ventures lasted long. After 1608, the success of the King's Men at Blackfriars demonstrated that the future of the private theatres lay with the adult companies. From then on, the Blackfriars was the most famous playhouse in London until, like all the rest, it was closed in 1642. In 1655 it was demolished.

The other two private theatres still in use when professional acting was put down resembled the Blackfriars in their main interior features. The Phoenix (1617) was built by Christopher Beeston, Shakespeare's former colleague, on the site of a cockpit, at Drury Lane – hence its alternative name, the Cockpit. Beeston, adept and none too scrupulous in company management, made it a great success. Before his death in 1638 it had become a rival to the Blackfriars. His son William took it over, but he did not have his father's touch. In 1640 he lost his 'governorship'.

The Salisbury Court Theatre (1629) was situated close to the Whitefriars, which it superseded, just to the south of Drury Lane. Built mainly of brick it was justly described as 'a fair new playhouse'. It was the home of both Queen Henrietta's Men and the Prince Henry's Men. After it was closed down, it attracted the especial fury of the triumphant Puritans and in 1649 its interior was wrecked by soldiers and a band of religious fanatics.

Briefly in 1660 William Beeston had hopes of reviving both those theatres, but the two royally-backed monopolists, Thomas Killigrew and William D'Avenant, soon put paid to that.

Before the introduction of purpose-built theatres, the innyards served in their stead; and the actors continued to make regular use of them long after they had permanent playhouses. A sizeable crowd could stand in the yard itself, while more spectators sat in the galleries that surrounded it. The stage might be a temporary platform set up on barrels or trestles. It might be a wheeled platform which the actors owned and which they moved from inn to inn. Such 'pageants', as they were called, had been used throughout the Middle Ages for the presentation of Miracle and Morality plays acted at religious festivals by amateur performers drawn from the various trade guilds. (They were still used for that purpose when Shakespeare was a boy.) Fitted with curtains and furnished with 'properties', and with a platform set up in front, they were very effective stages for skilled professionals.

The innkeepers encouraged the actors to visit their yards. Their presence greatly increased the sale of food and drink. The actors themselves liked their inn-theatres, especially in the winter. Inns regularly used for play acting included the Boar's Head, the Bull, the Red Bull, the Cross Keys, the Bell and the Bel Savage. It is known that the Chamberlain's Men were at the Cross Keys in the winter of 1594. After that year, however, the Privy Council decreed that plays must no longer be performed at inns. Two – the Boar's Head and the Red Bull – were then converted from inns to playhouses. The job involved no great problems. The inn yard and the surrounding galleries became the auditorium and the temporary platform became the permanent stage. The builders of the playhouses had the inn yard pattern much in mind. Food and drink, especially drink, continued to be sold in the converted inns, as they were in all the other playhouses.

Command performances at Court and one-night stands in great men's houses and lawyers' colleges familiarised the actors with yet another kind of theatre. Rectangular in shape, the auditorium held an audience seated on three sides of a stage erected in front of the wooden screen that crossed the width of the hall. The space behind the screen served as the actors' dressing room, and they came on stage from there, through doors or curtained openings in the screen. Depending on the lavishness of the provision made for them, they could cover the screen – which usually had an upper gallery – with hangings painted to symbolise the mood or the theme of the play. Generally, a hall performance included music and dancing – even fireworks and waterworks – as well as acting. Many a magnificent show was staged in Whitehall and in Gray's Inn, to name just two of the places where the players frequently performed for an educated and fashionable audience in the stately surroundings of a great hall.

Each kind of theatre the actors used contributed something to 'the Shakespearian stage'. No two, even of the same kind, had identical features, but they all had certain characteristics in common; and what they shared was always so much more important than any differences that the players were completely at home and confident wherever they happened to be performing.

The history of Shakespeare's own company illustrates that point very well. For example, when the King's Men decided to expand their activities by operating in a private playhouse, they saw no need to abandon their great public theatre. They continued to perform at the Globe in the summer after taking over the Blackfriars as their winter house. Shakespeare's last plays, written with the Blackfriars stage very much in mind, were also very popular at the Globe and an immense success at Court, too.

Again, no less than the plays of his middle and late periods, plays he had written before the Globe was built and before the Chamberlain's company was formed were acted to great acclaim at the Globe, at Court, at the Inns of Court and at the Cross Keys. To suit particular conditions, staging was adjusted and acting style modified, but the versatile players in his company were well used to that. Scripts were adapted; shortened here, lengthened there, to provide alternative versions suited to different theatres. That presented no problems to the company's dramatist. He supplied his actors with plays they could perform anywhere, an interchangeable repertory.

Since 1900, research into the features of Shakespeare's theatres and stages has been pursued vigorously. There was some earlier knowledge to build on. That great scholar Edmund Malone (see Chapter 1) had identified some of their characteristics. In the nineteenth century, too, there had been an occasional brave experiment in producing the plays more imaginatively so as to capture something of their essential speed and mobility of action. In 1844, for example, *The Taming of the Shrew* was presented at London's Haymarket Theatre in Shakespeare's original text and with only one change of scene – from an inn for the 'Induction' to a hall for the rest of the play. At about the same time, several attempts were made in German theatres to free his plays from the strait-jacket of picture-frame staging. The playing space was extended beyond the front of the proscenium arch to bring actors and spectators closer together, and only one set was used throughout the performance. A few pioneers had latched on to the essential fact that Shakespeare wrote for what they described as a 'space-stage'. In general, however, the nineteenth-century theatre was no nearer an understanding of how to stage Shakespeare than the eighteenth-century theatre had been.

The later breakthrough was initiated by the discovery of the famous 'de Witt sketch' of the Swan. Johannes de Witt, who lived in Utrecht, visited London in 1596. Like other foreign visitors at that time, he was greatly impressed by the playhouses. He made notes of what he saw. He also made a drawing of the interior of the Swan, which he described as 'the largest and the most magnificent' of all the theatres. (The Globe had not been built when de Witt visited London.) His original notes and sketch have been lost, but a friend copied them into his own notebook, which is still preserved in the university library in Utrecht.

The unique importance of de Witt's drawing was recognised at once. It is the only surviving contemporary illustration of the *interior* of a public playhouse of Shakespeare's day. Published in 1888, it gave fresh impetus to research and guided it in the right direction. All subsequent investigations have proceeded from that invaluable starting point. Its influence in the theatre was profound, for it proved to actors and directors that Shakespeare's plays, like those of his contemporaries, were not written to be performed behind a proscenium arch. De Witt's drawing made it plain that the Swan had a huge platform stage; that there was no scenery; that there was more than one acting level; and that the spectators watched the play from three sides of the stage.

De Witt was not a skilled draughtsman. Though the main features of the Swan's stage and auditorium are clearly depicted in his sketch, some details are obscure. Needing the clarify the doubtful points, researchers turned their attention to documents that had not previously been closely examined. New material was also discovered, and a great deal of information about the theatres and stages of Shakespeare's time was gradually unearthed. The observations made by other London visitors – notably Thomas Platter and Paul Hentzner – were studied. Philip Henslowe's diary and accounts provided a wealth of detail. The builders' contracts for the Fortune and the Hope specified materials and dimensions. Contemporary panoramic views of London showed where the playhouses were and what their outsides looked like. Wenceslaus Hollar's famous 'Long View', for example, depicted the circular shapes of the Globe and the Hope on Bankside.

The plays of the period were closely examined for clues as to their staging. Eyes opened by de Witt's drawing could see the implications of hitherto neglected stage directions: 'Enter on the walls King Richard, the Bishop of Carlisle . . .'; 'They place themselves in every corner of the stage . . .'; 'They march across the stage . . .'; 'Music of hautboys as under the stage . . .'; 'Above . . .'; 'Within . . .'. Such plain indications of multi-level action and flexible locations had previously escaped attention.

It came to be realised, too, that Shakespeare's texts contain within themselves specific instructions about stage positions and movements – as in this example:

Northumberland My lord, in the base court he doth attend
　　　　　　　To speak with you. May it please you to come down?
King Richard　Down down, I come, like glistering Phaeton.

What is more – and this had a tremendous influence – it became

apparent that effective productions of Shakespeare do not depend on
stage lighting and scenery. His words supply all that is necessary.
Most of the stage 'effects' once used when acting Shakespeare were
superfluous. Indeed, they were damaging because they came between
the audience and the language of the plays. Nowadays, that fact is
securely established as a basic principle of Shakespearian production;
but it took a very long time for actors and directors to realise that his
plays contain their own 'lighting' and 'scenery' – in the words he gave
his players to speak.

Used, as we are, to productions of his plays that encourage us to
listen, we find it strange that it was once thought necessary to
supplement Shakespeare's language with stage tricks. The essential
nature of his technique is now so well understood that only a few
examples need be given here:

> Look, love, what envious streaks
> Do lace the severing clouds in yonder east.
>
> *Romeo and Juliet*

>   Light thickens; and the crow
> Makes wing to the rooky wood;
> Good things of day begin to droop and drowse,
> Whiles night's black agents to their preys do rouse.
>
> *Macbeth*

> The sun doth gild our armour; up, my lords!
>
> *Henry V*

> *Oliver* Good morrow, fair ones; pray you, if you know
>   Where in the purlieus of this forest stands
>   A sheep-cote fenced about with olive-trees?
> *Celia* West of this place, down in the neighbour bottom:
>   The rank of osiers by the murmuring stream
>   Left on your right hand, brings you to the place.
>   But at this hour the house doth keep itself;
>   There's none within.
>
> *As You Like It*

Research continues, for by no means every detail has yet been settled.
The task is complicated by the fact that the theatres, whether public
or private, whether in permanent or occasional use, did not conform
in all particulars. For instance, it is questionable whether every public
playhouse had a trap door in the stage, leading to a 'space below'. Nor
is it certain that the 'discovery space' at the rear of the 'inner stage' was
used in quite the way that earlier twentieth-century scholars thought
it was. Indeed, some authorities today doubt whether the term 'inner

stage' is an appropriate description of the playing space towards the back of the big platform. Allowing for all that, however, the essential features are not in dispute. The description of the theatres and stages that now follows summarises the generally accepted facts.

The public playhouses could each hold a great many spectators: about 2500 – and that is a lot more than most modern theatres were (or are) built to accommodate. Circular or hexagonal in shape (like the bear-baiting arenas), they were constructed very largely of wood at first. Later, more use was made of brick. The auditorium was not roofed over, but much of the stage was covered by a wooden canopy (the 'heavens' or the 'shadow') which projected from the back wall and was supported at the front by two massive pillars. Ships' masts were sometimes used for that purpose. These wooden pillars, like the rest of the interior of the playhouses (and especially the underside of the heavens), were richly decorated. Some were cunningly painted to look like marble.

The auditorium was dominated by the huge platform stage (the 'scaffold') which provided a very large playing area – much bigger than in modern theatres. It was over forty feet wide; and as deep – or nearly – from back to front as it was wide. Very few modern stages are as wide as that and hardly any are as deep. It was raised high so that, as Thomas Platter reported, 'everybody could see everything very well'. Beneath that high stage there was ample room for the 'cellarage' – the 'space below' – reached by a trap door and made much use of. (In theatres that lacked that feature, the players improvised new movements, as they were well used to doing.)

The tiring-house (the actors' dressing room) occupied the back wall and had two doors, one at either end, through which entrances and exits were made. (Actors also came on stage from both sides, climbing steps that led up to the scaffold from the auditorium.) In the middle of the tiring-house wall there was a curtained recess which could be shut off or opened up at will. This was the discovery space.

Above the tiring-house and under the heavens there was a balcony or gallery, much used for action 'aloft' or 'above'. When the play did not require that additional acting level, the 'upper stage' could be used to house the musicians, though they generally occupied part of an auditorium gallery near the tiring-house. Sometimes, benches were put in to provide seats for well-heeled 'gallants' and 'lords' willing to pay extra.

Above the heavens there was a small room with a thatched roof. It was not part of the playing area, but it served important purposes. It housed the pulleys and ropes used to lower and raise gods and spirits or to assist warriors to storm battlements. There was a flagpole on its roof from which the theatre banner was flown to give notice that a performance would take place that day. At its door stood the trumpeter whose fanfares signalled that the play was about to begin.

The spectators came in by a common entrance at which they all paid the basic admission price. The 'groundlings' then made for the front and side standing room round the stage. Those who wanted seats paid the doormen or 'gallery-keepers' extra, and so obtained admission to the tiered galleries ranged round the walls. (Further details are given in Chapter 13.)

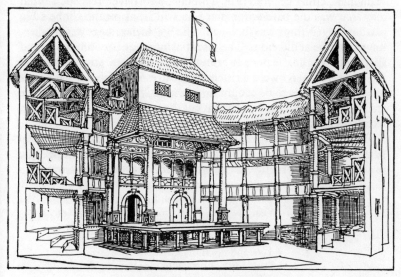

A Public Playhouse of Shakespeare's day
based on de Witt's drawing of the Swan

Those were the physical features of the public playhouses; but it must be emphasised that, throughout Shakespeare's career, neither inn yard nor great hall nor private theatre performances needed to differ fundamentally from those given in a public theatre. Wherever they were acting, the players were in a close – an intimate – spatial relationship with their audience. When measured against that all-important fact, the adjustments required to perform any of his plays successfully when moving them from the Globe to Court or from another great hall to the Cross Keys yard were minor matters which his company took in its stride.

On any of their stages – temporary scaffold, the Globe's huge platform, the Blackfriars' apron – the actors drew their audience in as joint partakers in the unfolding of the drama. What was happening on stage was never physically or emotionally distanced from the spectators. The innyard conditions, both of stage and auditorium, closely matched those of the public theatres. In a great hall, the screen was the front wall of the tiring-house. Its openings were the tiring-house doors and its gallery was the upper stage. The spectators, though all were seated, surrounded the stage on three sides, just as they did at the Globe. At the Blackfriars, it is true, there was artificial light (as in a hall) and probably a painted backcloth; but 'scene-setting' or any kind of stage illusion was always secondary. The 'hangings', either decorative or symbolic, were never 'realistic'. What mattered was the bare apron stage on which, as on the Globe's big platform, everything was focussed. The Blackfriars stage was smaller, but so was the auditorium. The essential intimacy between actors and spectators was unaffected. It cannot be too strongly stressed that all Shakespeare's plays were written for theatres in which the spectators felt for themselves to be caught up in the activity on stage. It was the arrival of the proscenium arch that cut the actors off, distancing them from spectators who watched passively.

Moreover, in Shakespeare's theatres, the audience did not expect a particular scene location to be graphically represented on stage. The place was readily accepted to be wherever the actors said it was:

> *King Richard* Barkloughly Castle call they this at hand?
> *Aumerle*   Yea, my lord. How brooks your grace the air.
>   After your late tossing on the breaking seas?
> *King Richard* Needs must I like it well. I weep for joy
>   To stand upon my kingdom once again:
>   Dear earth, I do salute thee with my hand.

Writing for this physically non-localised stage, the playwright was free from the constraints that so-called 'realism' imposes. He could 'set' and 'unset' his scene at will, its location and its atmosphere vividly embodied in the words he gave his actors to speak. So, to take just one example, in *Antony and Cleopatra* the action moves swiftly and unbroken from the luxuriousness of Egypt to the austerity of Rome, and back again. It is located now in Misenum, now in Syria, now in Athens. It passes effortlessly from Pompey's galley to a headland from which Antony sees his hopes destroyed in the sea fight of Actium; from the walls of Alexandria to Cleopatra's monument. The rise and fall of human destinies is played out on a stage spanned by 'the wide arch of the ranged empire'.

The scenic freedom, spaciousness and flexibility of the stage permitted the dramatist to fix and unfix time at will – clock time and calendar time alike. The hours and the seasons came and went as the drama required. Movement and grouping on the main platform presented simultaneous action in which past, present and future events could be juxtaposed: a crowded scene in which a monarch regally despatches state affairs while, on another part of the stage, a detached and lonely figure recalls past deeds, ominous in their implications for the future. The multi-level staging provided additional resources for 'flashback' and 'foretelling': conspiratorial whisperings 'above', while processional pomp confidently crosses the platform; lovers concealed 'within' overhear and comment on the plot hatched for their comic duping – the audience fully aware of all that is simultaneously unfolding. For, in Shakespeare's theatres, not only could 'everybody see everything very well', they could also hear everything very well – low-voiced comment no less than full-throated declamation; the whispered 'aside' no less than the ringing call to arms.

Neither having nor needing scenery or lighting effects, the playwrights and their actors spared no pains, nevertheless, to make their stages colourful and exciting. Elaborate properties were used as valuable adjuncts to the entertainment, so long as they were readily portable and could be got on and off stage without holding up the action. Henslowe's 1598 inventory of the properties he owned included the following items: the tomb of Dido, old Mahomet's head, Hell's mouth, a cauldron (Barabas perished in it in Marlowe's *The Jew of Malta*), lances, Cupid's bow, coffins, a chime of bells and a beacon. A man could be very convincingly beheaded in full view of the audience. A favourite bear from the Bankside Bear Garden came on stage in *The Winter's tale* to chase Antigonus to his death. Gunpowder smoke could arise through the trap. Smoky torches symbolised night scenes played in broad daylight. Processions marched, armies fought, battlements were scaled. The actors were skilled in music and dancing, jigging and juggling, rapier and broadsword duels and acrobatic feats.

They wore beautiful and expensive costumes – contemporary, not historical (Cleopatra commands Charmian to 'cut her lace'). An acting company spent lavishly to deck its monarchs and nobles and fashionable young men and women. Many a player wore a king's gorgeous robes on his shoulders and a rich crown on his head.

But nothing was allowed to interrupt the unfolding of the drama. Mobility and continuity were the paramount considerations in 'the two hours' traffic' of that stage, now thronged, now occupied by a single, soliloquising figure. (In so intimate a theatre, the soliloquy was an entirely 'natural' device). When the tempo could be so effortlessly quickened or slowed, the tension so swiftly tightened or slackened, the attention of the audience was rivetted to the action. Close study of Shakespeare's scripts reveals how deliberately he exploited the resources of a stage which demolished the barriers between actors and audience.

It was always the words that mattered most. Shakespeare wrote for a theatre in which language was king. Every means the stage afforded and all the skills at the actors' command were employed to get the words across. That lesson has been learnt in the twentieth-century theatre. Today's actors can perform his plays anywhere – as his own actors did – because they know that their spectators will listen attentively – as his own spectators did. Now, as then, it is recognised that no stage effects, and no actor's 'pitiful ambition', must be allowed to come between the audience and the language that Shakespeare wrote.

Asked to explain the principles that guide them when acting his plays, modern actors reply: 'Study the script; listen; trust the playwright; he tells you how to do it, for it's all there in the words'.

12

The Actors
and their Companies

ACTING HAS always been a hazardous profession, and it certainly was when William Shakespeare arrived in London to try his luck (see Chapter 5). It is doubtful, however, whether it was any more precarious an occupation then than it is now. By the time he made his start the commercial theatre was sufficiently well established to offer a talented and hard-working recruit a career in which, while many failed, many made a living – and some did much better than that. Then, during the twenty-odd years of his working life, the acting companies – his own, especially – developed into highly efficient organisations in which a 'hired man' could get regular and not ill-paid work and in which a 'sharer' could make a lot of money (see Chapter 7).

The legend that Shakespeare and his fellow actors were officially classed with 'rogues and vagabonds' dies hard. Despite conclusive evidence to the contrary, they are still sometimes described as having been social outcasts, now tolerated, now spurned, as they pleased or displeased their betters. It is true that they were regarded – and regarded themselves – as being socially inferior to their noble patrons; but so were all other commoners. There was no stigma in that. It is true, too, that their business was to please; but that was – and is – the business of all public entertainers. It was their audiences that the actors had to please; though, naturally, they wanted to retain the favour of whichever grandee had agreed to be their patron and had allowed them to be known as his 'servants'.

The truth is that the leaders of Shakespeare's profession occupied their own recognised and respectable place in the society of their day. They were esteemed for being 'excellent in their quality [their calling]', and there was nothing to prevent them from becoming prominent members of their local community while pursuing their occupation. An actor could well be a respected citizen. He could become a churchwarden, as Henry Condell did; or a sidesman in his parish church, as John Heminge did. When he prospered, his money was as good as anybody else's. He was not ostracised if he bought land

and became a gentleman, as William Shakespeare did. If he grew very wealthy he might turn to good works and munificent benefactions without incurring social disapproval for having been an actor. Edward Alleyn founded the 'College of God's Gift' at Dulwich; and though he made much of his money in other enterprises, he had been a player for many a year.

The false belief that acting was a despised occupation in Shakespeare's day arises from uncritical reading of the contemporary attacks made on it. People with ideological and personal reasons to sneer at and abuse the actors lost no opportunity of denouncing them. It is often wrongly assumed that their hostility represented the general view. Every Puritan preacher and pamphleteer had a go at the players. Disappointed and embittered playwrights, like Robert Greene, vilified them (see Chapter 6). Unscrupulous impresarios – Philip Henslowe, for example – attempted to justify their own conduct by maligning the actors they exploited (when, that is, they were not flattering them for their own ends). Glib satirists delighted to exercise their wit by contrasting the players' stage impersonations of royal and noble characters with their humbler status in real life. They were an easy target for self-appointed and self-opinionated moralists of all sorts.

The actors had more friends than enemies, however; and their friends included serious and eloquent writers ready to express their approval of acting and able to justify their support with weighty arguments. Intellectually, the theatre's champions were more than a match for its detractors.

The study of classical plays was given an important place in the curriculum of the grammar schools (see Chapter 4). Belief in the value of drama was embedded in the culture of the age, and educated opinion was on the actors' side. Their scholarly allies maintained that the theatre could, and often did, have a most beneficial influence. Audiences were uplifted when the players presented them with enactments of noble deeds and memorable instances of historical and moral truths. Some plays fell far short of the ideal, of course. Many were 'lewd'; but there were also many 'virtuous' plays to gain the approval of people whose opinions counted. A quotation from Sir Philip Sidney's *An Apology for Poetry* (1595) represents their views. Writing about *Gorboduc* (an early example of English tragedy, modelled on the Latin dramatist Seneca), he was severe on its artistic flaws; but he also praised it as being 'full of notable morality which it doth most delightfully teach'.

The actors themselves generally steered clear of theoretical discussions, but they – their leaders, at least – were well aware of the influential voices raised to justify the drama on moral grounds.

Scurrilously attacked by their enemies, they welcomed the knowledge that cultured people, who prized plays for their 'delightful teaching', did not regard acting as a dishonourable occupation. It is interesting to note that on the rare occasions when the playwrights offered any justification of their work (beyond the fact that it gave pleasure) they, too, argued that it served moral and social purposes. So, for example, John Webster declared that: 'By his action he [the actor] fortifies moral precepts with example; for what we see him personate, we think truly done before us'. Shakespeare (characteristically) made no direct pronouncement about it, but his Prince of Denmark had plenty to say. Hamlet describes the actors as being 'the abstracts and brief chronicles of the time'. He defines 'the purpose of playing', which is, he says, 'to hold, as 'twere, the mirror up to nature; to show virtue her own feature, scorn her own image, and the very age and body of the time his form and pressure [character]'.

Hamlet and Webster used the same argument: 'Drama is an imitation and an enactment of life. The actors present their audience with animated examples of virtue and vice, of good sense and of folly, and show them what is to be emulated and what is to be shunned'.

All the facts prove that the actors of Shakespeare's day got their living in a well-organised theatre industry and in circumstances quite different from those in which their predecessors, the strolling players, had worked. They had travelled from town to town, getting an audience where they could and competing for their scanty rewards with other itinerant entertainers – jugglers, tumblers, musicians, sword-players, prize-fighters, 'bear-wards' and 'ape-bearers'. Disliked and feared by parish authorities and magistrates as 'masterless men', threatened with the stocks and the whipping-post, they knew what it was like to be classed as 'rogues and vagabonds'. The situation of Shakespeare and his fellows must not be confused with theirs.

Because London was so much bigger than any other place, that was where the money was; and that was why the players were intent on establishing themselves permanently in the capital. For a long time, two factors made it difficult for them to do that. First, there was the hostility of the Puritan city authorities who opposed them, partly on religious grounds and partly because they charged the players with causing disorder. If they could have had their way, there would never have been any theatres in London or any regular acting venues such as the innyards. Fortunately, the players generally enjoyed the support of the Court and the aristocracy, and that enabled them to evade the restrictions imposed by the corporation.

The other handicap was the players' lack of organisation. Looselyassociated groups of actors coming together for tours and breaking up when the tours ended could not cope with the problems that had to be solved. There was a world of difference between getting a strolling band together and setting up and running a regular company with a permanent base in London. That was a large and ambitious enterprise, requiring an organised administration to formulate coherent policy and to provide continuity. A theatre or, at least, regular and dependable acting venues had to be obtained. Actors must be recruited and trained, plays and costumes bought, the repertory planned. None of this was possible without a source of working capital and a 'command structure' to plan and direct operations.

It was in 1572 (more than ten years before Shakespeare arrived in London) that the situation changed. In that year, Queen Elizabeth and her ministers put through Parliament the 'Act for the Punishment as Vagabonds'. It was designed to tackle the growing problem created by the roving bands of 'jugglers, pedlars, tinkers, fencers, common players, bearwards' who so often 'disturbed the peace of Her Majesty's subjects'. Its main provision was that all entertainers must obtain the patronage of 'a Baron of this Realm . . . or any other honourable Personage of greater Degree'. Those who did not and continued to perform were to be 'taken, adjudged and deemed Rogues, Vagabonds and Sturdy Beggars' and punished accordingly. (The Act of 1572 recognised a licence from two Justices of the Peace as an acceptable alternative to a nobleman's patronage, but that provision was struck out later.)

This gave the actors their chance to organise themselves into regular and permanent companies; and that they proceeded at once to do. With the patronage of a nobleman, they were safe. Their company bore his name. They wore his livery on suitable occasions. They were recognised as his 'servants'; and they were most certainly *not* 'rogues and vagabonds' to be 'taken up' and 'whipped from tithing to tithing'. They could perform anywhere in the country on tour. Best of all, they could acquire a permanent base in London, where the big and regular audiences were. As we have seen in Chapter 11, it was always better to place a theatre outside the Lord Mayor's jurisdiction; but for many a year after 1572 the actors also played at the popular inns within the city. The corporation could be a nuisance but it could not suppress the actors. After 1572 'My Lord So-and-So's Men' were pursuing their officially recognised and lawful calling.

One enterprising man, James Burbage, was quick off the mark. A letter he wrote to the Earl of Leicester in 1572 shows how eager he was to obtain the security then made possible. He requested the Earl to announce that he and his actors were Leicester's 'household servants'.

He made it clear that they were not asking for 'any further stipend or benefit at your Lordship's hands' beyond their liveries and 'your Honour's licence'.

There were other benefits too. A nobleman in royal favour could arrange Court performances for his 'servants'. Not only were they profitable, they also brought great kudos. Being summoned to entertain the monarch was something to shout about; and the crowds flocked to see players who had 'sundry times performed before Her Majesty'.

How well Leicester's patronage served Burbage and his company was amply demonstrated in 1574, when the Queen added her protection to his. Elizabeth commanded 'all justices, mayors, sheriffs, bailiffs, head constables, under constables, and all other our officers and ministers' to take note that James Burbage and his fellows, servants to the Earl of Leicester, were authorised 'to use, exercise and occupy the art and faculty of playing'. The Queen reminded the legal and civic authorities that the Earl's servants provided recreation not only for 'our loving subjects' but also 'for our solace and pleasure when we shall think good to see them'. She emphasised that their right to exercise their art applied to performances given 'within our City of London and Liberties of the same' and in 'any our cities, towns, boroughs . . . throughout our Realm of England'.

So much for the notion that the actors were classed as rogues and vagabonds! They had been freed from that slur many years before Shakespeare started his career.

The Earl of Leicester was not the only nobleman to give his name and his protection to an organised company of full-time professional actors. Lord Strange, eldest son of the Earl of Derby, had his company. (It was knows as Derby's Men after Strange succeeded to his father's title.) Lord Sussex was a company patron too. The company that James Burbage later created (the company that Shakespeare joined – see Chapter 7) was called the Lord Chamberlain's Men because its patron, Lord Hunsdon, was the Lord Chamberlain. Similarly, the company which Henslowe formed, and with which Edward Alleyn acted, was known as the Lord Admiral's Men because its patron, the Earl of Nottingham, held the office of Lord High Admiral of England.

In an age that valued the arts, when the monarch, her nobility and her courtiers delighted in drama, poetry, music and dancing, the patron of a leading theatre company took pleasure and pride in its achievements. It was no small addition to his fame to be so grandly connected with its writers and players; and if his company especially pleased at Court, he could generally count on receiving some gracious token of royal favour. At the very least, he basked in the reflected glow of his servants' triumph.

For these benefits, the patron was little out of pocket. He did not pay the actors' wages, nor was he responsible for their expenses. If the company that bore his name 'broke', either on tour or at home in London, he was neither responsible for its debts nor called upon to put it back in business. He paid for their livery because, on suitable occasions, his actors wore the 'uniform' worn by all his other retainers. When they put on plays for him at his town mansion or his country seat he paid them the appropriate fee. That, and the use of his name, was the full extent of his commitments. All in all, both sides – patron and actors – got a bargain that suited each.

In 1597, the actors' already strong position was further improved. In that year, the Lord Chamberlain and the Master of the Revels (both were Court officials) were given additional powers to regulate the London theatre. The City authorities' grip was loosened, and the actors were better able to make their views known to the royal officials.

Not that they had things all their own way – far from it. They could, and did, get into serious trouble with the royal authorities from time to time (see Chapters 6 and 8). Nor did the Privy Council and the Queen's officers turn down all the Lord Mayor's requests to have the players curbed. The royal government had little patience with religious bigots who wanted to make life hard for the actors; but when the City corporation drew attention to disorder in the theatres or the nearby streets and alehouses, its complaints were heard and understood. Nevertheless, throughout Shakespeare's working life the leading companies were in good shape and generally prospering under royal favour. Plague was their worst enemy; and there was nothing to be done about that. The theatres then had to close, and a handful of players from each company took to the roads, as their predecessors had done. Only now, they were licensed to do so; and the authorities did not hamper them while they tried to get their living.

The theatres did not belong to the acting companies. They were built by speculators, such as James Burbage (the Theatre), Philip Henslowe (the Rose and the Fortune) and Henry Laneman (the Curtain), who then let them to the actors. The theatre owner was responsible for the upkeep of the building (repairs and decoration) and also for paying a large fee to the Master of the Revels for licensing the theatre. As a rule, the owner also had to pay ground rent for the site on which the building stood. (James Burbage's difficulties with his ground landlord, Giles Allen, were described in Chapter 8.) In return for all this, the theatre owner received from the actors a share of the takings at each performance. Each side drove as hard a bargain as it could. Generally, the owner got a half-share of the daily gallery takings. That was worth a lot when a company was attracting big audiences. The theatre owner had a good deal of capital at risk, but his return on it was handsome.

Legally and financially, the acting companies were separate undertakings owned by their 'sharers', as they were called. They were not all organised in exactly the same way, but they had basic features in common. To comply with the law, as we have seen, each company had to have a noble patron. As we have seen, too, he took no part in the company's finances or management. An acting company was wholly dependent on its own resources; and it was an expensive business to be in. Plays must be bought. The repertory system demanded a constant supply of new ones, and each had to be licensed by the Master of the Revels, who charged a large fee for doing so. The theatre owner had to be paid. Costumes cost a lot, and that was an expenditure that could not be skimped. Rehearsals took up time. No money was coming in while they went on. There were musicians, bookkeepers (in charge of the play stock), costume-buyers, tire (wardrobe) attendants and 'gatherers' (door-keepers) on the pay roll. Above all, of course, actors had to be recruited, trained and paid.

Skilful management was no less important to success than having popular plays and good actors. It was no use playing to big audiences if the income they brought was not carefully accounted for and prudently handled. Current and future liabilities had to be the first charge on the daily takings. The profits were what was left over.

A company needed capital to get started. That was supplied by a small group of people who each put up money to buy a share. They were then responsible for the continuing management of the company. They were also entitled to its profits. The 'sharers' were usually actors, though there were a few exceptions. Cuthbert Burbage was a sharer in the Chamberlain's-King's company and he was not an actor. Nor was Philip Henslowe, and he had the biggest share in the Admiral's Men. The aim was to raise the required capital from as few sharers as possible. The more sharers there were, the harder it was to create a tightly-knit and coherently-directed organisation. Also, of course, there were more people to share the profits. The numbers varied from company to company and from time to time. In 1596 the Chamberlain's company had eight sharers. In 1603, when it became the King's Men, it had twelve. The Admiral's had ten sharers in 1597 (but Henslowe held the controlling interest).

When a sharer put his money in he bound himself to stay with the company for a minimum number of years (three, as a rule); and he agreed to be fined if he neglected his duties. Later, if he wanted to leave the company, he could sell his share; but he needed the permission of his fellows, and they could veto a prospective buyer of whom they disapproved.

However, if the sharers took the financial risk and accepted heavy responsibilities, they also stood to do very well. They were the joint owners of a valuable enterprise and their share of the profits made them prosperous. Theatre business in Shakespeare's day was very big business indeed.

Although each acting company was owned by its sharers, most were controlled by a dominant manager. For example, the Admiral's company was ruled by Henslowe, who was in an unchallengeable position because he had the biggest holding in the company and he was also the sole owner of the theatre it used – the Rose. (Later, he and Alleyn jointly held the biggest share in the Admiral's Men and jointly owned the Fortune.) He was, in effect, the owner-manager of the company, and his commanding financial advantage enabled him to control policy at all levels and in all fields and to exploit his playwrights and his actors.

The company to which Shakespeare belonged operated on different lines, having a collective rather than a despotic management. To a large extent, that was a reflection of the personalities of the leading men in the Chamberlain's-King's company. William Shakespeare, Richard Burbage, John Heminge and Henry Condell got on well together. They were friends as well as business partners and they worked closely and amicably. Even so, their cooperative relationship was fostered by a company structure that encouraged power sharing. Uniquely – no other company of Shakespeare's time was so structured – the leading actor-sharers in the Chamberlain's-King's Men were *also* the joint owners of the theatres in which they performed – the Globe and the Blackfriars. To use the term then current, they were 'housekeepers' or 'householders' of those two theatres. When the Globe was built in 1598/9 James Burbage's two sons, Cuthbert and Richard, put up half the money. Shakespeare, Heminge, Condell and two other actor-sharers in the Chamberlain's Men put up the other half between them. (Seven housekeepers in all.) When the King's Men took over the Blackfriars in 1608 similar arrangements were made; but this time the two Burbages, Shakespeare and the others became *equal* housekeepers of the theatre as well as being sharers in the acting company. The men in charge of the Chamberlain's-King's Men were truly partners. They took all the decisions (artistic as well as financial) collectively; and they shared the risks and the profits fairly.

Not only was it a happier system to work in, it proved more efficient, too. Shakespeare's company became pre-eminent primarily because it had the best plays and the best actors; but its outstanding success for so many years was also the product of the harmony that prevailed in its remarkable management team.

Writing in 1613, Johannes Rhenanus, a German visitor to London, commented on the thoroughness of the actors' training, and he was especially struck by their assiduous practice:

> As for the actors, as I noticed in England, they are given instruction daily as if at school; even the leading actors expect to take instruction from the playwrights.

We should not suppose that a star actor – Burbage or Alleyn, for example – would have allowed a novice playwright to interfere much at a rehearsal. We do know, however, that Ben Jonson was not slow to tell the actors how he wanted his lines spoken. (They joked about his fussiness.) We also know that Shakespeare attended rehearsals of other plays as well as of his own. He acted in most of them himself; and when he was not actually on stage he was in the theatre to give advice.

It is clear beyond doubt that the actors were highly-skilled professionals, engaged in a demanding and competitive occupation in which only the good ones survived and only the very best reached the top. Shakespeare's plays themselves afford still-living proof that they were written for performers who had mastered the technicalities of their art. (Many an amateur dramatic society has discovered the truth of that!)

The players had to be good to meet the demands the system made on them. In the season they performed six days a week, and it was rare for the same play to be put on twice in any one week. In one hectic season in 1594, for example, the Admiral's Men performed thirty-eight different plays, twenty-one of which were new. So, while they were staging seventeen plays they had acted before, they were also learning and rehearsing twenty-one others, bringing them into performance at the rate of one a fortnight. It was gruelling work, done at what modern actors – hard as they have to work – would consider a killing pace. Today, the Royal Shakespeare Company at Stratford is rightly considered to be fully stretched by a long season in which it typically performs five or six plays at the main theatre, another four or so at the Swan and three or four at the Other Place – thirteen or fourteen plays in all.

As a rule, an acting company of Shakespeare's time was made up of eight or so leading actor-sharers, about as many experienced and regularly employed hired men, and four or five boy actors (for the female roles). That – with doubling parts – sufficed for the cast of most plays. If more actors were needed, extra hired men could be engaged. (They tried to avoid that. It added to the expenses of a production, so they usually stuck to plays with cast-lists that matched their acting numbers.) Shakespeare, of course, wrote his plays to fit not only the Chamberlain's-King's Men's numbers but with parts to suit the aptitudes of the individual actors.

The actor-sharers had the company profits as their reward, but it seems that in some cases they were also paid the proper wage for acting. Experienced and reliable hired men got a weekly wage rather bigger than the going rate for a skilled workman in any other trade – a bricklayer or a carpenter, for example. Those with less experience were, of course, paid less. The best wage a hired man could get did not give him more than a decent living, but he had regular work – except when the plague (or some other 'inhibition', occasioned by riot, perhaps, or censored plays) closed the theatres. Then, if he was lucky, he went on tour – at half his London wage; and that only if tour takings were good. Such times were hard for everyone in the theatre. Housekeepers, sharers, hired men and all were up against it; but the housekeepers and sharers had their previous profits to tide them over.

With all its risks, however, the life had glamour. The lowliest hired man could dream of one day playing a Burbage or Alleyn role to the thunderous plaudits of a packed house. He could hope to become a sharer in due course, if his work was considered good enough – *and* if he could, somehow, put together the money to buy his fellowship. So great was the attraction of that distant and conjectural possibility that a few hired men were willing to put money into a bond when joining a company, as a guarantee of their intention to serve faithfully and long.

The boy actors were essential personnel in every company. They played all the female roles. (No woman was allowed to act on the professional stage in England – it was different on mainland Europe – until 1662, when D'Avenant received a royal patent consenting that 'all women's parts be acted by women'.) That accounts for the fact that the dramatic effects of trans-sexual disguise were so frequently exploited. In the comedies, some of Shakespeare's young women spend much of their time on stage pretending to be young men – which, of course, they were!

How skilful the boy actors had to be needs no emphasis. We have only to think of, say, Beatrice or Lady Macbeth – or *Cleopatra* ! So skilful were they, and so confident in their roles, that Shakespeare dared allow his Queen of Egypt to voice her abhorrence at the prospect of having 'Some squeaking Cleopatra *boy* my greatness' if she permitted Octavius Caesar to take her captive to Rome.

Although they were key performers, the boy actors were paid much less than the top hired men. They had career prospects to compensate them for low wages. Playing their female roles until their voices broke (became 'cracked within the ring', as Hamlet punningly describes it) they might then be kept on to play men's parts. By that time they were very experienced and thoroughly well-trained actors. Occasionally, an outstanding boy who was ready for adult male roles might be recruited from the children's companies (of the Chapel Royal or St Paul's). That was exceptional, however. The adult companies preferred to retain the boys they had taught. They were generally made of sterner stuff than young actors who had experience only of the more sheltered life of the private theatres.

The Chamberlain's-King's Men had particular reason for wanting to keep its own experienced boy actors, and its hired men, too. It had evolved its own distinctive acting style and, having trained them in it, it was reluctant to lose its players. Nor were many of them at all happy to move. Conscious of working for the premier company, they had no wish to join another which did not perform in the style they had been taught to value; and in which they were consequently unlikely to get the job satisfaction they were used to.

In comedy, Shakespeare's company had moved far away from the broad clowning that Tarlton had made so popular. Kempe's replacement by Robert Armin (see Chapter 9) had strengthened the hands of the other actor-sharers whose policy it was to establish a subtler comic style. In tragedy, they had deliberately distanced themselves from the melodramatic delivery, movement and gesture that characterised the earlier tragedians. Still in vogue in other companies – and well-enough suited to a popular 'roaring play' – it was crudely inappropriate to performance of the scripts that Shakespeare was writing. Even the great Alleyn's 'high-astounding' style was beginning to look distinctly old-fashioned in comparison with the acting method practised by Richard Burbage and his colleagues at the Globe and the Blackfriars.

In this, as in their collective management, the Chamberlain's King's Men were ahead of their rivals. They pioneered a more restrained, a more life-like, acting style: a 'naturalism' which was recognised as the hallmark of the company's excellence and in which its members took conscious professional pride. Hamlet's instruction to the First Player make a clear statement about what Shakespeare expected of his actors – *and*, of course, about how he himself, one of the company's most regular and most experienced players, approached his own performances on stage.

> Speak the speech, I pray you, as I pronounced it to you, trippingly on the tongue; but if you mouth it, as many of your players do, I had as lief the town-crier spoke my lines. Nor do not saw the air too much with your hand, thus; but use all gently; for in the very torrent, tempest, and, as I may say, the whirlwind of passion, you must acquire and beget a temperance that may give it smoothness. Oh, it offends me to the soul to hear a robustious periwig-pated fellow tear a passion to tatters, to very rags, to split the ears of the groundlings, who, for the most part, are capable of nothing but inexplicable dumb-shows and noise; I would have such a fellow whipped . . . pray you, avoid it. . . . Be not too tame neither, but let your own discretion be your tutor . . . with this special observance *that you o'erstep not the modesty of nature* .

Hamlet then tells the First Player to keep his comic actors under control and to make sure that they 'speak no more than is set down for them'.

The insistence that their actors (comic and tragic alike) must not 'o'erstep the modesty of nature' was the principle on which Shakespeare and his colleagues based the company's acting style. Just how much that principle mattered to them was demonstrated when they refused to allow that excellent but obstinate actor Kempe to defy company policy. (See Chapter 9.)

13

The Audiences

IT IS calculated that between fifteen and twenty per cent of Londoners regularly went to the theatre in Shakespeare's time. Some went frequently – once, twice, even oftener, each week. For others it had to be an eagerly-awaited holiday treat.

The public playhouses could each hold about two thousand five hundred people, and the private theatres about one thousand. A new play generally drew a good house; and the theatres always did a roaring trade at holiday times, Whitsuntide and Boxing Day being especially busy. Because they were sure of big audiences on festival days, the actors rarely put on a new play then. Nor did they often do so on a Monday, which was a very popular day in need of no extra boost. The theatres were closed on Sundays, so a lot of people were keen to see a play on a Monday, after their enforced abstinence. They also liked to stay away from work. It was much pleasanter to spend Monday afternoon at the playhouse and then start the week's labours on Tuesday. One of the complaints most often made about the actors by the City authorities was that they encouraged working people to be idle.

On *average* it seems that a public playhouse staging a well-liked play could expect an audience of about a thousand at each performance. (So, at least, Henslowe's *Accounts* suggest.) It is known, for example, that in 1595 the three playhouses then open (the Theatre, the Curtain and the Rose) had a combined weekly audience of about fifteen thousand. That gives each, on average, a daily audience of about eight hundred. The Theatre and the Rose would have had more than that, and the Curtain fewer. (It was an 'easer' for the Theatre – see Chapter 8.) By the end of Shakespeare's career, when the population of London had increased and there were more theatres, the average total audience had risen to twenty-five thousand each week.

It is known that a new play by Shakespeare guaranteed a full house. From the first, he knew how to please. When *Henry VI Part 1* opened at the Rose in March 1592 (the Chamberlain's Men had not then been formed, remember) Henslowe recorded gallery takings that staggered even that hardened operator. Because of the repertory system, the play did not come on again immediately, but it was staged a further thirteen times in the next three months. On five of those occasions its takings equalled those expected of a brand-new play; and its pulling power was such that in its first 'run' (March-June 1592) twenty thousand people paid to see it. His last sole work, *The Tempest*, filled the Blackfriars at its first performance and repeated that success at the Globe when it was put on there in the summer. As we have seen, it was also a successful Court play.

Public playhouse charges started at a level that working people could afford: 'whoever cares to stand below only pays one English penny' (Thomas Platter). A penny was about one-twelfth of a skilled London workman's daily wage, so it was not to be lightly spent. Since wives often accompanied their husbands to the play, their joint outlay was considerable. That is why so many had to save up between visits and go to the theatre as a holiday celebration.

The fact that they were willing to spend their money like that proves, of course, what keen playgoers they were. It should also prevent us from thinking of the groundlings as a rabble. Those who paid one penny 'to stand below' were not the mindless rowdies portrayed by writers whose fanciful descriptions of Shakespeare's audiences outrun their knowledge of the facts. An account of theatre goers' behaviour comes later in this chapter, but it is important to make clear now that most of the groundlings went to the theatre to see the play, not to fight with each other or to throw nuts at the actors. To get a good place in the standing room round the stage – often, to get a place at all – they had to arrive at the theatre well before the performance began and queue until the door was opened. They – by many the most of them at any rate – spent their leisure time and hard-earned money on theatre outings because they enjoyed watching a play, not because they wanted the opportunity of wrecking it.

Though the basic charge for playhouse admission was a far from trifling expense for a working man, it was not great compared with other pleasures. (A single pipeful of tobacco cost three times the minimum price for seeing a play.) The Bear Garden was the chief alternative source of public entertainment to which a man and his wife could go together and that cost as much as the theatre. It was much more expensive to drink in a tavern; and, in any case, women rarely did that.

Gambling dens and brothels were plentiful on Bankside, but the entertainment they provided was shunned by respectable working people. Law students and gallants and half-pay captains might racket about in the stews of Southwark when they were not in the dicing houses. Either of those pleasures cost them a great deal more than a visit to the playhouse – even though they paid more for their theatre place than did the steady artisans and shopkeepers who would have nothing to do with raffish entertainments. For them, the playhouse provided the family outing, and it was well worth the twopence it cost a couple to stand. If they felt very well-off, they might even double that expenditure.

People who wanted a seat in the theatre paid an extra penny for admission to the twopenny gallery. For yet another penny they could sit on a more confortable cushioned seat. Socially speaking, the very best seats were in the exclusive enclosures known as 'lords' rooms'. According to their position, they cost sixpence or one shilling (twelve pence). Only wealthy and noble patrons paid twelve pence to preserve their superiority; and they did not have as good a view of the stage as those in the cheaper seats. (The groundlings, it should be remembered, had an excellent view; but they had the discomfort of standing and because the scaffold was well raised up, they had to crane their necks.)

Thus ranging from one penny up to three pence for the majority of the spectators, with 'removed' sixpenny and twelvepenny places for the very well-to-do and the nobility, the public playhouse prices matched the purses of their patrons from every social level. Even the wealthiest and the most aristocratic could be suitably accommodated without rubbing shoulders with their inferiors. Only the really poor were excluded. (If there had been places to be had for a farthing – one-quarter of one penny – they could not, even then, have afforded to see a play.)

To judge from the available records, it seems that a public playhouse had standing room for about eight hundred people. Seats were available for seventeen hundred spectators in the twopenny and threepenny galleries. Quite a lot of skilled artisans were willing to pay twopence (fourpence, of course, for a man and wife); and quite a lot of prosperous shopkeepers and their wives, as well as lawyers, students and superior clerks, made for the threepenny galleries. Comparatively few took their seats in the lords' rooms; but enough to make a very handsome contribution to the total takings.

The private theatres charged much more; and their seating plan reversed the order of things that prevailed in the public playhouses, where the cheapest places were nearest the stage. (But, then, in a public theatre nobody was far away from the mighty scaffold.) Sixpence was the basic admission price at a private theatre. That bought a seat in one of the galleries. A place on a bench in the pit cost twelve pence (one shilling) or eighteen pence (one shilling and sixpence). A seat on the edge of the stage (much favoured by fashionable young men who wanted to show off their finery) cost two shillings. A box at the side of the stage cost two shillings and sixpence (half-a-crown).

Whereas prices were the same at all the public theatres (and changed little over the years) the private theatres varied theirs. A private theatre often had its own line in 'special seats'. At the Blackfriars there were 'twelvepenny rooms'. Patrons who paid that price there in the winter would pay the same for one of the lords' rooms at the Globe in the summer. In order to follow their favourite actors in their favourite plays, the King's Men's richer patrons were very willing to transfer their custom from the private to the public theatre and back again, according to the season.

On the other hand, the less well-off patrons of the public playhouses could not afford private theatre prices. A minimum admission charge at the Blackfriars Theatre six times that at the Globe kept the groundlings out. Few of the Globe's twopenny patrons were ready, except very occasionally, to pay sixpence for the comparatively remote gallery to which they were banished at Blackfriars. They were used to good seats at the Globe for a third of the price. The threepenny patrons could – and did – sometimes go to the Blackfriars Theatre, but many were reluctant to stump up four and five times the price of their Globe seats for the privilege of sitting with the 'nobs' in the Blackfriars pit.

The audiences at the two theatres liked the same plays, but only the well-to-do regularly patronised the private house. That was why the King's Men's decision to run the Blackfriars *and* the Globe was crucial. The company acquired a 'posh' audience, but it kept its mixed one at the Globe. Shakespeare continued to write for the audience he had always known how to please: an audience that included all social classes, from courtiers to working people.

Any reliable account of the behaviour of the audiences has to recognise that many contemporary descriptions were biased by the prejudices and axe-grinding of those who wrote them. Puritan bigots poured out a stream of denunciations of 'the Chapel of Satan', filled with 'young ruffians' and 'harlots utterly past all shame'. The well-established facts about the composition of the audiences simply do not tally with those lurid exaggerations.

The Lord Mayor and aldermen of London made the most of any disturbances that occurred in the vicinity of the theatres to argue that their patrons were a chief cause of riot and 'mutinous attempts'. There certainly were sporadic 'frays' between apprentices and 'young rogues that took upon them the name of gentlemen'; but they flared up in the streets near the theatres. There is no record that any disorders originated in the playhouses themselves in any of the years that spanned Shakespeare's working life.

The theatres were also denounced as the familar haunt of pickpockets ('cutpurses') and petty criminals of all kinds. There were – and are – pickpockets in any crowd; but (if the records of the law courts are at all reliable) very few indictable offences occurred in the playhouses. It seems clear from the case lists that there was little danger of being robbed or molested while watching a play, though the streets of Southwark and Shoreditch, like any other London streets at that time, could be dangerous.

The main (and genuine) nuisance caused by the theatre patrons was that they jammed the routes while making their way to performances and when they were going home afterwards. The streets became 'so stopped', it was reported, that people 'going about their necessary affairs can hardly find passage'. It was the inevitable consequence of the assembly and dispersal of a large crowd converging upon and then leaving a particular locality. Not even the bitterest enemies of the theatre ever suggested that its patrons formed themselves into an army of thugs intent on beating up law-abiding citizens. Indeed, one or two of the more reasonable moralists reflected wryly that, though they wished people were not so frivolous, playgoers might spend their leisure in worse ways. The time and money they 'wasted' at the theatre could have been expended on even greater 'mischiefs'. Stephen Gosson – no friend of the theatre – admitted that 'there come to plays all sorts, young and old, and it is hard to say that all offend'.

If the audiences had behaved in anything like the unbridled and licentious manner their enemies described, the theatres would have been suppressed by the authoritarian royal government. The Privy Council was quick enough to bring the players to heel when it chose to do so. (See Chapters 6 and 7.) If 'young ruffians' spoiling for a fight and 'harlots' seeking custom and 'penny stinkards' bellowing oaths at the actors had formed a sizeable proportion of the audiences, then respectable women of all classes and steady artisans and thriving shopkeepers and professional men and the gentry and the nobility would not have been regular playgoers.

The wholly misleading idea that it was considered disreputable for women to go to the playhouse has falsified the picture. Single men – students and gallants, mostly – formed a large part of the audiences; but women, many with their husbands but some unaccompanied, were present in all parts of the theatres. In 1607, for example, the

French ambassador and his wife were at the Globe to see *Pericles*. Platter noted that 'men and womenfolk visit such places without scruple'. The Venetian ambassador recorded with some surprise that ladies 'come freely and seat themselves among the men without the slightest hesitation'. In a letter dated 30 June 1614, a scholarly Londoner, John Chamberlain, informed a friend that he had called twice to see her married sister, but without success. He explained that on the first occasion she was playing cards at a neighbour's house, while on the other she had gone to the Globe.

As for the social backgrounds of the playgoers, there is abundant contemporary evidence that very nearly 'all sorts and conditions' of men and women were represented. To give just one example: in 1602 the Privy Council ordered the City authorities to make a swoop on 'playhouses, bowling alleys and dicing houses' and all other 'places of resort' to 'take up idle, loose and dissolute persons and such as cannot give a good account of how they do lawfully live'. Naturally, the City Fathers made a bee-line for the theatres, hoping for a good haul there. They left the brothels and taverns and gambling dens alone, but 'all the playhouses were beset in one day'. When the search was over, the zealous guardians of law and morality were left with egg on their faces. They had found in the theatres, not the unsavoury crew their prejudices had led them to expect, but respectable citizens and 'gentlemen and serving men, lawyers, clerks, country men that had law cases, aye, the Queen's men, knights, and . . . one Earl'!

Unlike the docile middle-class audiences of today, the spectators were apt to demonstrate noisily when a play did not please them; but they were quick and generous with their applause. The actors were left in no doubt about their opinions. Of course, 'some quantity of barren spectators' (*Hamlet*) might be present at any performance, and the playwrights were often provoked to make critical remarks about their audiences, or sections of them. Shakespeare's contemporaries – notably, Ben Jonson – had some bitter words to say about spectators who failed to appreciate their work. (Shakespeare himself never protested that any of his plays had been unfairly received or undervalued; but, then, he had no need to.) Such complaints, however, were occasioned by what disappointed playwrights saw as a lack of proper response to their merits. They did not constitute a general condemnation of audiences' behaviour.

One frequent source of complaint was the spectators' habit of cracking nuts while the actors were on stage. It was annoying, of course; but it was a customary – and expensive – part of the afternoon's pleasure. So, too, was drinking bottled beer. The actors complained about that as well – not because they objected to beer-drinking, but because the bottles hissed when they were opened. The theatre managers were themselves partly to blame. Platter observed that 'during the performance food and drink are carried round the audience'. There were good profits to be made by selling nuts and beer.

If the worst charge the playwrights could make was that their plays did not always succeed, and if the actors had nothing worse than noisy eating and drinking to contend with, then the spectators can hardly be accused of giving them a rough ride. There is evidence in plenty that the audiences could, and usually did, pay rapt attention to the comic, tragic and heroic dramas unfolded for their delight. Carried away by the actors' skill and the writers' talents, they quickly forgot their nuts and beer and every other immediate and personal consideration. Then (as the Venetian ambassador quoted earlier remarked) the vast audience was hushed, listening intently to every word.

But, when all is said and done, it is the plays that Shakespeare wrote for them that tell us most about his audiences. For all of the twenty years in which he got his living by providing them with entertainment, their enthusiasm for his work made him the most successful playwright of his day – and he had many greatly-gifted rivals. The people who flocked to the Globe to see his plays nearly four hundred years ago were Shakespeare's first critics; and time has confirmed that they were good judges. The dramatist who wrote to please them – *Romeo and Juliet* . . . *Much Ado* . . . *The Merchant of Venice* . . . *King Lear* . . . *Antony and Cleopatra* . . . the lot, all written for *them* – is now acclaimed, worldwide, as a genius.

Whatever Hamlet might say about the groundlings, it is quite clear that there was an unfailing rapport – a deep emotional accord – between William Shakespeare and his audiences. Their mutual understanding and confidence, tacit for the most part, is occasionally (very occasionally) made overt, sometimes in a turn of phrase, sometimes in a quite lengthy passage. Once or twice, using a character as his voice, he addressed his spectators directly. Then, there is no mistaking how he stood with them; how he understood them and how confident he was of his hold on them. We hear that assured, friendly note in *Henry V*, in the Chorus's 'Pardon, gentles all' and in the Epilogue. We hear it again in *The Winter's Tale*, in Time's eloquent 'apology'. Or listen to Rosalind's Epilogue to *As You Like It*, in which Shakespeare's relationship with his audience is so clearly revealed – and so frankly and deftly put to work. As Rosalind speaks, the long-gone Globe and its packed audience come back to us: the waning afternoon, the play done, and a crowd of people, who indeed *had* 'liked it', listening to the last words with which their favourite playwright sent them homewards.

It is not the fashion to see the lady the epilogue; but it is no more unhandsome than to see the lord the prologue. If it be true that good wine needs no bush, 'tis true that a good play needs no epilogue: yet to good wine they do use good bushes; and good plays prove the better by the help of good epilogues. What a case am I in then, that am neither a good epilogue, nor cannot insinuate with you in the behalf of a good play! I am not furnished like a beggar, therefore to beg will not become me: my way is to conjure you; and I'll begin with the women. I charge you, O women, for the love you bear to men, to like as much of this play as please you: and I charge you, O men, for the love you bear women – as I perceive by your simpering, none of you hates them – that between you, and the women, the play may please. If I were a woman I would kiss as many of you as had beards that pleased me, complexions that liked me, and breaths that I defied not: and, I am sure, as many as have good beards or good faces or sweet breaths will, for my kind offer, when I make curtsy, bid me farewell.

14

Foul Papers and Printed Books

TODAY, IT IS an advantage for dramatists to get their plays into print. Publication makes their work more widely known, and their royalties on the sales of the books are a welcome addition to their income from the theatre. It was not like that in Shakespeare's time. For the reasons set out later he did not show much interest in getting his plays printed. Some were, but even when they appeared in 'authorised' editions, he did not busy himself with them. He neither discussed the printing of the manuscripts nor corrected the proofs. (His apparent indifference to the printing of his plays is in sharp contrast to the close attention he paid when *Venus and Adonis* and *The Rape of Lucrece* were being printed. See Chapter 7.)

In 1623, seven years after his death, the First Folio was published. His old friends and colleagues John Heminge and Henry Condell collected the manuscripts and the previously printed plays, carefully sorting out and editing them to make up that great volume. It contained thirty-six plays (all he had written, except *Pericles*) and it ran to 907 large ('folio') pages printed in double columns. (Other Folio editions followed: the Second Folio in 1632, the Third in 1663 and the Fourth in 1685.)

In their 'Address' to their readers, Heminge and Condell declared that they had given Shakespeare's plays to the world 'as he conceived them', claiming that in their book his works were 'truly set forth according to their original'. As we shall see, that was too large a claim, but they did their work well. All subsequent editors of Shakespeare have been deeply in their debt. Indeed, but for Heminge and Condell half of Shakespeare's plays would have been lost; and some that survived would be garbled and incomplete, as they were when they began their task.

Even so, they were not able to establish a wholly satisfactory text. The First Folio includes some lines so obscure that it is hard to make any sense of them. It also includes some 'corrupt' passages. (They are called 'corrupt' because they are of doubtful authenticity. Some are interpolations – words written by somebody else and inserted in

Shakespeare's own text. Some are lines that have been so heavily altered by other hands as to bear only a faint resemblance to what Shakespeare originally wrote. To give just one example: in *Macbeth* Act IV Sc.1 Hecate's speech in lines 39-43 is corrupt.)

There are other mistakes: some lines have been omitted; some lines are repeated; some speeches are assigned to the wrong characters. We have only to compare the First Folio text of, say, *Hamlet* with the text of that play as printed in a modern edition to realise that Heminge and Condell did not fully achieve their ambition to get Shakespeare's plays printed 'as he conceived them'.

Though they were over-confident that they had solved them, they were well aware of the nature of the problems they faced. In preparing the text of their book for the printers, they had to sort out a vast quantity of material (some printed, some in manuscript) of varying authority.

Of the thirty-six plays they included, only nineteen had previously been printed. Six of those had appeared in what Heminge and Condell described as 'stolen and surreptitious copies, maimed, and deformed by the frauds and stealths of injurious imposters'. These 'pirated' versions of the plays had to be 'cured' and 'made perfect of their limbs', as they put it, before they were fit to take their place in the First Folio. (These are the plays printed in Shakespeare's lifetime in what are now known as the 'Bad Quartos'. The full meaning of that term is explained later.)

The rest of the previously printed plays were considered by Heminge and Condell to be faithful reproductions of what Shakespeare wrote. Having checked them against the manuscripts in their possession they instructed the printers of the First Folio to use them as their 'copy'. (These are the plays printed in Shakespeare's lifetime in what are now known as the 'Good Quartos'. The full meaning of that term is also explained later).

The texts of the seventeen plays not previously printed were obtained from the manuscript copies that Heminge and Condell had assembled. These manuscripts were of different kinds; and because they were not always wholly reliable they gave the editors a lot of problems.

In some cases they were able to use Shakespeare's own manuscripts, just as they were when he handed them over to his company – his own completed, handwritten texts. Although, as we have seen, he was renowned for supplying very 'clean' manuscripts ('we have scarce received from him a blot in his papers') it cannot be supposed that there were not some crossings-out, second-thought insertions and other revisions.

The term 'foul papers' was used to describe an author's manuscript in the state he left it when he had finished work on it. As the name (*'foul papers'*) implies, it was not a fair copy. It was a 'blotted' manuscript. The final draft of his work, it contained all the alterations – scorings-out, insertions, changes of every kind – that he had made while writing and when completing his last revisions before handing it over.

Shakespeare's foul papers may have been much more legible and error-free than those of most authors but, even so, they had to be prepared carefully for the press. However few 'blots' they contained, some of the 'copy' would puzzle the printers when they were setting it up in type, unless the editors could clarify every detail.

Sometimes, indeed, Heminge and Condell were themselves puzzled. To give just one example: in the First Folio text of *Henry V* (for which they used Shakespeare's foul papers) Mistress Quickly describes the dying Falstaff in these words: 'for his nose was as sharp as a pen, and a Table of green fields'. Most modern editors change that baffling utterance to read thus: 'for his nose was as sharp as a pen, and a' babbled of green fields'. In the 'secretary' form of handwriting (which we know Shakespeare used) it would have been easy to misread *a' babbled* as *a Table*. That, at any rate, is what it is thought they did – presumably the reading they supplied made sense to them. A few modern editors ingeniously argue that it does make sense; but most texts print *a' babbled*. (The emendation was first suggested by Lewis Theobald in his seven-volume edition of Shakespeare, published in 1733.)

Unfortunately, Shakespeare's foul papers cannot be consulted to settle editorial problems. They disappeared long ago. It is not known what happened to them after Heminge and Condell and the printers of the First Folio had finished with them. Nobody thought to keep them once they had been set up in type! Quite a lot of the sheets were probably used to pad out the bindings of other books – such was the fate of many seventeenth-century manuscripts.

Some of the other manuscripts used for the First Folio text had been written out by the book-keeper of the Chamberlain's-King's company. When he was given Shakespeare's foul papers the book-keeper prepared the play for performance. He marked it up with the actors' names, inserted stage directions, noted what properties and 'noises' were required and at what points in the action, indicated act and scene divisions, exits and entrances. Sometimes he did all this on the author's own manuscript; but more often he wrote out a new text, incorporating all the necessary instructions, to serve as a clear and workmanlike prompt-copy.

Yet another kind of manuscript was used by Heminge and Condell.

As we have seen, every play had to be licensed by the Master of the Revels; and that very important Royal Officer expected to be given a manuscript that was easy to read. (Plays were sometimes sent back with a stern reminder that the actors must supply 'fair-written' copies.) For that reason, a scribe was employed to make a copy of the book-keeper's manuscript, generally omitting his acting instructions. The scribe's copy was known as 'the book of the play'. It was, of course, a copy of a copy. However legible, it was two steps removed from the authority of the author's foul papers. As Shakespeare's original manuscripts were passed from hand to hand for copying, errors were likely to creep in at each successive stage.

Errors also occurred when the manuscripts, whoever had written them, were set up in type. Even today, with all the advantages of typewriters, word processors and vastly improved printing technology, the printed copy of an author's work is likely to contain mistakes and obscurities, even though the proofs are carefully checked by several readers. In the early seventeenth century, the likelihood of error was much greater. Apart from handwriting difficulties – both the 'secretary' and the 'italic' hands then in use made it easy to confuse certain letters – printing procedures created special problems. The printers kept only a small stock of type. Consequently, they did not 'set' a whole book at one go. They composed the type into words to print a 'gathering' of sheets. Having printed the requisite number of copies, they then broke the type up into its separate letters and used it to compose the words for the next sheets. In consequence, it was exceedingly difficult to correct any mistakes that escaped notice at an early stage of the printing.

Already faced with a very large quantity of manuscript material of varied quality, Heminge and Condell also had to cope with printing shop problems. It was an immensely difficult task to prepare the text of the First Folio and to see it through the press. That they succeeded as well as they did says much for their skill and devotion.

Their greatest asset was that they had worked with Shakespeare. They had been his closest colleagues and they had acted in all his plays. When they had to correct a 'stolen and surreptitious copy', when they had to decipher a manuscript, when they had to decide between different readings, they drew on their firsthand knowledge of their old friend's habitual ways of thinking and characteristic modes of expression. Some eighteenth-century editors were far too quick to 'improve' the First Folio; but for many years now it has been a sound editorial principle to leave it alone unless excellent reasons can be found for altering it. Our modern texts are far from being reprints of Heminge and Condell's, but the judgement of the only editors who knew Shakespeare and who had access to the theatre manuscripts of his plays is not lightly set aside.

To understand why Shakespeare himself made no effort to get his plays into print, we have to consider two matters: copyright; and the ownership of the plays. Copyright as we know it did not exist then. The author did not get a royalty on the sales of the books he had written. The bookseller (we would call him the 'publisher' today) bought the manuscript outright from its author. He paid the printer, and he was then entitled to sell the printed copies of the book and to pocket all the proceeds. However popular the book might prove to be, all the author ever received was what he got when he sold his manuscript to the bookseller.

Shakespeare was a very busy and a very successful man. He was drawing a large income from the theatre (as actor, housekeeper and sharer). Any extra money he could have gained by getting his plays printed would hardly have been worth the time and trouble involved, *even if* the decision to do so had been his to make – and it was *not*.

It was not for him to decide to sell his manuscripts to a bookseller, for this very good reason: he did not own them. Whereas other authors – poets and prose writers – sold their work directly to a bookseller, playwrights were in a different situation. The whole purpose of writing a play was to have it performed in the theatre, so the dramatist sold his manuscript to an acting company. Strictly speaking, he sold it to the sharers in the company. They jointly owned all the company's assets, and those included the manuscripts of its plays. The playwright received no further payment, however many times his work was performed. (Towards the end of Shakespeare's career a very well-known playwright might be given a 'benefit' from one performance if his work continued to draw the crowds, but that was an unusually generous arrangement.)

The company's play stock was its most valuable capital asset, and the sharers kept their manuscripts under close supervision. As we saw in Chapter 10, the manuscripts of Shakespeare's plays were not in his library at New Place when he died. They were in London, in the play chests at the Globe and the Blackfriars theatres. That was where they belonged. When Shakespeare handed the manuscript of a play over to his company, it ceased to be his property. His continuing financial and legal rights in it were those to which he was entitled by the fact that he was a company sharer. As the author of the play, he had no further control over it. As a sharer in the company, he took part in deciding how best to make profitable use of it – where, and when, and how often, it was to be performed, and whether it was to be printed.

The sharers saw no great advantage in getting their plays into print. True, the bookseller would pay them something, but not a lot. They might get about one-fifth of what it had cost them to buy the play from its author. Useful, of course, but not enough to be tempting. Certainly not enough to offset the risk of lower takings when it was performed. All the acting companies – the Chamberlain's-King's Men, especially – feared that the audience for a play would be reduced if people could sit and read it at home instead of having to pay to see it at the theatre. From such evidence as we have about the size of audiences for plays in print, it seems that their fears were greatly exaggerated. However, that is what they thought; and their attitude to the printing of their plays was coloured accordingly. Generally, they sold plays to the booksellers willingly only when, for some reason or other, they needed to raise ready money. For example, in 1594 (at the end of the long plague closure) and again in 1600 (when the Chamberlain's and the Admiral's had just built new theatres) many more plays went into print than usual.

Their attitude was entirely understandable. Their business was in the theatre. They made their money by finding and performing popular plays. Having those plays printed was a sideline; and not a profitable one. Once they had sold a play to a bookseller they had lost their exclusive control over a valuable piece of property – and for very little gain.

There was another very damaging possiblity to be reckoned with. While in manuscript and in the company's possession, a play could be kept safe from rivals. Only the company's own actors could learn it and perform it. Once in print, it was fair game. The rudimentary copyright system gave some protection to a bookseller's rights; but it gave no protection to an acting company. The sharers could not retain sole performing rights in a play they had allowed a bookseller to print. Very soon after it appeared in print, a popular play might be performed by another company, glad to cash in on its success without having had the expense of buying it from its author. It did not often happen, but the risk was real enough.

In all these circumstances, it is not surprising that Shakespeare and his fellow sharers were reluctant to have his plays printed. The question that does arise is why they decided to allow any of them to appear in book form.

Occasionally, as has been mentioned, they did it simply to raise money; but they were a thriving company and rarely pressed for funds. As a rule, they let the booksellers have their plays to reduce the harm already done to their interests by unauthorised – 'pirated' – printings; or to prevent the pirates getting in first.

Copyright regulation, as far as it went, was in the hands of the Stationers' Company. That was an association of booksellers and printers, incorporated by Royal Charter as far back as 1557. Except for the Universities of Oxford and Cambridge (also allowed to print books) the freemen of the Stationers' Company had the monopoly of printing in England. Membership of the Company included all the London booksellers and most of the printers, who were granted their privileged position so that the government could exercise control over the printing presses. Every book printed had to be licensed for publication by the officers of the Stationers' Company, who could then be held responsible if they allowed 'seditious' or 'depraved' books to appear.

In fact, many unlicensed books and pamphlets were printed. It was one thing to make regulations, quite another to enforce them. A good deal of 'mischievous' and 'mutinous' and 'lewd' material was in circulation. Still, from the government's point of view, it was better to have some control than none. Printers who dodged the censorship were severely punished – if they were caught.

It was also better for the booksellers to have some control over their trade than none. Most of them observed the correct procedures. To get the necessary licence to print a book, they entered its title in Stationers' Register, the official record of the Stationers' Company. It listed the titles of the books and the names of the booksellers publishing them. Usually – *not* always – it listed the authors' names too.

In theory, having entered a book in Stationers' Register (and having paid the fee for its entry and its licensing) the bookseller had established his sole right to have it printed and to sell copies. In theory, too, the manuscript of any book that was entered in Stationers' Register for publication had been honestly bought by the bookseller from its author, or in the case of a play, from the acting company sharers.

It did not always work out like that. As we have seen, some books were printed and sold without having been entered in the Register. Worse, from the sharers' point of view, some plays that were entered in the Register had not been honestly acquired by the booksellers. Hence Heminge's and Condell's bitter reference to 'stolen and surreptitious copies'. We shall see later how the booksellers managed to get their hands on the manuscripts of the plays they stole. First, however, the terms 'Bad Quarto' and 'Good Quarto' (used earlier when describing Heminge's and Condell's editorial problems) must be explained.

The term 'quarto' (like the term 'folio') is used to describe a book size. The pages of a quarto book are one-fourth (*quarto*) the size of the sheets on which the book is printed. A quarto page measures about twenty-three centimetres in depth and eighteen centimetres in width. The pages of a folio book are much larger than quarto pages. The sheets on which a folio book is printed are folded only once, so that a folio page is about forty centimetres in depth and twenty-eight centimetres in width. (Those measurements apply to a 'large' folio. Some folios are smaller than that; but all folios are larger than quartos.)

Heminge's and Condell's edition of Shakespeare's plays was, of course, a folio volume (and a 'large' folio, too); but each of the eighteen plays printed in his lifetime appeared in a quarto-sized book. (Nineteen in all had been printed before the First Folio appeared in 1623, but the quarto edition of *Othello* did not come out until 1622, six years after his death.)

The term 'Bad Quarto' is used to describe the 'maimed and deformed' editions that were printed by pirate booksellers. There were six Bad Quartos: *Henry VI Part 2, Henry VI Part 3, Romeo and Juliet, Henry V, The Merry Wives of Windsor* and *Hamlet*. Two of them were given incorrect titles. *Henry VI Part 2* appeared as *The Contention of the Two Famous Houses of York and Lancaster. Henry VI Part 3* appeared as *The True Tragedy of Richard Duke of York*. So bad were their texts, and so unlike the authentic versions printed by Heminge and Condell in the First Folio, that later editors considered that they were not written by Shakespeare. It was believed that he rewrote them and turned them into *Henry VI Parts 2 and 3*. We know better now – and so, of course, did Heminge and Condell!

Faced with these stolen plays, Shakespeare and his fellow sharers did what they could to limit the damage. For example, a year after the Bad Quarto of *Romeo and Juliet* appeared (in 1597) they authorised another bookseller to print the play and supplied him with an authentic manuscript. Similarly, the Bad Quarto of *Hamlet* (1603) was followed by a Good Quarto in 1604, for which the book-keeper's copy of Shakespeare's own manuscript provided the text. That Good Quarto, which is nearly twice the length of the pirated text of 1603, is the basis of modern texts of the play, though editors draw on the First Folio text as well.

Once a pirated edition of the play had appeared in print, the sharers knew that they might just as well let a bookseller have a good manuscript and publish an accurate text. The bookseller paid them something, and, more importantly, the publication of an authentic text protected the reputation of their playwright from the 'injurious imposters'.

Sometimes, knowing that certain very popular plays were threatened with piracy, they arranged with a bookseller to enter their titles in Stationers' Register, though they were not necessarily ready to let them be printed at that time. Entry did not guarantee that some other bookseller would not print stolen versions, but it made unauthorised publication more difficult. For example, in 1600 *As You Like It*, *Henry V* and *Much Ado* were all entered in Stationers' Register, with a note stating that they were 'stayed'. In other words, they were going to be printed – but not yet.

'Staying' the plays was not a wholly successful device. *Henry V* appeared in a Bad Quarto very soon after it was entered in the Register. On the other hand, *Much Ado* was printed in a Good Quarto, based on Shakespeare's foul papers. *As You Like It* did not get printed at all until it appeared in the First Folio (in a good text derived from the book-keeper's copy of the play).

Since the sharers valued their manuscripts so highly and kept them in the theatre play store, how did the unscrupulous booksellers come by the stolen versions they printed? A once-popular theory was that they employed shorthand-writers to attend performances and take down the speeches. More recent knowledge of the shorthand systems then available shows that they were much too crude to have been capable of doing that. Some words, some short speeches, might be recorded when delivered at acting speed, but nothing like a whole play.

It is generally held now that the 'surreptitious' texts were made up by actors, often to provide themselves with plays to take on tour. They then sold the manuscript of their botched-up play to a bookseller when they got back to London. Sometimes, hard-up actors would put a play together for the express purpose of selling it to a bookseller who would not ask questions about its origin.

Remembering their own parts well, the actors would have a pretty fair recollection of other parts, too; especially, of course, those spoken while they themselves were on stage and with which their own parts were cued. Between them, two or three actors could put most of a play together, even when they had taken only minor roles in it. What they could not remember, they made up. Many were quite capable of 'bombasting out a blank verse' – even if it was of poor quality.

The leading actors in the Chamberlain's-King's Men – sharers and regular hired men alike – would certainly not have had anything to do with this dishonest practice. It was detrimental to their own best interests and it was frowned on by professional players proud of their company's standing. But hired men who could not count on regular work with any one company had no reason to be scrupulous.

The belief that the pirated plays were derived from 'memorial reconstructions', as they are called, is reinforced by the fact that even a Bad Quarto often includes much material that is undoubtedly authentic. However inaccurate and incomplete the text is as a whole, the actors dictating the lines as the stolen version was written down remembered a great many of Shakespeare's own words.

Because Shakespeare did not prepare his own manuscripts for the press, the texts of his plays had to be established without any guidance from their author. Therefore, as we have seen, his editors were faced with a very difficult task – with consequences that have been of such lasting importance to Shakespearian students that a brief restatement of the main points is called for.

It was the uneven quality of their material (whether in print or in manuscript) that made Heminge's and Condell's editorial work so trying. Their printed sources included Bad Quartos and Good Quartos. Even a Bad Quarto might contain authentic lines. A Good Quarto might repeat errors made in the Bad Quarto which had provided some of its text. The later editions of a Good Quarto might contain mistakes not present in the first edition.

Their manuscript sources presented them with acute problems. When they were available, Shakespeare's foul papers were, of course, of prime authority; but, 'clean' as they were, they were not always easy to decipher. When they were not available, the book-keeper's copy was a generally reliable secondary source. Even so, it was marked up with stage directions and copious marginal annotations which frequently puzzled and confused the printers, who often had to guess what to print and what to omit. Nor, so many years afterwards, could Heminge and Condell themselves be sure of all the details. They had to try to remember how closely, if at all, Shakespeare himself had checked the book-keeper's copy of his manuscript. Was this word an amendment that the author had made? Was that line one of those he had meant to correct but had never got round to altering?

It has always to be remembered that Shakespeare's writings were theatre scripts. His original manuscripts were copied, marked, changed to suit particular performances. Finding in rehearsal that words, lines, whole passages could be improved, he did it there and then. Not the most efficient of book-keepers, the most careful of scribes, nor the best-regulated procedures could ensure that every alteration he made was clearly and accurately recorded.

Shakespeare – actor, sharer, housekeeper, dramatist – was far too busy to check that the manuscripts kept in the company's play chest were faithful texts of the plays 'as he conceived them'. Surrounded with pressing business, and with his next play on his mind, he simply could not find the time to 'oversee his own writings'. Had he done so, the labours of his future editors – Heminge and Condell and all their many successors – would have been greatly simplified. But that was not a consideration that occurred to him. He was preoccupied with his 'quick forge'.

Finally, it must be pointed out that this chapter has been no more than an introduction to a large and complicated subject. (Suggestions for further study are made in the Reading List.) However, even a brief description of how Shakespeare's manuscripts fared in the theatre and of how they found their way into print helps to explain something that puzzles many people. Although Shakespeare is the best-known dramatist of all time and although his plays are closely studied and performed the world over, yet the authenticity of certain words and lines – whole passages, even – is still doubtful. Readers armed with the information provided here will no longer be surprised that it is so.

Appendices,
Reading List
and
Index

Appendix 1

Shakespeare's Family Tree

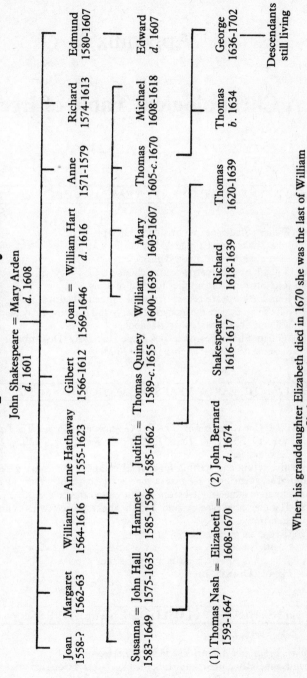

When his granddaughter Elizabeth died in 1670 she was the last of William
Shakespeare's direct descendants.

Appendix 2

A Chronological Table of Events

Period 1   THE FIRST TWENTY YEARS 1564-1584

1564 William Shakespeare christened (26 April).
1566 John Shakespeare made Alderman.
1568 John Shakespeare made Bailiff.
1569 William Shakespeare goes to school.
1576 John Shakespeare applies for coat of arms.
1577 John Shakespeare ceases to attend council meetings.
1578 John Shakespeare mortgages property and is excused paying poor relief.
    William Shakespeare leaves school.
1582 William Shakespeare marries Anne Hathaway (December).
1583 Susanna Shakespeare christened (26 May).

Period 2   THE EARLY YEARS IN LONDON 1584/5-1592

*Works: The Comedy of Errors, The Two Gentlemen of Verona, The Taming of the
    Shrew, Henry VI Parts 1, 2 and 3, Richard III, King John, Titus
    Andronicus*
Freelance acting and writing for several companies: Strange's Pembroke's,
Admiral's. Henslowe records runaway success of *Henry VI Part 1*.
Shakespeare's name made before plague closed theatres in 1592.
1585 Hamnet Shakespeare and Judith Shakespeare (twins) christened (2
    February).
1592 Greene's *Groatsworth of Wit*.
    Chettle's apology.
    John Shakespeare in danger of arrest for debt.
    Plague closes theatres.

Period 3   THEATRES CLOSED: THE NARRATIVE POEMS 1592-1594

Works: Venus and Adonis, The Rape of Lucrece
Spends much time in Stratford. Settles his father's troubled affairs. Briefly a

member of Southampton's circle. Dedicates poems to him. Oversees printing of poems in London. Prepares for reopening of theatres.
1593 *Venus and Adonis* published (18 April).
1594 *The Rape of Lucrece* published (9 May).
    His early plays back on stage as new theatre season starts up.

Period 4   FIRST YEARS OF THE CHAMBERLAIN'S MEN 1594-1598/9

Works: The Merchant of Venice, A Midsummer Night's Dream, The Merry Wives of Windsor, Much Ado About Nothing, As You Like It, Richard II, Henry IV Parts 1 and 2, Henry V, Romeo and Juliet
Writes two plays a year, the success of which establishes the Chamberlain's Men as the leading theatre company. *Palladis Tamia* testifies to his great reputation. Growing fame and fortune overshadowed by the death of his only son.
1594 William Shakespeare becomes sharer in Chamberlain's Men.
1596 Hamnet Shakespeare buried (11 August).
    John Shakespeare awarded grant of arms (20 October).
1597 William Shakespeare buys New Place (4 May).
1598 Francis Meres' *Palladis Tamia* published.

Period 5   THE CHAMBERLAIN'S MEN AT THE GLOBE 1598/9-1603

Works: Julius Caesar, Twelfth Night, Hamlet, Othello
With the building of the Globe in 1598/9 and their arrival on Bankside, the Chamberlain's Men become pre-eminent. Henslowe and Alleyn remove the Admiral's Men to the Fortune to get away from their competitors at the Globe. Shakespeare is a housekeeper in the Globe as well as being a sharer in the company. Competition from the children's companies at Blackfriars, but the Chamberlain's Men not seriously harmed.
1601 Essex's rebellion. Chamberlain's Men questioned about their performance of *Richard II*. Cleared of blame. Company plays for Queen at Court the night before Essex's execution (on 25 February). John Shakespeare buried (8 September).
1602 William Shakespeare buys land in Old Stratford (1 May) and cottage in Chapel Lane (28 September).
1603 Queen Elizabeth died (24 March).

Period 6   THE KING'S MEN AT THE GLOBE 1603-1608/9

Works: All's Well, Measure for Measure, King Lear, Macbeth, Antony and Cleopatra, Timon of Athens, Coriolanus, Troilus and Cressida
Very soon after James I's accession he appoints the Chamberlain's Men 'His

Majesty's Servants'. Known from now on as the King's Men, they are unquestionably the premier theatre company.

James requires a greatly increased number of Court performances, and pays much more for each than Elizabeth had done. Meanwhile, the Globe continues to do excellent business.

1603 William Shakespeare named in King's Men's royal patent (19 May).

1604 William Shakespeare receives scarlet cloth for his royal livery.

1605 William Shakespeare buys tithes on land near Stratford (24 July).

1606 Susanna Shakespeare listed as one who failed to receive Easter Sunday communion.

1607 Susanna Shakespeare marries Dr John Hall (5 June). Edward Shakespeare, son of Edmund Shakespeare, buried (12 August). Edmund Shakespeare buried (31 December).

1608 Elizabeth Hall, granddaughter, christened (21 February).
William Shakespeare and his fellows in the King's Men take over lease of Blackfriars Theatre (9 August).
Mary Shakespeare (Arden) buried (9 September).

Period 7   THE KING'S MEN AT BLACKFRIARS 1608/9-1612

Works: Pericles, Cymbeline, The Winter's Tale, The Tempest
The *Sonnets* were published in 1609, but are generally held to have been written between 1592 and 1598.

Keeping the Globe on as their summer theatre, the King's Men play at Blackfriars in the winter, greatly increasing their reputation and their profits. Shakespeare's new plays prove successful at both theatres and at Court, too. A housekeeper in the Blackfriars and in the Globe and a principal sharer in the company, he brings his working life to a triumphant conclusion.

1610 William Shakespeare completes purchase of more land in Stratford.

1612 Gilbert Shakespeare buried (28 January).
William Shakespeare gives written evidence in the Belott-Mountjoy lawsuit and describes his place of residence as Stratford.

Period 8   THE LAST YEARS 1613-1616

Works: Henry VIII, The Two Noble Kinsmen – in collaboration with John Fletcher

From 1612/13 onwards, Shakespeare spends more and more of his time in Stratford. The Blackfriars venture has been successfully established and John Fletcher has taken over as the company's principal dramatist. Shakespeare's attention is fully occupied with family affairs and with the consolidation and eventual disposal of his estate.

1613 Richard Shakespeare buried (14 February).
William Shakespeare buys property in Blackfriars.
Globe Theatre burnt down during performance of *Henry VIII* (29 June) – rebuilt in 1614 and open again by 30 June of that year.

APPENDIX 2

1614 William Shakespeare and Dr John Hall in London to negotiate in the matter of Shakespeare's tithes.

1616 William Shakespeare's will drafted (25 January).

Judith Shakespeare marries Thomas Quiney (10 February). William Shakespeare's revised will witnessed and signed (25 March).

Thomas Quiney appears in church court (26 March) and is sentenced. William Shakespeare died on 23 April and was buried on 25th.

Reading List

Read these books first. The order in which they are listed provides a progressive course of study, so follow it as closely as you can.

Peter Alexander: *A Shakespeare Primer*: Nisbet
S. Schoenbaum: *William Shakespeare, A Compact Documentary Life*: Oxford University Press
E.A.J. Honigmann: *Shakespeare: the 'lost years'*: Manchester University Press
Andrew Gurr: *The Shakespearian Stage, 1574-1642*: Cambridge University Press
Alfred Harbage: *Shakespeare's Audience*: Columbia University Press
C. Walter Hodges: *The Globe Restored*: Benn
J.L. Styan: *Shakespeare's Stagecraft*: Cambridge University Press
E.K. Chambers: *William Shakespeare, Vols. I* and *II*: Oxford University Press
W.W. Greg: *The Shakespeare First Folio*: Oxford University Press
W.W. Greg: *The Editorial Problem in Shakespeare*: Oxford University Press

The annual volumes of *Shakespeare Survey* (Cambridge University Press) are indispensable. Consult your local library.

You also need some reference books of your own. Some excellent (and inexpensive) ones are available, such as:
R.C. Bayley: *An A B C of Shakespeare*: Longman (York Press)
Gareth and Barbara Lloyd Evans: *Companion to Shakespeare*: Dent (Everyman)
Stanley Wells: *Shakespeare, An Illustrated Dictionary*: Oxford University Press
Stanley Wells (ed.): *The Cambridge Companion to Shakespeare Studies*: Cambridge University Press

Index

Note: WS = William Shakespeare

Act for the Punishment as Vagabonds
(1572) 182
acting companies:
  capital 185
  children's 69-70, 95, 121-2, 165
  composition 188
  and copyright 204
  demand for new plays 93
  and different locations 166
  and dramatists 74
  financial business 185-6
  legal status 185
  licences 163
  loyalty to 166
  management 185, 186
  plays, ownership 203
  privileged companies 116
  repertory system 93
  sharers 98-9, 185-6
  touring 72, 81-2, 90
actors: attacks on 180
  in comedy 117, 189-90
  and dramatists 187
  and London 181
  organisation 181, 182
  patronage 182-4, 185
  pay 179, 188
  and pirated plays 207
  professional training 54
  as sharers 188
  skills 187
  social status 179-80, 183
  style 80, 189, 190
  and theatre-owners 185
  touring 72, 81-2
  see also acting companies
actresses 188
Alchemist, The (Jonson) 120, 126
ale-tasters 22
Allen, Giles 94-7, 184
Alleyn, Edward: acting style 189
  as actor 67, 82

arms, grant of 109
  and Dulwich College 180
  and the Fortune 168
  and Henslowe 82, 90, 91
  rivalry 98
All's Well That Ends Well 94, 106
Alveston Manor, Stratford 140
Anne of Denmark, Queen of England
  115, 119
Antony and Cleopatra 120
  on drinking 64
  female roles 188-9
  location, changing 176
Apology for Poetry, An (Sidney) 180
Arden, Forest of 14, 20
Arden, Margaret (later Webbe) 28
Arden, Mary (later Shakespeare):
  children 25
  death 26
  legal transactions 24
  marriage 23-6
  status 22-3, 25
  widowhood 26
Arden, Robert 22-3
Armin, Robert 116, 117, 189
arms, Shakespeare's 108, 109
As You Like It 106
  actors in 117
  Arden in 14
  audience, addresses 197-8
  life as theatre 79
  Marlowe in 68
  school in 40
  'staying' 207
  WS acts in 102
Aston Cantlow church 23
Aubrey, John 55, 57, 63-4, 107, 154
audiences: applause 196, 197
  behaviour 194-5, 196-7
  cost of seat 192-4
  daily average 91, 204
  dispersing 195

219

in galleries 175
groundlings 175
at holiday times 191
involvement 175-6
social class 84, 118, 122-3, 162, 165
women in 195-6
Avon, River 11, 13, 20

Bacon, Francis, as 'Shakespeare' 7
'Bad Quartos' 200, 205, 206-7, 208
bailiff, powers of 16
Bankside: Bear Garden 82, 97, 192
Globe theatre 97, 98
liberties 97
Barnard, Sir John 156
Beaumont, Francis 123, 126-7, 132
Beeston, Christopher 55, 63, 101, 169
Beeston, William 55, 169
Bel Savage (Ludgate Hill) 67, 170
Bell, The (Gracechurch Street) 67, 170
Belott, Mary, see Mountjoy
Belott, Stephen 63
Belott-Mountjoy suit (1612) 9-10, 63
bequests, WS's 143-51
Bernard, Sir John 156
Billington, Michael 130
Birthplace, The, see Henley Street
Birthplace Trust, The 157-8
bishop's court, transactions 52
Bishopsgate, WS in 62, 64
Blackfriars Gatehouse, WS buys 133-4,
138, 147
Blackfriars, Liberty of 165
Blackfriars Theatre 95, 100, 121-2
audiences 125
auditorium 176
children's company at 95, 121-2, 169
closure 161
demolition 169
King's Men at 120, 122, 124-5, 131
lighting 176
plays 125, 126-7, 130, 131-2
prices 194
scenery 176
stage 176
The Tempest at 192
in winter 171
Boar's Head, The (Whitechapel) 67, 170
Book of Common Prayer 17, 18, 36
'book of the play' 202
bookseller: control over 205
dishonest 205
and plays 203, 204, 205
boys: as actors 188-9
education 32-3

Bristol, in Tudor period 19
Brooks, Baldwin 155-6
Bull, The (Bishopsgate) 67, 170
Burbage, Cuthbert: and Blackfriars
Theatre 95, 121, 124
and the Globe 97, 99, 168
as manager 122
as sharer 99, 124, 168, 185
skills 90, 91
and the Theatre 96-7
Burbage, James:
buys Blackfriars Theatre 95, 125
patronage 182-3
skills 90-1
as speculator 92, 184
and the Theatre 67, 69, 94-5, 96, 166
Burbage, Richard:
as actor 82, 90, 91, 101
bequest to 150
and Blackfriars Theatre 95, 121, 124
and the Globe 97, 99, 168
and Kempe 118
and Love's Labours Lost 119
satirised 121-2
and the Theatre 96-7
Burbages, rivalry with Henslowe 90-1
business, family in 24-5

Caesar 37
Cage, The (Stratford) 142
Cardenio 131
Catechism, Church of England 36
Cecil, Robert 115
censorship 70, 205
Chamberlain's Men – see Lord
Chamberlain's Men
'Chandos' portrait 154
Chapel Lane cottage 113, 147
Chapman, George 124
Charles I, King of England 139
and King's Men 161
Charles II, King of England:
and the theatres 161-2
Chettle, Henry 77
Children of the Blackfriars 124, 125,
126, 127
Children of the Chapel Royal 169
Children of the Queen's Revels 95,
121-2, 124, 125
children's companies:
competition from 69-70, 95, 121-2
private theatres 165
Church of England 17, 18
Catechism 36
as Established Church 45

INDEX

Cicero 37
Clopton, Sir Hugh 15, 64, 110
Cobham family 103, 104, 105
Cockpit, The 169
College of Heralds 23
Collins, Francis 113, 143, 144, 145, 149
Combe, John 148-9, 154
Combe, Thomas 148-9
Comedy of Errors, The 76, 93, 94
comic acting 117-18, 189, 190
command performances 165, 170, 171
Condell, Henry 101, 121, 124
  bequest to 150
  in Cripplegate 62
  edits First Folio 102, 117, 154-5,
    199-203, 206, 208-9
  in King's Men 116, 117
  social status 179
*Conspiracy and Tragedy of Charles Duke of
  Byron, The* (Chapman) 124
*Contention of Two Famous Houses of York
  and Lancaster, The* 206
Cope, Sir Walter 119
copyright 203, 204-5
Coriolanus 120
  imagery 42
coronation honours, Charles I 139
costumes, cost 185
Cottom, John 56
Court, command performances at 165,
  170, 171
Court of Common Pleas 47
Coventry: Mystery plays 59
  in Tudor period 19
Cowley, Richard 116
crime and the theatre 195
Cripplegate, WS in 62-3, 64
Cross Keys, The (Gracechurch Street)
  67, 170
  Lord Chamberlain's Men at 170, 171
Curle, Edward 102, 103
Curtain, The (Shoreditch) 64, 67, 69
  audience 191
  Lord Chamberlain's Men 95-6, 168
Cymbeline 128-9, 130

Daniel Deronda (Eliot) 10
'Dark Lady' of the Sonnets 51
D'Avenant, William 169, 188
de Witt, Johannes 18, 171-2
Dekker, Thomas 121
Dennis, John 105
Derby, Henry Stanley, 4th Earl 56, 57
Derby's Men 183
Dickens, Charles 54

discovery space 173, 174
Dover Wilson, John 5
Dowdall, Mr 153
Dowden, Edward 5, 129-30
drama: Elizabethan 84
  ephemerality 84
  London-centred 58, 60, 67, 90
  and the plague 72-3, 81-2, 118
  popularity 84
  study of 180
  value of 180-1
dramatists: Elizabethan 67-9
  exploitation 74
  scenic freedom 176-7
  technique 176-7
Drayton, Michael, visits WS 135
drinking: cost 192
  during plays 196-7
Droeshout, Martin 154
Drury Lane Theatre 71
Dulwich College of God's Gift 180

Earl of Worcester's Men (later Queen
  Anne's Men) 98, 116
Earle, John 65
'easer' theatres 96, 191
Eastward Ho! (Chapman et al) 124
education, Elizabethan 33-44, 50, 180
Edward VI, King of England 16, 17, 19
Elector Palatine, see Frederick V
Eliot, George 10
Elizabeth I, Queen of England:
  death 106
  and drama 84
  education 43
  enthusiasm for WS 105
  at Kenilworth 59
  and Lord Chamberlain's Men 103,
    115
  and *Merry Wives of Windsor* 105-6
  patronage 183
  and religion 17
  and *Richard II* 70
  as 'Shakespeare' 7
  and Southampton 88
  and the theatre 70
  thrift 115, 118
Elizabethan period, prosperity 20
enclosure, in Stratford 136
England in Tudor period 9
entail: broken 157
  creation 146, 147
Essex, Robert Devereux, 2nd Earl 70
Essex's Men 60
Evans, Henry 95, 121-2, 124

Every Man in his Humour (Jonson) 55, 101
Exchequer Court 47, 48
executions, public 65

Falstaff, name 103-5
family as 'firm' 24
Faustus (Marlowe) 67
Feldon 14, 20
female roles 188
festival days, theatre-going 191
Field, Jacqueline 62
Field, Richard 38, 50, 62, 87, 88, 89
First Folio (1623) 199-203, 206
   actors, list 117)
   completion 154-5
   corrupt passages 199-200
   frontispiece portrait 154
   introductory pages 3, 42, 102, 154, 199
   text 199-200
   uneven quality 208
Fletcher, John 123, 126-7, 132
   with King's Men 127, 131-2
   writes with WS 131-2
Fletcher, Laurence 116, 117
Florio, John 88
'folio' 205, 206
Forest of Arden, see Arden
Fortune, The (Finsbury) 98, 123
   builder's contracts for 172
   Lord Admiral's Men at 168
   owners 186
'foul papers' 201, 208
Fourth Folio (1685) 199

gardening, WS's interest in 113, 134-5
Garrick, David 71
Gastrell, Francis 109
German theatres, staging 171
Gillom, Fulk 56
girls, education 32-3
Globe, The (Bankside) 69, 98-100
   audiences 122, 123, 124-5
   closure 161
   destroyed 98, 131
   housekeepers 98, 99
   Lord Chamberlain's Men at 166, 168
   origins 97-8
   plays performed 62, 124-5, 126
   prices 194
   profits 100
   running costs 98
   as summer theatre 171
   The Tempest at 192

gloves, as status symbol 21
'Good Quartos' 200, 205, 206-7, 208
Gorboduc 180
Gosson, Stephen 195
grave, WS's 152-4
Greek, study of 38, 39
Greene, Robert 68, 73-7, 180
Greene, Thomas 136, 140
Greene's Groatsworth of Wit, Bought with a Million of Repentance 73-4, 77
Greenhill Street house 49
Grooms of the Chamber 116
groundlings 175
   charges to 192
   view 193
Guild of the Holy Cross 16, 19, 33
Guild of the Holy Cross, The 15-16, 19, 33
Gunpowder Plot (1605) 138

Hall, Elizabeth (later Nash) 140, 141, 146, 155
   marriage 156
   will 156
Hall, John: *Casebook* 139, 154
   death 155
   inscription on WS's grave 153
   knighthood, refuses 139
   legacy to 146
   religion 139, 140
   and WS 140
   as WS's doctor 151-2
   as WS's executor 140, 144, 148
Hall, Sir Peter 130
Hall, Susanna, see Shakespeare
hall performances 84, 165, 170
Hall's Croft, Stratford 10
Hamlet 64, 106, 118, 196
   on actors 59, 181, 189-90
   admirable qualities 32
   Bad Quarto 206
   child actors in 69
   First Folio text 200
   Good Quarto 206
   gravediggers 108-9
   mangled versions 163
   personality 151
   Stratford in 11
   theatre, references to 79-80
   WS acts in 102
Hamlet, Katherine 11
Hampton Court, King's Men at 119
'Harey the vj' 76, 91
Harrison, Anthony 48

INDEX

Hart, Joan, see Shakespeare
Hart, Mary 157
Hart, Michael 148, 157
Hart, Thomas 148, 157
Hart, William 26, 113, 148
Hart, William (nephew) 148, 157, 161
Hathaway, Anne (later Shakespeare)
   50-3
  death 155
  legacy to 150-1
  marriage 50-1, 51-3
  widowhood 51
Hathaway, Richard 51
Heminge, John 99, 101, 121, 124
  arms, grant of 109
  bequest to 150
  in Cripplegate 62
  edits First Folio 101, 117, 154-5,
    199-103, 206, 208-9
  in King's Men 116, 117
  social status 179
  WS visits 133
Henley Street house 22, 24, 25-6
  bequeathed 147, 148
  and family misfortunes 49
  parents in 110, 113
  in trust 157-8
Henrietta Maria, Queen, at New Place
  156
Henry IV 94, 106, 128
  Falstaff in 103-5
  Part 1 31
  Part 2 42, 96, 121
Henry V 62, 104, 106
  audience, addresses 197
  Bad Quarto 206, 207
  characterisation 5
  at the Globe 62
  national unity in 66
  'staying' 207
  text, editorial problems 201
Henry VI Part 1, audiences 191-2
Henry VI Part 2: Bad Quarto 206
  pirated 75
Henry VI Part 3: Bad Quarto 206
  pirated 75
  satirised 74
Henry VII, King of England 14
Henry VIII 98, 131
  on Elizabeth I 20
Henslowe, Philip:
  accounts book 172, 191
  and Alleyn 82, 90, 91
  competition with 90, 91, 97-8
  exploitation of dramatists 74

and the Fortune 168
and Greene 77
and *Henry VI* 76
as manager 186
properties, theatrical 177
and the Rose 67, 68, 82, 168
as sharer 185
as speculator 184
touring companies 166
Hentzner, Paul 172
Hero and Leander (Marlowe) 68
Hesketh, Sir Thomas 56-8
Hoghton, Alexander 55, 56, 57
Holland, Aaron, 168
Hollar, Wenceslas 99
Hope, The 168
  builder's contracts for 172
Horace 37
housekeepers, householders 98
  profits 188
Hunsdon, Lord, patronage 183

imagery 31, 41-2, 134-5
inner stage 173-4
Inns of Court performances 84, 165, 170
inn yards as theatre 165, 166, 169-70
Isle of Dogs, The (Jonson) 70, 96

Jackson, John 133
James VI & I, King of England:
  and children's company 124
  coronation 118, 119
  and King's Men 116-20
  and religion 17
  and the theatre 115-16
  uniforms, provision of 3-4, 116
Jenkins, Thomas 35
Jew of Malta, The (Marlowe) 67
Johnson, Gerard 153-4
Johnson, Joan 63
Johnson, Samuel 71
Johnson, William 63, 133, 134
Jones, Davy 58
Jonson, Ben 55, 58, 124, 130
  and actors 187
  on audiences 196
  at Blackfriars 126
  in First Folio 154
  in prison 70
  reputation 121
  satirises Chamberlain's Men 121
  visits WS 135
Jonson, Ben: on WS 101, 158, 165
  on WS's education 42-3, 55
Julius Caesar 98, 106, 128
Juvenal 37

Kempe, William 99, 117-18, 189, 190
Kenilworth Castle, pageants (1575) 59
Killigrew, Thomas 169
Kind-Heart's Dream 77
King John 76, 94
  patriotism in 66
King Lear 120
  actors in 117
  language 31-2
  Nahum Tate's version 163
  pessimism in 4-5
  WS's beliefs in 4-5
King's Men: acting style 189
  and Blackfriars Theatre 120, 122,
    124-5, 131
  collective management 186-7, 189
  and competition 121, 133
  friendships within 186
  as Grooms of the Chamber 116
  housekeepers 186
  and James VI 116-20
  plays for 119-20, 125-7
  popularity 119
  pre-eminence 187
  sharers 185
  touring 120
  in two theatres 124-5, 128, 131, 170-1
  unity of 117
  WS in 9, 120, 124, 129, 130, 133,
    186-87, 133
King's New School of Stratford-upon-
    Avon 33, 34, 35
Knight of the Burning Pestle (Beaumont
    and Fletcher) 127
Kyd, Thomas 76

Lady Elizabeth's Men at the Swan 168
Lamb, Charles 163-4
'Lancashire connection' 57-8
Lane, John 140-1, 156
Laneman, Henry 95-6, 168
  as speculator 184
Langley, Francis 168
Langrake, James 48
language 31-2, 173, 178
Latin, study of 34, 35, 37-9, 42
Law Against Lovers, The 163
legacies, WS's 143-51
Leicester, Robert Dudley, Earl of:
    patronage 182-3
Leicester's Men 60
  at the Theatre 166
Liberty of Paris Garden 62, 97, 165
Liberty of the Clink, Southwark 62, 63,
    64, 97, 165

licences, acting companies 163, 202
lighting, stage 162
Lily's *Short Introduction to Grammar* 35,
    37
literature, Elizabethan 84
location, representation of 176-7
Lodge, Thomas 68
London 64-7
  acting centres 166-70
  actors in 181
  'Long View' 99
  plague 72, 81, 90
  private theatres 169
  theatre 58, 60, 61, 67, 90
  Tudor 19
  WS in 9, 10, 62-4, 83, 111
'Long View of London' 99
Lord Admiral's Men 116
  and Chamberlain's Men 98
  competition 91
  at the Fortune 98, 168
  and Marlowe 67, 68
  name, origins 183
  at Newington Butts 168
  plays written for 106, 187
  at the Rose 166, 168
  sharers 185
  touring 82
  workload 187
Lord Chamberlain, and the theatre 92, 184
Lord Chamberlain's Men 55, 92, 116
  acting style 189
  articles of association 99-100
  become King's Men 116
  and Blackfriars Theatre 95
  and censorship, political 70-1
  and children's companies 69
  collective management 186-7, 189
  at the Cross Keys 170, 171
  at the Curtain 168
  and Elizabeth I 115, 118
  friendships within 186
  at the Globe 62, 166, 168
  housekeepers 98, 186
  name, origins 183
  at Newington Butts 91, 93, 168
  plays written for 93-4, 100, 101, 106
  private commissions 103
  sharers 98, 99, 185
  success 103, 105
  supremacy of 116, 187
  at the Swan 168
  at the Theatre 166
  WS in 76, 77, 92, 93, 186-7

INDEX

Lord Strange's Men, see Strange's Men
lords' rooms 193
Love's Labours Lost 76, 85, 94
  on education 41
Love's Labours Won 94, 106
Lyly, John 68

Macbeth 120
  corrupt passages 200
  life as theatre 79
  WS's beliefs in 4
Malcontent, The (Marston) 125
Malone, Edmond 7, 171
Manningham, John 102, 103
manuscripts:
  difficulties of 200-3, 208
  ownership 148, 203
Marlowe, Christopher 67-8, 73, 77, 91
  as 'Shakespeare' 7
marriage: importance of 138
  regulations 51-2, 52-3
  roles in 24
Marston, John 105, 124, 125
Mary I, Queen 17-18
Massinger, Philip 132
Master of the Revels 71-2
  licences 202
  and the theatre 184, 185
Measure for Measure 94, 120
  mangled versions 163
medicine, Elizabethan 139
Merchant of Venice, The 94, 106
  on moneylending 48, 49
Meres, Francis 85-6, 93-4, 106
Mermaid Inn 63, 133
Merry Wives of Windsor, The 24, 106
  Bad Quarto 206
  on education 34
  as royal commission 105-6
Meyrick, Sir Gelly 70
Midsummer Night's Dream, A 94, 106
  mangled versions 163
  plays in 58
Miracle plays 169
Mondays, theatre-going on 191
moneylending 48
Morality plays 59, 169
Mountjoy family 62-3
Mountjoy, Christopher 63
Mountjoy, Mary (later Belott) 63
Much Ado About Nothing 106, 128
  actors in 117
  on education 34
  Good Quarto 207
  as *Love's Labours Won* 94

popularity 71
'staying' 207
Watch, comic aspects 28
WS's beliefs in 4
Mystery plays, Coventry cycle 59

narrative poems 83, 85, 86, 87
Nash, Anthony 113, 149, 156
Nash, Elizabeth, see Hall
Nash, Thomas 155
  marriage 141, 156
Nashe, Thomas 68, 73, 76
  evades arrest 70
National Theatre 130
New Place 109, 110
  Anne at 51
  bequeathed 147
  building of 15
  gardens 134, 135
  Halls at 140
  Henrietta Maria visits 155
  purchase of 9, 10
  in trust 157
  WS at 40
Newington Butts theatre:
  Lord Admiral's Men at 168
  Lord Chamberlain's Men at 91, 93, 168
  Lord Strange's Men at 166, 168
Nicholas Nickleby (Dickens) 54
Norwich, in Tudor period 19
Nottingham, Earl of, patronage 183
nuts, cracking during plays 196

Oberon (Jonson) 130
Old Stratford:
  property investments at 113, 147
  in trust 157
Oldcastle, Sir John 103-4
Othello 120, 128
Ovid 37, 85, 88
Oxford, Edward de Vere, 17th Earl, as 'Shakespeare' 7

pageants 59, 169-70
Palladis Tamia: Wit's Treasury (Meres) 85, 93-4
Paris Garden Stairs 97
patrons 87, 88, 89, 182-4
  duties 183-4
Paul's Walk 65
Peele, George 68, 76
Pembroke's Men: and the plague 82
  at the Swan 168
Pepys, Samuel 163
Pericles 128, 196, 199

Philaster (Beaumont and Fletcher) 127
Philip II, King of Spain 17
Phillips, Augustine 70, 99, 116, 117
Phoenix theatre 123, 169
Pierce Pennilesse (Nashe) 76
pirated plays 200, 204, 206-7
pirates, literary 74
plagiarism 75
plague, epidemics 27, 72-3, 81-2, 90, 118, 125
  and the theatre 184
Platter, Thomas 98, 172, 174, 192, 196, 197
players, see actors
playhouse, see theatre
plays: amateur performances 58-9
  buying 185
  continuity 177
  duration of run 93
  and idleness 191
  as incitement to riot 81, 194-5
  licensing 185
  mobility 177
  ownership 203
  pirated 200, 204, 206-7
  popularity of 165
  printing 203-4
  publication 90
  scenic freedom 176-7
  'staying' 207
  tempo 177-8
playwrights, see dramatists
Poetaster (Jonson) 121
poetry, Elizabethan 84
  permanence 84-5
Pope, Thomas 99
Popham, John 70
Porter's Hall 169
prentice riot, Southwark (1592) 81
Prince Henry's Men 169
  origins 116
printers, procedures 202
printing, monopoly 205
private theatres:
  audiences 118, 121, 122-3, 191
  children's companies 166
  closure 161
  in London 169
  prices 193-4
  profitability 168
  size 191
privileged companies 116
Privy Council:
  and actors 195
  and Blackfriars Theatre 95

censorship 70
closure of theatres 72, 81
  and Stratford 112
  suppresses plays 96
  and the theatre 184, 196
proscenium arch 164, 171, 172, 176
Protestantism 17, 18-19
  as Established Church 45
public executions 65
public records: Stratford in 11-12
  WS in 3-4, 6, 52, 53-4, 62, 110
public theatres: audiences 122, 123
  closure 118, 161
  competition 165
  de Witt sketch of 172
  in London 166-8
  physical features 174-5
  popularity 168
  prices 192-3, 194
  profitability 168
  size 191
Puritans: and actors 180, 181
  and plays 58
  and theatres 161, 165, 194

'quarto' 205-6
  'Bad' 200, 205, 206-7, 208
  'Good' 200, 205, 206-7, 208
Queen Anne's Men, origins 116
Queen Henrietta's Men 169
Queen's Interluders (later Queen's Men) 60
  at the Red Bull 168
Quiney, Adrian 22, 30, 33, 34, 111-12, 141
  civic duties 38, 48-9
Quiney, Judith, see Shakespeare
Quiney, Richard 28, 141
  education 33, 34, 38-9, 41, 50
  in London 110, 111, 112
Quiney, Richard (nephew) 155, 157
Quiney, Shakespeare 155, 157
Quiney, Thomas: death 157
  excommunication 142
  immoral conduct 142-3, 157
  marriage 141, 142
  penance 142
  and WS's will 144, 147
Quiney, Thomas (nephew) 155, 157

Rape of Lucrece, The 83, 85, 86, 87-8, 89
  printing of 38, 62, 199
recusants 45
Red Bull, The 123, 168, 170
Red Lion, The (Whitechapel) 67
religion, national policy 17-19

Repentance of Robert Greene, Master of the Arts, The 73
repertory companies 93, 192
Restoration theatre 162
Revels Office 72
Reynolds, Humphrey 22
Reynolds, William 149
Rhenanus, Johannes 187
Richard II 94, 143
  as political propaganda 70-1
Richard III 76, 94
  WS acts in 102-3
Robinson, John 144
Rogers, Philip 113
Roman Catholic Church 17
Roman Catholics, as potential traitors 45
Romeo and Juliet 94, 106
  Bad Quarto 206
  Good Quarto 206
  imagery 31
Rose, The 97-8
  audience 191
  Henry VI Part 1 at 191
  and Henslowe 67, 68, 82, 186
  Henslowe and Alleyn at 90, 91
  Lord Admiral's Men at 166, 168
  Lord Strange's Men at 81, 168
  Tamburlaine at 67
  touring companies at 166
  Worcester's Men at 98
Rowe, Nicholas 6, 49, 89, 101, 134, 135
Rowse, A.L. 5
Royal Shakespeare Company, workload 187
Russell, Thomas 149
Rychardson, John 52

Sadler, Hamnet 53, 138, 144
  bequest to 149-150
Sadler, Judith 53, 138
Sadler, William 53
St Helen's parish, Bishopsgate 62, 64,
St Paul's Cathedral 65
St Paul's Churchyard 63
Salisbury Court Theatre 123, 169
Sallust 37
Sandells, Fulk 52
Satiromastix (Dekker) 121
scenery 162
Scourge of Folly, The 102
scriveners 34
Second Folio (1632) 199
Sejanus (Jonson) 101, 120
Seneca 180

Shakeshafte, William 56, 57
Shakespeare coat of arms 108, 109
Shakespeare family tree 213
Shakespeare name, variants 56
Shakespeare, Anne (sister) 136
Shakespeare, Anne (wife), see Hathaway
Shakespeare, Edmund 137
Shakespeare, Edward 137
Shakespeare, Gilbert 136-7
Shakespeare, Hamnet 83, 136, 138
  birth 53
  death 107
Shakespeare, Henry 21, 49
Shakespeare, Joan (1558) 27, 136
Shakespeare, Joan (1569) (later Hart)
  26, 27, 113, 136
  legacy from WS 146, 148
Shakespeare, John (father) 21-26, 110
  as alderman 29, 214
  as ale-taster 22, 28
  arms, grant of 23, 83, 107-9, 215
  as bailiff 17, 29-30, 60, 214
  as burgess 29
  career 21-2, 27-30, 46-7
  as chamberlain 28-9, 33
  children 136-7
  civic duties, withdrawal from 45-6
  as constable 28
  death 26, 113
  education 34
  as glover 21-2, 27
  lawsuits 47
  marriage 22-6
  misfortunes 30, 31-2, 44, 45, 46, 49, 83
  moneylending 48-9
  property investments 22, 46, 47, 49
  prosperity 20, 22, 25 27-30, 46-7
  recovery, financial 83
  religion 17, 18, 19, 27, 45-6
  social status 15, 23, 28-30, 48-9
  wool trading 27, 46-7
  and WS's marriage 51, 53
Shakespeare, Judith (later Quiney) 83, 113
  birth 53
  death 156
  humiliation 143
  legacy from WS 144, 146, 147
  marriage 141-2
Shakespeare, Margaret (1562) 27, 136
Shakespeare, Mary, see Arden
Shakespeare, Richard (d.1613) 137
Shakespeare, Richard (grandfather) 21, 23

Shakespeare, Susanna (later Hall) 50,
  83, 113
  character 139, 140-1
  christening 53
  death 156
  Henrietta Maria visits 155
  inheritance 146, 147
  literacy 138
  marriage 139
  at New Place 51
  as non-communicant 138
  religion 138-9
  slander case 141
Shakespeare, William: **Life**
  birth and childhood 9, 17, 27, 30
  education 33-9, 40, 42-4, 55, 214
  as apprentice glover 49-50
  marriage 3, 50-3, 150-1
  'lost years' 53-4, 55-7
  acting career 54, 58, 61, 80, 82,
    100-1, 120
  in London 62-4, 214
  early plays 76-7, 82, 88, 214
  poetry 83-9, 215, 216
  in Chamberlain's Men 76, 77, 92, 93,
    186-7
  and The Globe theatre 100, 106, 215
  in King's Men 9, 92, 120, 124, 129,
    130, 133, 186-7
  and Blackfriars Theatre 127-9, 216
  last plays 128-31, 171, 216
  writes with Fletcher 131-2, 133, 216
  withdrawal from theatre 92, 133, 216
  death 151-4, 217

  abstemious habits of 64, 68
  acting roles 102
  anecdotes about 5-7, 54, 102-3
  appearance 153-4
  as artistic director 129
  audience, rapport with 197-8
  biographies of 5, 6, 7, 8
  business matters 112-13, 120-1, 134,
    135-6, 146
  charitable nature 145-6
  and company business 120-1
  creativity 32, 120
  chronological table 214-17
  as dramatist 164
  Elizabethan plays 106, 214-15
  experimentation 127, 129
  and family matters 112-13, 134,
    135-6, 137
  family tree 213

  and father's misfortunes 30-1, 32,
    49-50
  financial affairs 53, 100, 111, 113-14,
    133-4, 135
  friendships 158, 186
  and gardening 113, 134-5
  health 143, 144
  heirs 113, 136, 146, 147, 155
  imagery 31, 41-2, 134-5
  information, sources 3-8
  Jacobean plays 106, 216
  language 31-2, 173, 178
  lawsuits 3, 112
  location, representation of 173, 176-7
  manuscripts 148, 200-3, 208
  personality 4-5, 32, 77-8, 103, 150-1
  plays, printing 199, 208
  popularity 71, 76, 104-6, 128, 163,
    191-2
  property investments 3, 38, 100,
    109-11, 113, 133-4, 147, 155
  at rehearsals 187
  religion 17, 18, 145
  reputation 163
  social status 9-10, 15, 30-2, 108-10,
    111, 135, 180
  stage directions 172-3, 176
  stage technique 173, 176-7, 178
  themes 31
  tragic period 106
  training, dramatic 101
  versatility 171
  visitors to 135
  will 51, 53, 143-51, 155, 217
sharers 98, 185-6
  obligation 185-6
  ownership of plays 203, 207
  pay 188
  printing plays 204
  rewards 186
Shawe, Julius 144
Shoreditch 97
  WS in 63-4
shorthand-writers and pirated plays 207
Shottery 51
  property investments at 111, 157
Sidney, Sir Philip 180
Sly, William 116, 124
Snitterfield village 21, 23, 27, 49
social class, and audiences 84, 118,
  122-3, 162, 165
Somerset House, King's Men at 119
Sonnets (1609) 85, 86, 87, 89
  Dark Lady of 51

Southampton, Henry Wriothesley, 3rd
  Earl 87-90
  allusions to 89
Southampton, Lady 105
Southwark: prentice riot (1592) 81
  WS in 62, 63, 64, 97
'space below' 173, 174
space-stage 171
Spain: peace with 115, 119
  struggle with 65
Spanish Tragedy, The (Kyd) 76
speculators and theatres 184
Spenser, Edmund 65
stage directions 172-3
stage, Elizabethan 164-5
stage lighting 162
stage, Shakespearian 166, 170
  location, representation of 176-7
  research into 164, 171-4
Staple, merchants of the 47
Stationers' Company 205
Stationers' Register 205, 207
'staying' plays 207
Strachey, Lytton 129-30
Strange, Lord 56, 57
  patronage 183
Strange's Men 54-5, 56, 57, 58
  at Newington Butts 166, 168
  and the plague 81
  at the Rose 168
  touring 81
  WS with 82-3
Stratford-upon-Avon: bailiff 16
  church court 18
  Corporation 16, 19, 22
  Guild Chapel 15-16, 29
  Guild of the Holy Cross 15-16, 19, 33
  history and development 11-18
  importance 19-20
  influence of 10-11
  links with 9, 15
  name, meaning of 12
  plague 27
  in public records 11-12
  town council 16-17, 28-30, 45-6
  town plan 13
  WS in 83, 107-10, 120, 131, 133
Street, Peter 96, 97
strolling players 181
Stuart, Elizabeth 128
Sturley, Abraham 38, 111-12
Sussex, Lord, patronage 183
Swan, The 97
  De Witt sketch of 168, 171-2
  Lady Elizabeth's Men at 168

Lord Chamberlain's Men at 168
Pembroke's Men at 168

Tamburlaine (Marlowe) 67
Taming of the Shrew, The 76
  at Haymarket (1844) 171
Tarlton, Richard 60, 117, 189
Tate, Nahum 163
Taylor, John 154
teachers, portrayal of 41
Tempest, The 128-9, 130
  audiences 192
  ephemerality of drama 84
Thames, River 65
Theatre, The (Shoreditch) 64, 67, 69
  audience 191
  Burbage at 90-1
  demolition 96-7
  lease, problems with 94-5
  Leicester's Men at 166
  Lord Chamberlain's Men at 166
  purpose 166
theatres: balcony or gallery 174
  changes in 161, 162 163
  charges 192-4
  and the Civil War 161
  closure 72-3, 81, 125, 161-2, 184
  and crime 195
  design 162, 177
  discovery space 173, 174
  Elizabethan 164-5
  as fomentor of disturbance 81, 194-5
  ground rent 184
  and idleness 191
  inner stage 173-4
  inn yard pattern 170
  in the round 162, 172
  intimacy 176
  licensing 184
  lighting 162, 176, 177
  location 165
  lords' rooms 193
  multi-level staging 172, 174, 176
  owners 184-5
  properties 177
  proscenium arch 164, 171, 172, 176
  Restoration 161-3
  scenery 162, 176, 177
  shape 162, 174
  size 162, 174, 191
  stage 172, 174, 176
  tiring-house 174
  touring 72, 81-2, 90
  trapdoors, stage 173, 174
  twopenny galleries 193

upkeep 184
see also audiences; private theatres;
    public theatres
Theobald, Lewis 201
Third Folio (1663) 199
Thorpe, Thomas 85, 86, 89
Timon of Athens 120, 121
tiring-house, the 174
tithes as investments 112, 113-14, 136
Titus Andronicus 76-7. 94
    title page 90
Town Ditch 65
tragedies 106
trapdoor 173
Troilus and Cressida 94,106
*True Tragedy of Richard Duke of York,
    The* 206
Twelfth Night 106
    actors in 117
    pageant 59
Two Gentlemen of Verona, The 76, 93-4
    pageants in 58
    schoolboy imagery 41-2
Two Noble Kinsmen, The 131, 132
twopenny gallery 193

University Wits 68
usury 48
Utrecht university library 171

vagabonds, actors as 179, 182, 183
Venus and Adonis 83, 85, 86, 87-8
    printer of 38, 62, 199
Vereiken, Ludovick 103
Vertue, George 110
Virgil 37
Volpone (Jonson) 120

W.H., Mr 86, 89
Walford, John 47, 48
Walker, William 16, 150
Warwick, Earl of 59
Webbe, Alexander 28
Webbe, Margaret, see Shakespeare 28
Webster, John 181
Welcombe tithes, investment 113-14,
    136, 138, 140, 147
Whatcote, Robert 144
Whateley, Anne 52, 53
Wheeler, Margaret 142, 144
Whitefriars theatre 169
Whitehall, King's Men at 119
whittawers 21
Whittington, Thomas 111
Wilmcote 23, 49, 53, 157
Wilson, John Dover, see Dover Wilson
Wilton House, King's Men at 119
Winter, Samuel 13
Winter's Tale, The 60, 128-9, 130
    audience, addresses 197
    bear in 177
    death of son in 107
    disguise in 58-9
    gardening imagery 135
    wool in 47
women: in audiences 195-6
    on stage 188
wool trading 46-8
Worcester archives 52
Worcester's Men, see Earl of Worcester's
    Men
Wordsworth, William 4
Wriothesley, Henry, see Southampton

York in Tudor period 19